River Kids

Growing up in Oyster Bay

1938 – 1958

By Jennie Linnane

Fiction, drawn from an anecdotal memoir.

Most names and some characters are fictitious.

For Paul

Also by Jennie Linnane:

Behind the Barbed Wire Fence

Yarns from Yabby Creek

Framing Charlie

Ironbark Hill

TABLE OF CONTENTS

1 Oyster Bay 1

2 A Good Sort 13

3 The Margo 27

4 The Race 34

5 Next Door 42

6 Condensed Milk...50

7 The Passionfruit Thieves 56

8 Josephine Mary...67

9 Herbie and Frecks 72

10 The Farm..78

11 Jack the Joker...84

12 Adding On 95

13 The Wireless 99

14 Starlings 108

15 The Accident..114

16 Bedtime stories 117

17 Grandma Carrington 132

18 Daisy..139

19 Cracker Night...147

20 The River 160

21 Nana and Grandpa Hughs......................................172

22 Uncle Charlie 186

23 Christmas 196

24 The Gift..205

25 Rusty and the Neighbours......................................212

26 Playgrounds 229

27 When the Rain Came 239

28 Dunnies..246

29 Word Games 254

30 Quids, Bobs and Pennies 264

31 Bathurst..270

32 A boatload of Firewood 279

33 The Home Dentist..287

34 Biddy's Calf...297

35 Uncle Owen 301

36 Johnno..310
37 Mr Toobey 321
38 Molly Martin...331
39 Little Siblings..342
40 The Chook-house School...354
41 The Three Kings 364
42 Herb's Wheels 368
43 Best Friend Ruthie 379
44 The Humpy 395
45 Sister Agatha..412
46 The Convent Ball...421
47 The Bus Driver 429
48 The Pie Shop..440
49 Puppy Love 457
50 Devoted Parents 469
51 Fast Fred's wintering 476
52 Towards Sixteen 487
53 Heartthrob Johnnie Ray 495
54 Growing Up 501

1 Oyster Bay

In the distant past, Oyster Bay had been established as a small, primitive holiday settlement, appropriately named for its abundance of oysters. The first roads that connected scattered cottages to a single store were mere tracks, barely wide enough for the passage of carts, making it difficult for the horses to pick their way around potholes and to dodge the overhanging wattles and gum tree branches. As year piled upon year, the community grew, and by the time the family Hughs arrived the tracks had become roads. Oyster Bay had gained the status of "village".

Oyster Bay Road ran past Jack and Margo's house. Jack, with a fund of creative words always awaiting his command, looked upon its name with scorn. 'Not much imagination there!' he scoffed in criticism of the person or people who had deemed the name fitting and wonderful. He declared quite logically that it should have been called Serpentine Road.

Margo always reminded her husband that names were not significant. It was the location that mattered, and he could not complain about that without denying his love of bush, boats and fishing – and oysters. Herbie and Annie, still youngsters in those old days when very few vehicles travelled Oyster Bay Road, regarded the section near their house as a playground. They did not care what the road was called so long as they could ride around over its dusty surface with their scooter and tricycle and throw a stick for their puppy, Peggy.

The first three Hughs children were war babies, third generation Australians of Irish, German and English ancestry, all born at Sydney's St George Hospital. Herbie's arrival engendered much family jubilation, but this was soon dampened by the declaration of the Second World War. The news of Annie's birth was similarly overshadowed by the grim reality of Japan's attack on Pearl Harbour.

The next baby, Lorraine, was born with a condition then termed "hole-in-the-heart" and lived for only two weeks. Jack, cooking for the soldiers far away on Thursday Island, was granted compassionate leave. He stayed with Margo until after the funeral and then, absolutely distraught, went back "to the war".

Herbie understood that "war" meant men fighting somewhere a long way from Oyster Bay and had drawn from an adult conversation the frightening fact that some aeroplanes dropped bombs. Every time an innocent passenger plane crossed their "bit of sky" he would scoop up Peggy, grab Annie's hand and hurry them inside to shelter in the impenetrable fortress of the small fibro house, snug under its invulnerable corrugated iron roof.

Apart from that, the children knew nothing about the war. They did not know that a man named Hitler was implementing a maniacal plan to exterminate Jewish people. They had no idea that Japan had given Darwin a pounding and had sneaked its mini-submarines into Sydney Harbour. And no one knew that America was about to drop the largest of all bombs that would wipe out two Japanese cities.

At pleasant Oyster Bay, the Hughs children were insulated, and therefore it was nothing to them that many commodities were rationed, or impossible to obtain. Margo fed them very well, and had she told them they were eating sheep's brains or the stomach tissue from cows, they would not have cared – it was all just dinner to Herbie and Annie. And anyway, the breadcrumbs coating the brains, the tripe's white sauce with parsley and the liver's rich gravy made those foods taste especially nice.

Fathers too were rare commodities at Oyster Bay. Little Annie Hughs had known nothing of hers until a man called Daddy wearing big boots and dung-coloured clothes walked joyously into their house, as though he owned it, and immediately took embracing possession of her suddenly very happy mother.

Herbie, with his head, almost lost in the hat with the side turned up, proudly remembered and responded to this big soldier as he knelt on one khaki-knee and spoke gently to his children. As there had been no memory in Annie's head of "leave" visits, it took longer for her to accept him and even more time before she would not scowl upon his audacious claim to her mother's big bed, to which she and Herbie had always enjoyed exclusive rights.

The war ended, and Paul Hughs was born. The other two children had become quite used to seeing their mum waddle around with a big belly, and it was a great surprise, after her ten days in the hospital, to observe her new slimmer figure. Jack, carrying the baby, helped her carefully to mount the steps of their house where Herbie and Annie, bursting with excited chatter, waited with Nana Carrington. That occasion established itself in the Hughs' family history as an exciting, happy event: a young soldier and his wife in the youthful years of their united life journey destined to embrace the smooth and bumpy trek of more than six decades.

The post-war children of mid-twentieth century Australia were the last, or at least the second-last generation to enjoy the freedom of an idyllic environment; clean, friendly and safe. The wide area over which the growing Hughs kids roamed, especially during summer, comprised a landscape of hills, gullies, cliffs and caves; encompassing rivers, bays and creeks – all natural stimuli for children's fancy – and they knew it all intimately.

The entire district of Oyster Bay, Jannali and Como, each about a mile distant, was to them an adventure-land of inestimable delight and they explored it to their hearts' content. The miles slipped away unnoticed under bare feet or sandshoes, hot boulders warmed when rest was needed, the smooth bark of a gum tree cooled as they climbed and always they breathed the sweet, fresh air beneath the canopy, lofty and blue. As they grew, the young and adventurous Hughs children increasingly cherished the bushy location with its tall gum trees and native flowers. But most loved of all was the river.

They were river kids. The Georges River, which spilt every day into the mud-bottomed gullies of Oyster Bay, was their favourite playground. They learnt to swim in it; paddled canoes built by their own hands and simple ability from sheets of old flattened roofing iron – and very often sunk in it. The mangrove island out in the middle beyond the channel was an exciting maze of sprawling trunks and branches, the labyrinths among the trees just sufficiently broad to allow the navigation of all their flimsy homemade rafts and canoes.

When the tide retreated, the scallywags still could be found there frolicking in the gloriously soft black mud and catching dozens of small crabs, which they cooked along with periwinkles over a riverbank campfire. Every rock had supported scampering limbs, every cave had echoed the chorused treble of voices, every climb-worthy tree in the vicinity had at least been attempted. And into the pithy bark of the loftiest gum, initials were etched as high as arm and penknife could reach; conquests recorded as triumphantly as the plunge of the flagpole upon Mt Everest.

At Christmas time the moon's gravitational pull swelled the tide towards the trees and caves. The children drew particular delight from this glorious manifestation of nature. It was novel to walk on the wharf, calf-deep in the smooth and glassy expanse which completely transformed the riverbanks. To Herbie and Annie, this phenomenon was itself a magnificent celebration of the Christmas holidays. The air under the high summer sun had a fresh, salt-tasting zest to it, exciting and enticing, and the stirring breezes, which blew shoreward, carried the frequent plaintive piping of seagulls. They needed no calendar to tell them Santa was nigh.

Oyster Bay, in those early days after the Second World War, was still small and reasonably self-contained. The black bitumen road, Oyster Bay Road, came from the west into the geographical and social nucleus of the village, itself cradled maternally by bosomy hills. From this point, between the post office-store with its red phone booth, and the grocer, greengrocer and butcher shops on the opposite corner, the gravelled "tail-end" section of Oyster Bay Road continued eastward. Like a brown reptile, it twisted this way and that. It climbed and descended amongst the houses, bush and rocks on the mitten-shaped body of land and halted abruptly at The Point.

The Hughs' house was not far from the shop. Even in summer, the children could be sent off to buy ice creams for the family and, with tissue paper atop and impatient tongues licking dribbles from hands, they could deliver the treats reasonably intact in about five minutes. Their backyard, like most others, followed a gentle declivity to meet the cliffs overlooking the bay. From there, steps and pathways led down to the water and the waiting green rowing boat.

The sons and daughters of Jack and Margo Hughs were reared beneath the additional shelter of the Catholic faith with its mysteries, rituals and taboos and the perennial practice of self-denial. To be sure, it was an enormous hardship, leaving the warmth of bed on a stinging-cold winter's morning to attend Mass, their stomachs sometimes growling in protest against the prolonged fasting required before receiving Holy Communion.

Additionally, there was the well-enforced abstention from eating meat on a Friday. During Lent children were encouraged to practice self-sacrifice: the renouncing of a particularly relished food, for instance, or the abandoning of a pillow at night, or the forgoing of a wireless serial – the ultimate sacrifice. One objective of the imposed deprivation was to help children to strive for a stronger moral character, but the striving was very hard for them.

Diligently, they avoided committing sins of the mortal variety which, they believed, had the power to dispatch them directly to hell should they perish before confession. The well-instilled fear of the Devil and the associated warm reception, the true meaning of eternity and limbo, even the threat of being banished to purgatory to work off lesser sins, were usually a most effective means of tethering young feet to the unbending, thin path to glory.

7

At school, after the daily recitation of the rosary, pupils were reminded to recite it again at home in a family group. This command was supported by the familiar mantra: "The family that prays together stays together". Annie Hughs always shrank in her seat the next day when Sister asked whose family had said the rosary last night and all the obedient flung up their arms and looked around to see how many heathens were now hell-bound.

It was useless trying to induce Jack to say the rosary for he fiercely resented what he perceived to be religious tyranny and was hostile to the imposition of activity he regarded as merely an automatic repetition of the Hail Mary prayer.

'I thought I'd finished with rosaries the day I left Marist Brothers!' he protested. However, he later complied, once, when his father, beloved Grandpa Hughs, passed away. Apart from that single concession, the family did not chant the rosary every night and yet managed to stay together.

Over the years, Grandma Carrington occasionally stayed at the house to keep the children alive while Margo was in the hospital having another baby, but sometimes she looked after them at her own place at Marrickville. Herbie and Annie mistakenly believed that Grandparents Carrington were rich. They had a black telephone and a floral-patterned carpet; the bathroom was tiled and a gas water-heater, positioned above the plug-end of the bath, trickled out hot water. Best of all, there was a pull-the-chain lavatory adjoined to the rear brick wall of the house – a stark contrast to the Hughs' old fibro "dunny" down the backyard holding up the wild choko vine with its donging progeny. Or perhaps the vine was holding up the dunny!

The Hughs' house, an unpainted fibro dwelling of one bedroom, differed in every respect from that of the grandparents. The Hughs ate only in the kitchen, whereas the Carringtons had a choice of rooms, dining or breakfast. The Marrickville lounge room was furnished with a comfortable lounge suite, and also, to Annie's delight, an upright piano with a pile of music books and a metronome on top suggesting much musical learning. By contrast, the Oyster Bay lounge room was small and had to accommodate the double bed and the other bedroom furniture.

When Margo started knitting again and wearing her floral skirt-and-smock suit; when she began painting the cane pram glossy white after Pauly had migrated to the cot, the older children knew that the next baby would soon be a cuddly, noisy reality.

Margo had grown immense. She walked slowly, leaning back to counter-balance the weight of the baby, hands massaging her lower back muscles, and she sought a chair often. It was not long before a mustard-coloured ambulance arrived at the house. Jack helped Margo to walk along the path. She paused several times and then advanced over to the vehicle where two ambulance men assisted her to settle onto the narrow bed.

9

The ambulance moved away with careful slowness over the corrugated road, and Jack stood there watching until it had disappeared down the hill. He ran a hand through his hair, turned and sauntered worriedly over to Grandma and the three children. Though mere youngsters, they could see he was unhappy. They had realised by their mother's groans and by the way her features had distorted during those pauses on the path that she was in a great deal of pain – of intensity unimaginable to them.

Tony could not wait to get to the hospital and breathed his first in the ambulance while it screamed across Tom Ugly's Bridge. When Annie received this dramatic news, she wished with all her heart to have been there. Knowing nothing about the pain and struggle of birth, she just wanted to have experienced the thrill of travelling in the speeding, wailing ambulance and of being present when the new baby arrived.

Now, there were six people in the family, snowy nappies on the line again and a squawking, red-faced baby in the pram next to Margo's side of the bed. Eventually, when Tony had grown large enough to go into the cot, Pauly was promoted to a bed in "the kiddies' room". The three beds were positioned in a nicely convenient row, perfect for their springing antics – leaping like grasshoppers from one to the next.

Margo had developed an efficient rotation system that operated like an invisible conveyer belt. Arriving home from the hospital, the newborn was deposited in the pram next to Margo's side of the bed. The previous occupant had been moved into the roomier cot, which itself had been vacated to make way for it. But the old wooden cot was still in the parents' room. There, the infant remained until strong enough to shake loose the nuts and bolts.

From that place, the little wrecker was conveyed to the children's room to share one of the single beds. By this time, the conveyer belt system was once more proving its efficiency. The repaired cot was again occupied, and another newborn had been settled into the newly painted pram. Later, to make more room, Jack closed in the front veranda for older boys, Herb and Paul.

At home, the Hughs children were allowed to be little hobos, the boys in their patched overalls and Annie in her frock made from dyed calico flour bags. But sometimes, Margo dressed them up nicely. After donning her best dress (an overcoat in cold weather), she would secure her hat with a long pin and draw on her gloves. Lastly, she'd settle the baby into the canvas *Cuddle Seat*, worn in front and held up by straps over her back, and merrily they would all set off in bus and train to visit Grandma Carrington at Marrickville.

Naturally, Grandma's place reminded the older children of all the things they lacked. It also evoked a feeling of restriction – neighbours' houses hugging close, busy road out front and an absence of bushland. But one advantage always belonging to them was the pleasing ambience of their own area.

They had a spacious backyard with a vacant bush block on each side. They had fruit trees and vegetable gardens and a fowl yard full of cackling life, and from the back veranda, they could see the beloved river with the treed-hill over the other side. Thus, returning from Grandma's place, Herbie and Annie felt a renewed appreciation of everything about the Hughs' tiny bit of Australia and wished to stay forever in "Our Little Joint", as Jack affectionately called their humble fibro house.

2   A Good Sort

During the early years after World War II when money was particularly scarce, Margo and Jack were dreaming about far-away house extensions. They were still using the lounge area as their bedroom. By day the double bed, the family's casual leisure place, was often strewn with newspapers, comics, toys, rusks, apple cores and fragments of *Arrowroot* biscuits. It also was the place where Margo changed the baby's nappy. Protesting siblings occasionally opted to flee from the miasma to breathe again in the sweet, uncontaminated air of outdoors.

Jack was a heavy sleeper and snored vibratingly. His afternoon nap was taken lying on his back with arms folded, descending into the deepest slumber within seconds. One afternoon, Annie was busy on the communal bed arranging the hair of her bride doll, Princess Elizabeth, resplendent in white finery for her forthcoming marriage with the Duke of Edinburgh. The responsibility of The Royal Hairdresser had entirely absorbed her until her father came in to lie down.

'Aah … throw-the-bones time,' he said with a huge sigh, and he reached over to the dressing table for a comb. 'Here you are love, comb Dad's hair, itputs me to sleep.' Annie abandoned the doll and turned her attention to the pleasurable duty of sliding the comb straight back from her father's manly forehead in the gentle, caressing manner she had often seen her mother use.

Margo was a barber to all of them, and Jack was to be her next customer. Naturally, to a young aspirant hairdresser, his wealth of hair presented an irresistible temptation. Happily surrendering to it, Annie carefully drew up tufts, tying each one in a bow with the narrow ribbons Margo had given her for her dolls. After much delicate twisting and tying, bows of yellow, blue and red sat brightly all over Jack's head – the back, saved by the pillow.

Sitting there contentedly, the girl could see her busy mother in the kitchen wiping over the old ice chest. Margo had baked that morning and traces in the air of *Anzac* biscuits began to exert a powerful influence. Annie almost succumbed, but the desire to witness her dad's reaction to the hair-do when he awoke triumphed and she remained in her improvised salon. The afternoon was quiet and dreamy, except for Jack's rhythmical snoring and Margo's humming, until the front gate screeched open and Peggy started barking.

There was a rapid knocking on the door. Jack awoke, got to his feet, swayed sleepily, and in the manner of a robot moved forward to answer it. What bad timing! Annie worried that the hair artistry, prematurely discovered by an astounded, possibly incredulous, outsider would anger her father and spoil her joke. In this state of apprehension, she listened intently. There came the rise and fall of a man's voice, brief silence, the higher intonation of a short laugh, and then he was gone. Jack, paying no attention to the pamphlet he held, stood staring wonderingly into the middle-distance. The "hairdresser" relaxed and waited.

Margo, now mopping the lino near the ice chest, did not pause in her to-and-fro movement as she called out, 'Who is it, Jack?'

Pondering at the front door, Jack was beyond Margo's range of vision but well within Annie's. 'Well, I'll be buggered!' he said dismayed, his eyes following the man's retreat.

'Have they gone? Who was it?' Margo asked again as she mopped.

Jack, perplexed and still unaware of the pamphlet he grasped, turned and covered the few steps that brought him into the room. His other hand went up to scratch the back of his head – discovery so tantalisingly imminent! Margo, now positioning a mat in front of the ice chest, had not yet glanced up; she assumed the caller was merely another salesman. But Annie's eyes were riveted on the hairdo. The bizarre sight of her rugged father in singlet and shorts, head liberally adorned with colourful frivolity, was threatening to destroy the control she had been struggling to maintain.

15

Jack raised his eyebrows and looked towards the kitchen. 'Well … he was some sort of delivery bloke.' Now aware of the catalogue, he glanced at it for a second, tossed it down and went on, 'Strange kind of joker – didn't say much, just grinned like a Cheshire cat. Weird!'

That got Margo's attention. Frowning, she came into the room and looked at him. Her brow lifted immediately. Her face opened, and a high squawk erupted from her throat. Wobbling legs stole balance, and she flopped heavily onto the bed where her whole plump body shook with laughter.

Jack stared at her in astonishment. She flung an arm towards the dressing table. 'Look– in – the – mirror!' she squeaked out and fell into wet-eyed hysteria.

He turned then and saw the reason for the hilarity. '*G-a-a-wd!*' he exclaimed and began plucking the offending bows from his upstanding little ponytails. He looked over at smug Annie sitting there laughing merrily next to her mother. 'Come here you little brat,' he said, reaching out with feigned menace. She shrieked as he tickled until her mother cried out for them to "pipe down", even though still in her own paroxysm, wiping eyes with her apron and groaning that her sides ached.

Jack recovered from the shock, the mirror and the "little brat" had inflicted upon him and he lay back on the bed and gave way to laughter. The joke was such a treasure of a triumph for

Annie. Too often the children and even Margo had been at the mercy of the jester's practical jokes, and it was satisfying for once to change roles.

Sometime after that, Margo began bestowing critical reviews upon the leaking ice chest. It had served the family reasonably well for many years, but now there was not enough room in it for everything. Moreover, in summer the ice did not last long, and the weekly ice-delivery was too infrequent.

One of the icemen who used to deliver to the Hughs' place was nicknamed Fast Fred. Margo and the children were quite accustomed to seeing him trot up the steps at the sideof the house, along the closed-in back veranda, which took him past the laundry-bathroom, and into the kitchen. A hessian bag draped over his shoulder eased the discomfort of the large block of ice, secured with sturdy tongs. Margo always held the ice chest lid open, ready for him to lower the block into the top compartment, and he did so with undisguised relief for his youth was fast forsaking him; cragginess of features seeming to increase his actual sum of years.

Fast Fred, a marathon talker, was a cheery, good-natured fellow and, like Jack (who later enjoyed Margo's account), believed a liberal amount of exaggeration bestowed honour upon a good story. After Margo paid him for the ice, he said: 'Goodoh Mrs Yooz,see ya next week,' and began his departure – which was

17

never swift. Indeed, they all knew he would pause at the bottom of the steps and fall into a friendly, relaxed attitude, the prelude to a spell of yarning.

'By the jingoes, this little'un's growin' fast ain't he?' he marvelled one "iceman day". Before Margo could tactfully deflect the conversation, nostalgic recall of his own fast-growing days began to evoke scenes in Fred's mind, lifting his tone and softening the lines of the weathered, sun-browned face. His pleasure was evident for all to see as he gazed squint-eyed into an invisible distance wherein, awaiting selection, were the cherished chronicles of his library of yarns.

'I 'member when I was just a bit of akiddie like this one here,' he said, ruffling Tony's blond hair. The little fellow beamed up at him as they listened to the next "rip-snorter" instalment of his childhood farm-life story.

'Me dad used to blast stumps outa the ground with dynamite, y' know. Blast 'em to bugg– whatameantasay ... it'd blast 'em t' kingdom come, it would. And I dunno where the crikey they ever landed – that's how bloomin' high they went! And the dogs'd run helter skelter out inta the bush like blue-arsed flies– – ah, whatameantasay Mrs Yooz – very fast, very fast – and wouldn't come back till next Sundy!'

While Fred continued his yarn, Pauly asked Herb, 'Is a fly with a blue bum faster than a fly with a black bum?

18

Big brother laughed and told him, 'Well, it must be, 'cause everyone always says it'.

The comic iceman regularly paused for breath and a quick stoking of memory embers. 'And another thing I 'member too – *the mice!* I seen the ground *ab*-so-*lute*-ly alive with 'em! Rabbits too. And talkin' of rabbits, Mrs Yooz, do y' know the rabbit plague wiped out enough pasture to feed forty million sheep? Forty *million!* And all because of some rich joker, –Tom Austin, or sumpthin'– bringin' 'em inta the country a century ago for sport. *Sport!*' He swayed his head ruefully. 'Y' wouldn't read about it, would ya?' And then his features lifted into a sunshiny smile. 'Well ... acshully I *did*. That's how I know!' he chuckled.

Annie was only a child but well able to discern Margo's growing restlessness at this point, and she perceived that although her mum enjoyed the entertainingly delivered humour, she fervently wished him gone. But kind Margo Hughs was fond of the happy-hearted country boy beneath the worn exterior and respected Fred's earnest, colloquial way of speaking and, unwilling to sabotage his precious memories, she bore it all with kindness and fortitude.

Yet, her attention became increasingly distracted as she turned an ear to the house wondering if their latest baby had awoken for her next feed. The wireless was turned on, and she could hear someone singing about a red-nosed reindeer.

'Go and check on bubby, pet,' she said quietly to Annie.

At this point, Margo began sauntering along the path towards the front yard so that the dear storyteller would drift along with her and soon leave. Only then, would she be able to tie up the gate again to ensure that nomadic toddler Tony could not stray onto the road.

Eventually, to Margo's relief, Fast Fred's thoughts returned to the present and to the melting ice awaiting delivery to his next customer. He made a quick touch to the forehead, the little farewell salute so belonging to him, and said, 'Well, hooroo Mrs Yooz, seeya next Fridy arvo!' and off he trotted towards the cart, dripping now behind the patient Clydesdale. Margo was always so glad she was not at the end of Fast Fred's ice run!

The baby's name seemed strange at first – 'Josephine *this*' and 'Josephine *that*' – until the full name curtsied to its diminutive and everyone began to sense that Josie and Hughs truly belonged together. Annie lavished her abundance of premature maternal devotion upon the precious baby, irresistibly cuddly in the pretty clothes Margo had knitted. And always emanating from the tiny bundle was the fragrance of baby powder, greatly enhancing little Josie's sweet appeal.

The Hughs family had grown to a crowd of seven. The old ice chest, humbly assisted by the *Coolgardie* safe hanging on the back veranda, could no longer contain all the food that required chilling and so Jack bought a *Silent Knight* Kerosene refrigerator.

On the day of the delivery, the children crowded around inspecting it, faces alive with awe and admiration. They marvelled over the perceived paradox it presented, for they had no understanding of the complex scientific principle behind tangible proof that a small flame burning underneath could keep things cold and even produce ice. Margo made ice cream and ice blocks, and she had no trouble with the operation of the fridge, except occasionally when the wick wore down causing a thin spiral of black smoke to rise from the chimney.

It was an amusing quirk of Jack's nature that the only colour of the spectrum he claimed able to see was green. (Margo joked that it was the influence of his mother's Irish blood.) He was not colour-blind but often asked in feigned wonder: 'Well, what other colour *is* there?' and thoroughly enjoyed the howls of protest. Therefore, happy he undoubtedly was that the fridge complied with his little idiosyncrasy.

But Annie's heart sank with disappointment. She surveyed it critically, wishing they could exchange it for cream or a white one, or even light grey. She screwed up her face. 'Why does everything have to be *green*?' she moaned.

'Don't complain, dear,' Margo replied in her usual practical manner. 'If it makes Dad happy to be surrounded by green, that's something to be glad about, isn't it?'

Annie knew that Pollyanna Mum had something there. It was taught at school that in nature the colours green and blue are synonymous with repose and harmony. Thus, the green fridge inside their green house beside the green bush and river under the vast blue sky ought to have kept the blue-eyed Hughs family in repose and harmony for the rest of their lives. Jack drew fulfilment from this fundamental law, but it had entirely eluded Annie.

However, the shining green glory in the kitchen had scarcely made its acquaintance with repose and harmony when a minor disaster was thrust cruelly upon the gentle mother. As with anything new, the fridge was guarded almost reverently against even the slightest threat of damage. Margo was often seen proudly and happily wiping its gleaming front with a soapy dishcloth to remove little *Vegemite* finger-marks and other deposits of various unidentifiable substances.

But one disastrous morning, Tony staggered past the refrigerator with a metal aeroplane zooming along at the end of his arm. He was not accustomed to the fridge being in his flight path, and the result was a long trail scratched across the middle of the green door.

Margo gasped, slapped a hand over her mouth and stood there in shocked rigidity staring at the scar. 'Oh **NO**!' she cried, and similarly, all the kids dropped their jaws and stared.

'Struth!' Herbie yelped, 'LOOK at it!' (Which they all happened to be doing just then.)

'It's scratched the paint off!' pointed out observant Pauly.

The certainty of paternal anger reduced Annie's voice to a foreboding whisper. 'Golly!' she exclaimed. 'Glad Dad's not here!'

Margo for a moment was rendered mute, but when the first shock receded, she threw herself into action. Searching through her sewing basket, she drew out a piece of floral-patterned fabric and cut from it a small part that almost matched the sacred hue of the refrigerator. She handed it to Herbie.

'Run down to the shop and ask for a small tin of paint as close as possible to this,' she told him, pressing the material into his hand. 'Ask Mr Gumm to put it in the book – and hurry back dear, *please,*' she added in an imploring voice as he shot down the back steps.

Lady Luck proved gracious that day. The paint was reasonably close to the colour of the fridge, and Margo wasted no time getting started. To the onlookers, she presented a most incongruous sight: their honest and trustworthy mum down on her knees applying masterful subterfuge to the awful scratch. When finished, she sat back on her heels and surveyed her handiwork.

'There!' she said, relief and satisfaction softening away the worst worry lines from her face. 'You'd hardly know there was a scratch there at all now,' and she got to her feet and sent her tribe outdoors so that the paint could dry un-finger-printed.

When Jack came home, the camouflaged mark flashed like neon to the subdued kids and Margo spent much time loitering in front of the fridge while she listened to the breadwinner's account of his day at the restaurant. All was revealed startlingly, however, when Pauly pointed to the green door after Margo had left it momentarily unprotected. 'Mum painted the fridgerata, today Dad!'There were audible gasps and communal cessation of breathing within the room.

Surprisingly, *astonishingly*, Jack's first response was as mild as frowns and mumbled exclamations could be, and soon he even was complimenting his smart wife on her artistic handiwork! The children pondered this unexpected change in his character and looked speculatively at one another. It was apparent that their usually explosive father had something else on his mind that day for he appeared happily excited, despite the maimed fridge.

As "little piggies have big ears" the children were always banished from the kitchen after tea when their parents were speaking privately. Usually, they did not want to listen anyhow, but this was different – and intriguing. Naturally, they eavesdropped as often as dared using ingenious pretexts, such as thirst, to enter the kitchen. Presently, while easing her suddenly parched throat, Annie observed that her mother had the budget book lying open on the table and similarly her father was studying the bankbook.

After retrieving a ragged old comic from the table, Pauly reported importantly: 'They're doing sums in the writing pad.'

Herbie, returning *again* from the lavvy, heard such snippets as: 'That can wait till next month,' and 'Could stretch that a bit further,' and 'This one's not urgent,' and 'Might just be able to do it!' – all so puzzling to the young masters of espionage.

After a while, Margo rose from the table and stepped over to the kiddies' room where they had been listening at the door. She smiled at the spying little group huddled there with wide open eyes focused on her, and said, 'Come into the kitchen now, Dad's got a big surprise for you.'

Jack turned in his chair and grinned as his children eagerly gathered around. After protracting and enjoying the moment of their almost painful expectation, he asked, 'I don't suppose you'd all like to go for a picnic on Sunday, eh?' his feigned indifferent attitude turning it into a contrary assumption.

A picnic! Well … a beaut idea and a shout of enthusiasm erupted from Pauly. But to Herb and Annie, a picnic hardly constituted a "big surprise", and they knew their father would not have so lightly disregarded the damaged fridge on the prospect of a little picnic.

He beamed at the two-fold reaction and, unable to hold back any longer, said, 'Well kids, there'll be lots of picnics from now on.'

Always the actor, he paused, lending a touch of drama to his enigmatic intonation. When his children were sufficiently paralysed with suspense, he announced, 'Tomorrow I'm going to Como to buy something very special. I want you kids – Mum and bubby too – to be waiting down on the wharf about lunchtime, because … guess what? (He was about to throw them into a chorus of soprano rhapsodies.) 'Because I'll be bringing home – a beautbig launch!'

3   *The Margo*

Jack took the bus to Como the next morning, and Margo sent the children outside to play until it was time to go down to the wharf. After a while, she came out to where Paul and Annie were playing marbles under the clothesline. She put down the laundry basket and looked around in sudden wide-eyed wonder.

'Where's Tony?' she asked and stared at the blank faces. They were supposed to be minding him but had become distracted by the intriguing sight of ants carrying off their recent toenail clippings.

A quick, alarmed search in the near vicinity did not locate the little fellow. Margo saw that the front gate was still securely tied. She returned indoors, repeatedly calling for Tony, and then hurried down the backyard. Paul and Annie followed. They looked in the cubby, behind the chook-house, under the mulberry tree, behind Jack's trellis of climbing beans – no Tony. And then they saw that the distant back gate was gaping open. Margo's fear leapt across to the children, and they began running towards the scrub and the cliff beyond.

'*No!*' Margo called out. 'If he's there you might frighten him.'

And so, slowing their pace and willing Tony to be behind the next bush or rock, they sent hopeful, searching glances in every direction until the cliff was clearly visible. And there he was.

Margo's grip halted the children's natural impulse to run forward. 'Now, *don't* call out. Stay here, and I'll go and get him.' She was equanimity personified: Tony was inching closer to the edge of the precipitous cliff; now leaning, the better to see something over to his right. Margo called out with entreating inflexions: 'Tony, come here to mummy, darling.'

At the sound of her voice, the child half-turned, chuckling and pointed his chubby arm out to the mud flat near Birtles's wharf. 'Look dat funny man!' he said and turned back to watch the man's activity. But in turning, he swayed as his centre of gravity slightly shifted. They all gasped. Annie and Paul stopped breathing for a long moment. Margo, now within a hairbreadth of panic, continued talking and moving closer, quietly and with more haste.

'Come to mummy now darling and see what I've got in my pocket for you,' she said as she advanced, infusing winning temptation into her calm voice. Yet her heart was banging. Hurriedly, the frantic mother made her way around the obstacles of rocks and prickle bushes, gaining ground, arms out, hands ready. She prayed he would not start pumping his little legs up and down, as was his habit when excited. 'Look what I've got here for you,' she repeated – the most forgivable of fibs.

Tony was not looking at his mother, but he wanted her to see what he was laughing at. 'Dat funny man, Mummy – dat man widda shubba!' He turned then, to check that she could see the man in a big hat extracting worm-bait with a shovel.

She got there. Her arms shot around Tony, and she swiftly drew him away from the cliff ... and Pauly and Annie could breathe easily again. The incident etched itself deeply into the memory of both children and was made even more memorable by the poignant sight of their courageous mother kneeling on the ground well away from the cliff, her arms wrapped around bewildered Tony, and tearfully rocking him.

The contrite pair received a most energetic reprimand that morning, and they were to be deprived of wireless serials for a full week. Furthermore, to ensure their negligence was not lacking in proportionate punishment, many additional jobs were imposed, mostly, rightfully on Annie, the elder. But at least they did not have to forgo the launch-welcoming. The excitement of that event drew a forgiving veil over the previous unhappy episode and pushed it all the sooner, albeit temporarily, into the past.

As midday approached, Margo closed the back door behind her. With baby Josie cradled in one arm and tightly grasping Tony's hand, she led the way along the path and then slowly down the stone steps to the wharf. On that magic noon, when the launch first came into view, the excited kids grew ecstatically noisy. *Oh boy, here she comes! Wooo-hoo!*

The vessel appeared larger as it drew nearer and turned to leave the channel route to head home. Jack eased the throttle. The launch slowed, and the high motor surge was reduced to a gentle idling throb. The air became heavy with the smell of petrol fumes and churned salt water; a scent which, to the Hughs after that, always triggered the happy thought of picnics.

Jack tossed the rope to Herb and carefully manoeuvred the launch alongside the wharf. The grey-and-white wonder-boat was home. Captain Jack wore a perpetual grin that perfectly matched his children's. Margo, too, smiled exultantly and several times exclaimed over the size of the boat and the width of the seats. And Jack, keeping it steady against the stone wall while his noisy family boarded, enthusiastically recounted how well it had ploughed through the Georges River and around into Oyster Bay.

After the happy day of the launch's homecoming, and a when a run up the river as far as the Como railway bridge had satisfied the initial yen for seafaring, Jack fell into the habit of referring to the launch as "she" and "her". He told his family that in a previous life she had been a sailing yacht. He was justly proud of her – they all were – and soon she became much like a living entity to them.

One warm twilight as they gazed at the launch rocking gently in the water with the small rowing boat snuggled alongside, Margo remarked, 'She looks for all the world like a whale with her calf.' That image pleased Jack, and he hugged Margo for thinking of it.

Fanciful thoughts aside, practical Jack anticipated the maintenance requirements by laboriously excavating earth and rock from the incline, which extended to the water's edge, to provide a sheltered, raised base upon which to build a slipway. Herb assisted in this huge undertaking, and it was accomplished without the aid of machinery.

Jack honoured his wife by naming the launch *The Margo,* and he later secured an elegant nameplate. To the younger children, the new acquisition was simply "the put-put boat", obviously for the sound it produced when leisurely cruising. The full-throttled surge sounded quite thrillingly different.

And so, whenever Nature kindly bestowed high tide and beautiful weather upon Sundays, they became picnic days for the Hughs. Off they would go in Jack's launch, occasionally all the way up the river, but more frequently across the choppy expanse to Botany Bay. There was a good stretch of sand there called Towra Beach where no one else seemed to go. It offered privacy and uninhibited freedom – the kind of picnic spot Margo and Jack Hughs always sought.

In the distance, they could see the dark, geometrical shape of the Bunnerong Power Station, which provided much of Sydney's electricity. People disparagingly christened it the "Bunger-on, bung-er-off" power station because of the recurring blackouts caused by the coal strike in the 1940s. The Hughs and everyone else at Oyster Bay were familiar with the hurried routine of lighting lamps and candles. They knew the disappointment felt when the wireless went off in the middle of *Larry Kent* or Jack Davey's *The Dulux Show*, or Bob Dyer's *Pickabox* or *Yes What* with characters Percy Pimm, Greenbottle and Mr Snoodles.

But the picnics! Great was the excitement and laborious the preparation with much careful planning, mainly for the food required. Margo always spent several hours of the previous day baking so that they could look forward to a feast of picnic fare. The practical mother also packed lavvy paper and *Band-Aids*, jumpers, hats and raincoats ... preparing for a day out was always an epic manoeuvre for the Hughs mob.

Over time, the Sunday picnics fell into an established routine. Upon arrival at the beach, after Jack had stopped the engine, Herb would jump out to pull the launch's bow until it wedged itself into the shore, and to embed the anchor firmly into the sand. Shortly afterwards, Jack and Herb would rig up the tarpaulin to provide shade for Margo and the little ones, and then set up the campfire to which she would later set a match.

With great exuberance, the bigger kids always ran off along the beach in search of shells to add to their collection. They also picked up smelly, dead puffer fish to hurl at one another. Usually,

Jack and Herb took the launch out again to the deep, there to catch a few bream. When they saw the smoke signal rising from under the billy, they headed for shore and then at last everyone could enjoy the scrumptious picnic lunch.

4 The Race

Humphrey Smithers, whom Jack had nicknamed Smitto, was an irritating know-all and not popular in Oyster Bay. Chatting in the shop or at the bus stop, for instance, he would delight in stating some obscure fact, fully counting on the listener's ignorance. Once that was assured, he would embark upon a lengthy authoritative explanation, which had the victim wondering why he was imposing his knowledge upon such indifferent ears.

This person also liked to take a firm stance in justifying his own opinions, which had nothing to do with the subject debated and everything to do with his principle of always seizing upon the opposing view. Percipient, Jack Hughs recognised this as an attempt to make others feel inferior because, he said, Smitto secretly believed himself so.

Although Mr Smithers was the owner of a fine launch, he often exhibited by various maligning comments an obviously painful envy of *The Margo* and always sought to race it. But the cumulative effect of many failures increased his frustration until the quest for victory assumed obsessive proportions.

The Margo was capable of exciting speeds if her master felt inclined to give freedom to the throttle, which he did whenever another boat appeared to be inviting a race. Jack's launch, with her grand history of sailing, was endowed with beautiful lines of design which facilitated the smooth, seemingly effortless glide through the water. It was easy to apply imagination and view her as a racing yacht, with youthful billowing white sail, moving swiftly forward against the horizon and the merging blues of sea and sky.

Whenever Smitto was on the river, Jack would allow him to catch up – 'To give the poor bugger a bit of hope,' he'd say with perfect condescension. He would then open up the throttle a little so that *The Margo* steadily gained the lead, even though she was well down in the water laden with all the bulky gear and a crowd of Hughs in different coloured sunbonnets, canvas hats and caps.

It was humiliating for proud Mr Smithers to be left struggling along in the powerful wake; all the more so because he knew that Jack Hughs had no specialised training in the mechanism of engines, yet he privately acknowledged that his rival was quite capable of operating them. Naturally, Smithers believed himself to be in a position of advantage, hence infinitely more qualified to meet successfully any boat-racing challenge, begrudgingly allowing the exception of a speedboat.

Nevertheless, all his self-confidence was wasted, for he became The Perpetual Vanquished. Such races were triumphs to the Hughs tribe, and especially to Jack. Seated astern with hand on the rudder, he would chuckle away to himself while maintaining a disciplined eye to the bow – the best of captains. He even affected a teasing unawareness of the competition. Smitto, however, suspected somewhat uneasily that if *The Margo* were allowed her full potential, he would be forced to acknowledge her superiority.

This irascible person, having suffered defeat so often, became much upset about it and this prompted him to buy a larger, more powerful engine for his launch. He felt satisfied that he now had the absolute advantage and was disinclined to admit the remotest possibility after that of losing *any* race. He cruised invitingly up and down the river, his revitalised launch proudly cresting the small waves.

It was apparent Smitto was hoping that irritating Jack Hughs would take out his 'upstart of a bloody barge' (his term, often flung at *The Margo*) and give him a "burn". Jack protracted the contender's anticipation by making him wait until a suitably fine Sunday when the family was ready to set off for another picnic.

'Righteo Herb,' he said, 'get the maggie (magneto) out of the shed and we'll give old Smitto a good thrashing.' These were thrilling words to his river kids, for at that time their competitiveness was almost as innate as breathing.

From a short jetty, farther along past clumps of mangroves, Smithers watched out for Jack Hughs and his mob. As soon as he spied them congregating on their wharf with the rolled-up tarpaulin, the picnic gear and the "maggie" in its box, he hurriedly boarded his launch to have it warmed up and ready to teach complacent Hughs a well-deserved lesson. His eagerness made obvious the fact that he believed it was going to be his day of sweet victory and he wanted to get started as soon as possible.

'Champing at the bit,' Margo quipped to Jack.

The family boarded and settled into their usual places: the youngest ones in the middle next to Margo, and Pauly with Annie on cushions under the bow to avoid the spray which they knew would fly up later when their father applied the speed. When the magneto was in place, Herbie untied the rope, stepped in and sat at the stern where he could man the rudder until Jack took over.

By this time, Smitto's launch was throbbing away over at his wharf, sounding alarmingly powerful to Herb and Annie. Imperturbable Jack dismissed their anxieties, explaining that it was merely an echo bouncing back from under another cliff shelf producing the powerful resonance. He had full confidence in *The Margo*. Annie was still anxious though, and Herbie appeared unhappy and doubtful as he watched the other launch glide sleekly away from the bank and out towards the middle of the glassy bay.

Nonchalant Jack Hughs betrayed no indication that he was aware of any difference in the performance of the other launch. He only deigned to look briefly at its owner to offer his usual genial salute, and Smitto, envisaging himself as the sure victor, magnanimously waved back.

37

'All this sudden friendliness!' Annie scoffed.

To Herb and Annie, it began to seem that their father did not care about the race. They became increasingly impatient because of the casual manner he displayed in taking so long getting the boat going and guiding it ever so slowly towards the middle. There, finally, he would be able to increase the speed and follow the channel out of the bay. (Jack said later that it felt a bit like a plane carefully taxiing and aligning before the exciting, powerful take-off.) Margo was sensitive to her children's agitation and assured them that their father was just teasing Mr Smithers, who was obviously most eager to display the full speed of his launch with its new engine.

As soon as they were level, both launches headed out towards open water. Smitto's loudly, powerfully chugged away, looking so empty with only one person aboard while Jack's was well weighed down and seemed barely able to keep up. In fact, *The Margo* appeared to be falling miserably behind. Annie could hardly bear it. Herb too looked worried and impatient.

Happy Smitto however, kept turning his broadly grinning face, immensely enjoying the sorry sight of the "upstart bloody barge" barely tagging along. Even so, Jack, a picture of superiority with his iron attitude of invincibility, kept his eyes staring serenely ahead and his frustrated kids wondered why he was smiling.

Herb's impatience met its limit. 'When will you give it full throttle Dad?'

Exasperating Jack replied calmly, 'All in good time, Herbie … all in good time.'

Margo became caught up in the excitement then, and after an impatient, restive moment she reached over and tapped his boot. 'Oh, come on Jack … let her go!' she urged.

And so, spurred by Margo's excitement, Jack gave full rein to *The Margo*. With a new surge of power, his launch drew level with Smitto's and effortlessly cruised on past leaving him to ride the waves.

Spontaneous jubilation arose: 'Ooh, gawd! Good on ya Dad! Oh, you little beauty! Whacko, whacko!'

After a moment, they again looked back. Smithers had turned his launch for its homeward retreat. It was indeed the nadir of his store of defeats and several healing months were to pass before he would again speak to Jack Hughs – briefly and reluctantly.

Jack, the master of understatement, said blithely, 'It seems Smitto's a bit of a bad loser.'

But Margo, casting aside her intense dislike of the man, replied with sad inflexion, 'Poor Mr Smithers! Poor fellow!'

She always felt sympathy for the losers of competitions, Snakes and Ladders, Ludo or Rummy, but especially for those who came last in a race. She was responding to residual influences of childhood when she had an injured foot and was always left trailing behind her many siblings. Margo often reminded her children to be gracious in defeat.

Family pride and exaltation had been very much in evidence on the day of the race. Afterwards, however, the Hughs' cup sufficiently overflowing, they were able to spare a little reflective compassion for the strange, proud man who could never win a race.

Later, Jack winched *The Margo* onto the slips and rewarded her for her excellent performance with a good clean and also a loving polish of the nameplate. With help from Herbie, he treated the launch to a fresh coat of paint, capriciously disregarding a lifetime of allegiance to a particular hue. She emerged wholly transformed, a dignified chocolate brown with bright red trim.

Some years later, reminiscing about that particular race, Annie asked her father about the blasé attitude he had so teasingly displayed.

'Heheheh!' he chuckled softly. 'You know Annie, I really wanted to beat the bastard that day. I *had* to win. If he only knew that I was even more obsessed with that race than he was!'

'But you never showed it,' Annie commented amusedly.

'No, well, that was just a bung-on in case his launch beat us. Had to kid I couldn't care less, y'see … not that I thought he had any chance against *The Margo!*' he added loyally.

Jack sadly swayed his greying head; the old yearning for the river settling back in his blue eyes. 'But the winning was goodoh, wasn't it love,' he said.

'Yeah, it sure was Dad,' Annie responded, and she grinned admiringly at him. 'And so were you, Captain Hughs.'

5 Next Door

Apart from Smitto, there were very few people in Oyster Bay whom Jack Hughs did not like. Jack and his family were well regarded in the neighbourhood, contented and happy most of the time. Their north-facing house was reasonably secluded, shouldered by vacant blocks. The eastward had a light scattering of gum trees with scrubby undergrowth and some large rocks, but the westward was thick with bush.

These two blocks significantly extended the children's play area, especially when Jack cleared a bike track on the bushy one. Herb, Annie and Paul spent much of their free time tearing around it, Herbie on his bike and the other two on their scooters with Thumper (Peggy's successor) panting out every circuit of this strangely illogical human activity.

The kids thought the track was "bonzer", and so did their friends Ruthie and Billy and a few others from Oyster Bay. Margo was pleased because she always knew where her children were and that relieved her of the usual voice-throwing, roundup-call from the back veranda when daylight began to yield to the veiling dusk.

But the fun came to an end the day a man and woman alighted from a taxi and proceeded to walk around the track. Being fiercely territorial creatures, the Hughs kids resented this sudden invasion. They were forced to quell their indignation though when informed that the trespassers actually owned the property. What was worse, the couple intended to build a house there and shift in as soon as possible.

What a blow! Herbie and Annie grumbled endlessly about it. They would not have minded if the new people had a few kids they could play with, but Mrs Brownleigh told Margo she was unable to have children. However, she stressed defensively that she loved her three small dogs as though they were her babies.

Diminutive Thumper resented these yappy white fluff-balls and frequently vented his animosity at the fence by indulging in his favourite fantasy that he was a German shepherd, blasting them furiously with his "Blitz Krieg". That outrage incited the first of many complaints against Margo and Jack; against their 'mischievous brats, their mongrel dog and their noisy, bloody rooster' – which last was guilty merely of commanding the hens to wake up and get on with laying the eggs.

The new neighbours themselves made a great deal of noise, although only what was to be expected while building a house. During the months of hammering and sawing the Hughs became more acquainted with the Brownleighs. One evening, as Jack's family sat at the table enjoying potato chips and freshly caught mullet, Annie commented, 'That lady never smiles at *us* Mum, only at her little dogs. Yeah, and she talks real lah-di-dah too.'

Later, in response to this observation, Margo advised her daughter to be kind to their neighbour, explaining that it was a great sorrow to a woman to be deprived of children – in her opinion, the direst of fates. With her intuitive compassion, Margo had read suffering in the woman's face and wondered if other problems existed. Annie imagined how she would feel if deprived of her dolls, and a stirring of sympathy for the stern-faced neighbour immediately arose in her child's breast. It came to her then, that if her mum could tolerate the lady's "snobby" ways, she would overlook her serious face and the lah-di-dah nonsense.

That night, drawing upon her Roman Catholic means of support in times of worry, Annie knelt by her bed and whispered a prayerful hope to Our Lady, the Immaculate Conception, that the lady next door would adopt some girls. While on the subject she asked God to send another girl-baby to her mum to establish better gender balance to the Hughs family.

Thus continued the poignant nature of her nightly prayer until it was superseded by alarm for her father after hearing him talking about the war in Korea; specifically, Menzies' statement that 3,000 Aussie men would be sent there. *'Please God, don't let Dad go there!'*

Margo, anxious that the privacy of her side-located back door would be compromised, kept an eye on the various building stages of Brownleigh's house as she went to and fro, and was glad to discern that the front entrance would face the road. Eventually, the house was finished, and although the cessation of building noises brought relief, a different irritation began to manifest itself.

After moving in, the husband fell into the habit of sitting on a bench at the sunrise side of his house, directly opposite the Hughs' side entrance, and with a beer, in hand, he looked up every time Margo emerged. Often it was his loitering at the fence which upset her as he ostensibly inspected his "garden".

'Garden?' scoffed Margo. 'Huh! A clump of thistles, dandelions and cobblers' pegs ... and him standing on them and all the time watching us!' She sighed, 'And I used to love the bush being right there ... the birds, wildflowers ... and all the kiddies on their bike track ...' Her voice trailed off in a wistful tone, 'and the sunset over the trees.'

Jack, glancing at the paper one morning, remarked that the headline story reminded him of a recent traitorous comment the "bloke" next door made concerning Prime Minister Chifley. Margo was scrutinising the fine-toothed comb for lice as each time she withdrew it from Pauly's hair. Although piqued by the mention of the neighbour, she replied in a desultory, abstract fashion, 'Well, there must have been some that liked him ... forty thousand were at Bathurst for his funeral.'

But the resurrection of neighbour-irritation agitated her, and she became less abstracted: 'You know, he sits there nearly all day!' she protested, indulging in a good measure of hyperbole. 'It's a darn nuisance and very annoying. And *that!*' (a hand-flap here at the fly-wire door which always treacherously announced her), 'Would you oil the jolly hinges, Jack?' Margo's compressed lips and the sudden way she turned her kindled features to glare across at the new house clearly revealed how utterly fed up she was with the man next door.

Over the weeks Margo economised in her emergences from the side door, keeping her eyes averted from the neighbour's gaze and her ears closed to his greeting. She learnt that her reluctant 'hello' invited an over-the-fence, mean-natured litany of complaints: of the offensive, steaming heap of manure the baker's horse had dropped near the gate; a denigration of the council for the state of the gravel road after rain, and even the tardiness of the walking postman.

'He's always critical and always boring. Small wonder his wife never smiles!' Margo said one frustrating day. Jack looked at her intently. She was changing. By nature, happy, easy-going Margo Hughs had never been one to complain. Now she went on in an almost breathless commentary to reveal that it was nearly impossible to avoid being observed with all the occasions of descending the steps to go around to the backyard.

She listed the details of her trips carrying baskets of washing, her visits to the vegetable garden, her regular checks on Josie in the playpen and many other incidental excursions to the backyard, which she undertook during the day, not the least of which were the treks down to the lavatory. 'I can't even go *there* in privacy!' she exclaimed in a teary, defeated tone.

Margo's mood ignited Jack's and, as the listening children all knew, once fired his anger was not quickly extinguished. 'The bloody pervert!' Jack growled and after that coloured every reference to the neighbour red, and every object as well. He slapped down the newspaper. 'Right! Time to get cracking!' This sudden announcement meant opening up the back wall of the house for the installation of a new doorway and moving the steps around to there – something he had intended to do for quite a while. But first, to silence the screeching (red) screen door, he strode off to the (red) shed for the (red) oil can. And so, with a sudden boost of energy, Jack began the big project of relocating the side entry to the back of the house.

The excited household was astir early that special day and all stood around watching the action. Jack cut through the fibro (*asbestosis* generally unknown then) and the hardwood studs to create a large opening in the kitchen wall, and everyone rejoiced as the light flooded in. The sight of the enormous wall-hole elated Margo – blessed privacy! She stood there, unobserved at last, and surveyed the pleasant domestic view of her backyard, the broader scene of the riverboats rendered toy-sized by distance, and the salient points of the bushy hill beyond.

Amid the noise of excited kid-chatter, Jack became the recipient of much praise and hugging from his lady-love who, after a week of inconvenient front-door-exiting, exclaimed that the new access was wonderful. But, sparkle-eyed, she teased that it would be *even more wonderful* when the steps were reconstructed so that she could actually go *in* and *out* of her new doorway. She applied comical voice emphasis and hand gestures to these little prepositions, and Jack responded with an amused quip about men's slavery under feminine tyranny. He imprisoned her in one of his rough bear hugs.

Laughing, she said, 'Oh, careful Jack, mind the baby.' That was Hugh's number seven, Clivey – before he had hair.

Earlier that week a truck had delivered a load of sand for the cementing job and naturally upon this tempting dune the children were forbidden to trespass. Grandpa Hughs arrived at the weekend to help, and when at last the new steps and the first, and solitary, section of concrete path had dried they were christened with much exuberant ingress and egress of the novel back entrance.

The men then built a linen cupboard into the newly available space at the end of the closed-in veranda where the door used to be, and Margo was delighted to see another of her creative ideas become a reality. She was renowned for her practicality. Her sometimes-brilliant plans usually had short gestation and quickly grew to maturity, for the blessed man who loved her was always pleased to grant her wishes.

6 Condensed Milk

The Hughs' front and side fences were constructed in the standard design of squared post, hardwood rail and chain wire. The eastward divider between their house and the vacant block was twice the length of the front fence, the width of the upper rail a temptation for small, agile bare feet. The children often trod the rails, slowly at first with arms extended to aid balance, heads down-bent and eyes gauging the distance for the next cautious step.

Herbie and Annie became adept tightrope walkers on the smooth rails and learnt to shorten the time it took to half-run from the letterbox to the chook shed. There, the posts and rails terminated at the high enclosure of chicken wire.

Annie, practising this activity one morning, wondered if she should join a circus one day, but at present, she was just glad to escape the washing up and the screeching baby, Clivey. She needed time, also, to recover from her mother's smacks after being caught raiding the tin of condensed milk, which, as she well knew, belonged exclusively to the baby, metered out via a dummy.

Entirely alone for once, Annie decided to increase the speed of her rail walking, all the while plotting to spend next week's pocket money on her very own tin of the heavenly stuff and to hide it where it could be enjoyed illicitly at her leisure.

Moreover, she would cut the lid wide open as her mum *used* to do, thus allowing the dummy to be promptly coated for the impatient baby.

But that was before Margo noticed how fast the tide had gone down. After buying the next tin of the delicious milk, she displayed typical mother-cunning by merely puncturing the top with opposing holes, one for air and the other only wide enough to allow the thick, sweetened milk to dribble onto the dummy. After that difficulty was imposed, the Hughs kids had to suck hard and fast to get even half a mouthful before the sound of their mother's approaching footsteps sent them scurrying to safer precincts.

Annie had been standing at the dresser on the fateful morning of the smacks, blissfully indulging in this regular little theft (not yet smart enough to remove herself from the scene of the crime while she pilfered) when her complacency was rudely disturbed by Margo's triumphant exclamation: 'Aha! Caught you!' Annie nearly dropped the tin in fright.

Her mother had the presence of mind, the naughty girl noticed, to rescue the prize and return it safely to the dresser before bringing her hand down three times on Annie's bottom – WHACK!

'That's for what you've guzzled.' Whack! 'That's for being sneaky about it.' (Was *child sneaky* worse than *mother cunning*? Annie later pondered.) Margo paused a second and then brought her hand down again. Whack! 'And that's for the times I *didn't* catch you,' she said, satisfied to have found justification for a third smack. 'Now go outside and think about that, or I'll find jobs for you'.

She shut the thin plywood dresser door with an excessive firmness implying complete inaccessibility – chained, locked and bolted.

More jobs! Feeling vulnerable and being particularly free from popularity just then, Annie thought it wise to heed the maternal advice and make herself scarce. She hurried on her snivelling way down the back steps before her mother remembered that the washing up was still waiting. After applying mental balm to wounded emotions, she mounted the lofty refuge of the fence – where mothers fear to tread – and began walking the planks.

Annie's imagination became occupied with the compensating fantasy of an entire crate of tins of *Nestlé's* Condensed Milk safely concealed beneath her bed (quite forgetting her mother's invading broom) when her foot made a slight miscalculation which sent her hurtling to the ground. There she lay, prone and severely winded.

Her throat emitted loud animal sounds, the gasps exploding hideously as her lungs struggled to recover the expelled air. When breathing became easier, she lay groaning, too alarmed to move and realising the full meaning of the idiomatic phrase "a close shave".

But what a waste of a job-avoiding expedient it was! If only her mum had come outside just then or looked from the window during the terrible death-rattle noise! Annie seemed afflicted by a mean twist of fate: when she did not want her mother in her vicinity, there she always was, but when her sympathetic, forgiving presence was required – not a sign!

It was characteristic of Annie's bad luck that the accident happened at the house's virtually obscure side, greatly diminishing the chance of rescue and she wished instead to have flopped off the front fence in full view of family and sympathetic neighbours. Minutes passed. Annie became annoyed with her potential saviour for her tardiness, and she bemoaned the fact that not one of the pesky boys was around to discover her there, suffering tragically.

'Well, where is everyone? Am I going to lie here all day and catch ammonia and die anyway,' she dramatized, now irritated with herself as well.

It was very boring lying there, Annie thought. But the waiting at least provided ample time for her to speculate on the possible benefits the situation may engender: Her mother would be so thankful that precious daughter had come back from the close encounter with death and aeons of Purgatory that she would regret her previous hasty judgement and the harsh punishment. Annie expected that her mother would offer her a good swig of the ambrosial condensed milk and allow her to lie in bed for the rest of the day and read comics. As well, she would almost certainly let her off her evening jobs.

She was enjoying these comforting little thoughts when her nuisance conscience nudged contentiously. In a trice, she was back in the classroom with permanently red-faced Sister Joseph, in the middle of yesterday's "debate" about why she could not choose her long-dead baby-sister's name Lorraine as her Confirmation name.

As the girl understood matters, if you died without ever sinning, you were a saint. Sister said that everyone is born with Original Sin staining the soul, bequeathed by Eve. Annie argued, 'Well, how did Saint Bernadette became a saint, then?'

Sister had grown impatient, that day, with her wilful pupil's apparent obtuseness. She made a dismissive gesture, which meant: 'Oh go away bothersome brat!' and told her to choose another name – and so, Bernadette became Annie's Confirmation name.

As these thoughts wafted through the sufferer's brain, they rendered her oblivious of the shifting sunlight, until the rattle of the Fruito's old truck coming up the hill brought her back to the passing moment and the memory of last weeks' squashy, succulent persimmons. Suddenly, a burst of brothers dashed out of the house followed by her inattentive parent carrying the wash-up dish for the specked fruit the kind man always gave them.

The fence casualty, Annie Hughs, jumped up with an agility quite remarkable, considering her death-knell experience. Lamenting briefly the poignant scene that might have been and the forfeit of the job-holiday which should have followed, she threw off her martyrdom in a wink and ran out to the truck to compete with the boys for the best of the bounty awaiting.

Margo, glancing at the girl shuffling in close to her brothers at the back of the truck, reached into the dish and handed her a persimmon. 'There you are dear, I saved your favourite for you,' she said, smiling her lovely sunshine. And Annie forgave her.

7 The Passionfruit Thieves

With the door installation completed and Margo contented, Jack became eager to get back to his other love – gardening. He dug a trench along the west fence and then upended the lavvy pan there. Into this receptive womb of fertility, he planted two passionfruit vines.

The children had a hand in tending the vines, watering and weeding, and proprietarily they watched for the first flower buds to appear. Eventually, the high wire fence was enshrouded in leaves and pretty Catherine wheel blooms, well inspected by bees and culminating as nature intended in delicious purple fruit. Annie, Pauly, and sometimes Herb, began spending more time there biting open the skins and sucking out the sweet pulp. The prerequisites for this activity were sharp teeth, the lavvy handy and, after occasional bee stings, the blue-bag their mother used to whiten the washing.

One blissful morning, after gorging themselves to repletion on all the ripest fruit, they collected a paper bagful for the kitchen. Annie turned to leave, thereby allowing the vine to get on with growing more fruit, but Pauly had spotted some beauties on the other side of the fence, so he slipped his hands through to grab them.

At once, a sharp staccato clapping and an abrasive voice shattered the quiet morning: 'Yoo-hoo, *away!* Get away!' Mrs Next Door was standing on her back veranda energetically waving the children from the trellis. The outraged squawks startled them, and they stood there, gape-mouthed and struck mute by the bewildering spectacle – after all, it was their fruit!

'What's up with *her?*' Annie protested when her jaw had relaxed sufficiently for speech.

Pauly, peering at the woman through a gap in the tangle of the vine, pulled back his blond head and replied, 'Yeah, they're not hers – *bummy* old witch!'

They raced along the path, up the new steps and into the house, eager to report the absurd injustice, fully expecting their mother to scoff and exclaim: 'The hide of *her!*' and send them back to the vines. But Margo did not respond that way at all. She shook her head in grave admonition and muttered in a low voice, 'Ooh, that *blessed* woman!' The children knew she was not conferring veneration or divinity upon "Her Highness", as Jack had labelled the unpleasant person. Margo then stunned them with the revelation that the passionfruit on the neighbour's side of the fence was theirs, by law.

Theirs! *Theirs?* That shock produced embittered protests from Paul and Annie, but Margo was adamant in this most confusing defence of the neighbours' rights, and after voicing a few more querulous exclamations the two protesters gave up.

Their wise mother soon overcame her first indignation and applied the parental guidance to the baffling concept of fences being common property. Nevertheless, after further reflection her face grew stormy and seemed to mirror her children's thoughts: 'How petty of her to make a fuss about such an innocent little thing!' She glared with icy hostility at the house next door wherein the lofty presence dwelt, and then gazed softly upon her maltreated loved ones – who found the contrast most gratifying and consoling.

Presently, Paul and Annie were called upon to mind Tony. They gathered up a collection of toy cars and ventured out to the used sand heap – now a sand-*flat,* and no longer sacred. There, they built roads, bridges and tunnels, all the while muttering little hypothetical "we oughta" plots, conspiring to get even with the Minister for the Protection of Passionfruit.

They felt justified in their plotting, being partly influenced by Jack's earlier scornful comments about the neighbours whom he referred to as "typical whingeing poms". Margo, as usual, bore the responsibility of modifying Jack's vehement outbursts, which were always too loud, and too near the "ear-flappers". She sought to imbue her children with fair-mindedness; to teach them that the Brownleighs were not representative of the whole and that every country had its share of complainers, not just England. She issued a timely reminder, also, that quiet, gentle Grandad Carrington was English.

Jack, however, voiced the last word regarding the people next door: '*He's* a violent alcoholic, and *she's* too mean to throw a shadow!'

Inquisitive Pauly had never encountered that particular idiom and questioned, in effect, the ability of a human body to govern its own shadow. Jack laughed and ruffled his son's hair … and the mystery remained so.

The sunny morning wore on. The coppery-crowned neighbour with a shopping basket in hand, left the dogs to continue their grief-stricken yapping and, her prime interest in life being passionfruit, detoured across to the sand-flat. Displaying hostility entirely disproportionate to recent events, she pushed up her just-sucked-a-lemon mouth and said pettishly: 'I've counted them'. After a cautious glance at the Hughs' house, she lowered her voice, curled her lip and warned, 'and you'll get a slap for each one you *steal.*'

That verb was a stab to children who, although not angelic, had never been guilty of stealing. Satisfied now, she stalked off down the hill towards the shops. The childless, disgruntled woman might have aroused charity and compassion in some folk, but there was an overwhelming scarcity of those qualities that day at the Hughs' address.

As soon as the sunhat and olive dress had dragged their grudgingly thrown shadow down the hill, Paul and Annie ran back to the vine, Tony innocently trailing along in their vengeful wake. Their ingrained trait of honesty submitted to the higher power of revenge and they divested the vine on the hostility side of the fence of every passionfruit.

Monumental mistake! Was this not an act of premeditated, malicious theftabove which their saintly characters had been so elevated? The kids knew they were acting provokingly, but knowingit did not prevent them from sinking deeper by the minute into venial sin, bordering dangerously on the mortal.

Maternal wrath descended swiftly upon them that day, and Margo's blue eyes no longer seemed tenderly loving. She assured her children that she was fed up with their misbehaviour: 'You're always giving the neighbours reasons to complain about my "mischievous brats",' she scolded. Paradoxically, in deference to a past illness that the woman had suffered, she made sympathetic excuses for her. More forcefully she added, 'And you must learn to keep the peace and stop irritating them!'

Their mother's distorted attitude jarred painfully, and they tried to put it right: 'It's *them* who irritates *us*!' they chorused indignantly. Pauly whinged and Annie sulked, and both wished never to have met the people next door. They longed for life to be restored to the good old days when there was a bush block there and bike track to whiz around on.

Margo, setting the table for lunch, waved away a droning blowfly, shook her finger at the two villains and said, 'You'll just have to get used to it. Like it or not, those people *are* our neighbours – Thumper, *outside!* – and if you pick any of *their* passionfruit you'll both get a good hiding.' (A hiding was always defined as "good".) She pointed the fly-swatter at older and should-be-wiser, Annie. 'And you'd better watch your step, miss.' The sullen girl had been weighing the merits of protesting and offering a further defence, but her mother's glare and the intimidating fly-squasher prompted her to shut her libellous mouth.

Thus, Margo laid down the law and Annie's enfeebled capacity to negotiate became extinct. BUT, when belatedly she remembered to apply the positive stimulus of the woman's threat to slap them, the focus changed instantly. Up went Margo's querying brows and, hand on hip, she stared at her endangered darlings.

'*Oh!* Is that so?' she exclaimed, and added in deadly tones almost to herself, 'Well, we'll see about *that!*'

Her hand dropped from her round hip, and The Precious Threatened began to feel pleasurably solaced as she swished about from dresser to fridge and plonked bread, butter and tomato sauce upon the table as though they were the cause of her wrath.

Savagely, but with well-practised exactitude, she sawed slices of bread for the cold sausage sandwiches.

'Meat!' Annieexclaimed aghast to her brother. 'Mum forgot that it's Friday!' she whispered. But Annie was hungry, and they both loved sausages ... and anyhow, next week's visit to confession would take care of the terrible sin.

When the initial force of indignation was half-spent, and the flush of anger had receded; when she had marshalled her thoughts and allowed wisdom supremacy, Margo, with her steadfast allegiance to principle, made ready to face the ordeal of confronting her irascible neighbour. This was unnerving for her. By nature, she was averse to any manner of disputation. Wrapped up in her family and reigning magnificently as wife and mother, she had neither the time nor inclination to glance beyond her own nest.

On this particular occasion, however, still incensed, still smouldering, she placed a generous number of passionfruit in a paper bag, removed the apron from her plump, motherly form and returned stray brown wisps to the confines of her hairnet. She drew in a deep breath and with heavy, almost vibrating expiration said, 'Well ... better get this over with,' and ventured ruefully but determinedly forth to try to unite civility and courtesy with the implied warning: 'You'll slap my children over my dead body!'

Meanwhile, the newly-enrolled members of the Honourable Society of Passionfruit Thieves scampered out excitedly to spy at the fence, their faces alive with expressions of eager expectancy – absolutely lusting for drama.

Upon opening her door, the woman stammered a surprised, wary greeting. She half-extended an arm hesitantly towards her front room from where, a second later, a stir could be heard. Was it the crash of an overturned chair? Was His Lowness surfacing, affected by the excesses of the night before? Was he struggling now against the punishing authority of gravity and sadistic soundwaves? Margo hoped so.

She certainly did not feel overburdened to accept the invitation to enter. She just handed over the fruit – not through a wish to appease the neighbour, but because it was the proper thing to do. Margo Hughs never compromised her integrity.

Reluctantly, Mrs Next Door received the bag, her staring, frowning face displaying annoyance that she was forced to accept the offering as fair recompense, thus depriving herself of issuing a further pleasurable complaint.

The iniquitous duo crouched by the fence, crushed lavender threatening betrayal with its strong scent riding the breeze and listened intently, willing greater amplification of their mother's voice. She spoke, however, in her usual quiet, and on this occasion, deceptivelycalm accents but added gravity. Her pre-selected words conveyed the most inoffensive yet effective censure possible, warning Mrs Next Door of the *unacceptable* (Margo's euphemism for "perilously dangerous") practice of threatening another woman's children.

The advice was delivered in a shorter time than the spies had wished. It was not the number of words Margo spoke which commanded attention, but the quality. It was not with noise she enunciated them, but with quiet, controlled tones of unmistakable caution.

Paul and Annie, honing their hearing acuity behind the lavender, caught only several responding 'humphs' from *that blessed woman*, the words 'unauthorised trespassing', 'delinquents' and a few feeble exclamations of protest or retaliation, but overall, she appeared to have been crushed into silence. And suddenly spotting the thieves standing up boldly now at the fence (Aesop was right: it is easy to be brave at a safe distance), she fixed upon them a blizzard glare, which promised: 'You'll regret this!' They didn't, however.

When the unpleasant duty was concluded, and when Mrs Brownleigh had been ensconced firmly outside an intangible but impenetrable child-protecting barrier, the Hughs lioness paced back to her own territory with a serene air. Victoriously, she entered her sanctum with cubs, exuding lavender, trailing admiringly.

Her mood and the smiling weather being now in happy equilibrium, Margo took the kettle to the brown teapot, that friendly symbol of domestic comfort. After a few moments' pondering upon all that had happened and speculating what may still occur, she poured a soothing cuppa and sat on the front veranda where her nerves could reclaim their natural tranquillity.

Abruptly, she squawked out a short laugh. 'Ha! "*Unauthorised* trespassing"! Well let me know, Mrs Nasty, when it's authorised,' she gloried to the window, 'and I'll send my so-called "delinquent brats" over to exploit your generosity!' Thus, Margo unwound into grinning reflection – and Annie resolved to quiz her later on that perplexing little outburst.

Ten contemplative minutes passed, and when she emerged from her introspection and became more … *Mum* again, she roused Annie and Paul from their absorption in *Ginger Meggs,* and *Donald Duck* and spoke with gentle guiding influence of their meanness in committing such an outrage upon the vines solely to spite the neighbour.

To close the subject, she issued a brief, edifying finale on the unwise, the unworthy, the unrewarding policy of seeking revenge. Annie saw her mother glance briefly across at next-door and, noticing the upturned chin and triumphal air, the girl perceived how pleased, appeased and satisfied her mum had become.

The Hughs family knew a relative time of peace after that episode, although it had sown the seed of discontent which sprouted over the years and advanced to fruition in the eventual selling of the house. Meanwhile, when the next crop of passionfruit beckoned, the children exercised unwilling restraint in removing only those on their side of the vines, resentfully regarding this sacrifice as an impingement on their rights.

Annie had lived in that beloved fibro house since age three; had watched it grow as it watched her and vowed to stay there forever. Even so, eventually she did fledge the nest. Decades later a nostalgic Annie asked her mother if she also had been sorry to go.

Margo's reply came without hesitation. 'No', she said, 'I never really liked it there after the Brownleighs came … they were the main reason we moved – that and … and Paul,' she added sadly.

8 Josephine Mary

Jack brought home a friend and co-worker, Mr Gerard, accompanied by his wife. Mr Gerard was French, his wife Australian. They were contrasts: he, so dark-haired and olive-skinned and she, light-complexioned with blonde hair worn in the stylish French roll – very apt. The reason for their visit was to meet Margo and discuss a child-minding proposition with her, the object being to provide Mrs Gerard with the freedom to return to work.

The Gerard child was eighteen months old, and Margo expected that he would be the ideal company for her toddler, Josie. The Gerards were pleasant people, and Margo enjoyed the visit. The agreement was reached, the details concluded, and a few days later the Hughs family met cute little Jean-Paul, his father pronouncing the name with French inflections.

Annie was very much in awe of this good-looking man from far-away France who had pronounced Josie's name *Josepha* and with the French-softened initial. When asked her own name (Annette) she withheld the usual diminutive and modified the end: 'Annetta', she replied, for some strange reason believing it sounded more in keeping with his important presence. She managed to ignore her father's little chuckle and was glad Herbie was not there to snigger and reveal her nickname, "Frecks".

'Aah, ma Cherie *Annet-tah*!' Mr Gerard exclaimed, nodding and smiling, and Annie just *loved* the way the sound breathed out over those exotic French vocal cords.

On the first day of the new venture, Margo began to wonder why the little fellow out there in the playpen with Josie, often burst into a fit of crying. She had made several trips down the back steps and over to the playpen to pick him up from where he had apparently fallen and to soothe him before returning to her housework.

But after yet another such episode, she became concerned and decided to stand by the window and watch for a moment to ascertain the reason for his distress. She did not have to wait long. Just as Jean-Paul succeeded in struggling up to clutch the side of the playpen, sweet and gentle, Josie began clobbering him with her doll. Once more, down he went. '*Oh*, so that's—!' Margo rushed out to separate the two toddlers.

It was unsurprising that the child-minding arrangement was short-lived. Initially, Margo had agreed to take care of Jean-Paul only because it represented an advantage in that two children did not require much more effort than one, provided that they proved to be entertaining companions. As well, the remuneration was most welcome – and undoubtedly well-earned. However, Margo had not previously encountered her little daughter's fierce sense of ownership and territoriality and was surprised by the discovery.

Josie, in fact, was incensed that the interloper possessed the audacity not only to trespass onto *her* mat in *her* playpen but also to take the liberty of grasping *her* toys, which she had assembled into a well-guarded corner. The attitude expressed so clearly in Josie's usually angelic, but now coldly staring face might well have been summed up thus:

'*You* have invaded my space! This is *my* castle; *I* am the elder. Therefore you must be subservient to me at all times. If I *must* tolerate your presence, stay in *that* corner and make yourself as small and as insignificant as possible. And ***stop that snivelling!*** Otherwise, I will be forced to continue the punishment until such time as you learn appropriate respect and reverence! Got that? – And stay away from my mother!' Sweet Josephine Mary was only two.

Margo had expressed admiration for Mrs Gerard's composed demeanour and her elegance, likening her to Grace Kelly. When Jack enthusiastically agreed, adding a keen comment about the French-roll hairstyle, Margo began to feel a little dowdy by comparison. Pondering this, she decided to do something with her own hair and went off to the Jannali chemist.

After a few more days of shoring up courage, she did what many women do when needing a lift of spirits – dyed her hair. This action was unprecedented for Margo and before opening the bottle she underwent periods of painful hesitation, for a dye is a dye and

69

would allow no turning back to tresses of natural brown. And so, it was with relief that she, at last, began the brave transformation. But the promised ash brown turned out maroon!

About the same time, Pauly, who had been sent to post a letter, threw a stone at a crow. He missed the cawing black target and hit the passing bus. Margo was yet to learn of this accidental vandalism, and all her concerns were still focused on frantic attempts to remove, or at least subdue, the stubborn dye.

The driver, Clarrie, whom the Hughs had known for "donkey's years", ordered Paul aboard, turned the bus, with its cracked window, off the tarred road and drove it up the hill to the Hughs' place. It was an exceptional event and drew neighbours, notably Mrs Next Door, into their front yards to look, wonder and speculate.

Startled Margo hastily wrapped a towel around her much-washed head and ventured out to the gate where the driver stood with contrite, ground-studying Pauly held prisoner by a firm hand. The bus carried quite a few passengers that day, and all eyes stared. Wisps of maroon hair began straying down around Margo's brightly flushed face. The white towel, providing cruel, stark contrast, started slipping and her hands went up, desperate to secure it. She lamented later, 'I wanted the ground to open up and swallow me!'

When Jack came home, there was more punishment. His initial startled response, predictably dramatic, evolved into laughter and joking. Margo wondered if she would ever be allowed live it down and took to wearing a scarf all day. However, always philosophical, she remarked that her hilarious hair at least served to deflect some attention from Pauly's offence.

It was a cruel quirk of fate that the only time Josie had ever caused an emergency dash to the doctor's happened during the early days of the maroon hair. For some reason known best to her little self, Josie decided to shove a shirt button up her nose, and when the frantic tweezers-fishing produced no button, Herbie was sent over the road to ask Miss Gilbert to telephone for a taxi.

Margo that day pulled her felt hat down as far as it could go to cover her newly cut maroon hair, the effect being unkindly comical. She was relieved to be home again with red-nosed Josie, both safe from further curious scrutiny and barely concealed smiles, but she wondered what her next trial would be and when it would vindictively present itself.

9 Herbie and Frecks

Paul was not always his sister's partner-in-crime; very often they battled each other. Annie fought with beloved Herbie, too – in the bad old days before regarding him as beloved. The two eldest Hughs kids squabbled about everything, especially when brother teased sister with her hated nickname. He, the smarter, reigned victorious for he was not easily provoked, could run faster and had the infuriating habit of laughing at her feeble efforts to strike fear into him.

'GawdYou're a drongo, Frecks!' he'd laugh during disputes as Annie's features contorted instead of screaming crudities at him, which really only emphasised her frustration and defeat.

Herbie's good looks, his tanned, freckle-less skin, and his apparent disregard for incidents, calamitous to Annie, comprised the attributes she admired in him and yearned to possess. Naturally, she loved her brother and vigorously defended him against the slightest hint of outside criticism, but there existed the absurd contradiction in sisterly love and the sometimes-overwhelming desire to shove him off the nearby cliff.

Margo believed that to ignore the irritation was to hasten its oblivion and, frantically busy, became exasperated with her daughter's snivelling complaints. 'For heaven's sake, just ignore him!' she exclaimed whenever Herbie teased, but the girl's head was too lacking in sense for such wise restraint.

'Oo-wah! I'm gunna tell on you, Herbie,' Annie wailed one day, and immediately did so. 'Mu-um! He's throwing dog poo at me.' Hastily she stowed her own cache of sun-dried ammunition under a shrub. The cause of the fight was petty, as usual, but at some time during a moment of low meanness, Annie threatened to smash to smithereens her brother's balsa-wood model aeroplane.

It was only a bluff, but it filled her with a novel feeling of empowerment … until his threat to inflict a "Chinese burn" on her arm caused a sudden shift in the precarious balance of power which sent her streaking indoors, Herbie in pursuit. In her reckless haste, she knocked over the saucepan stand, and the subsequent burst of babe-squawking sent Annie's expectation of mother-protection into oblivion.

Margo promptly appeared and slapped the squabbling pair. 'Now, pick them all up!' she demanded. Paul and Tony stood quietly out of the way by the dresser, their eyes wide and wary as Margo stomped off to rescue the startled infants. In a minute, she returned with teething despot Clivey whinging in his pram and toddler Josie eyeing her role models disdainfully from under her frowning little brows.

A rigorous lecture followed, Margo's air-slicing finger emphasising her words. 'I'm jolly well fed up with the pair of you!' she declared and pointedly lifted her gaze to the mantelpiece clock, a tacit reminder of their father's homecoming. Silenced, at last, they were reduced to using thought transmission, but Margo intervened even in that.

'Now look! If you two can't play outside without trying to murder each other, I can soon find plenty of jobs for you.'

She ceased rocking the pram, spread her fingers and began listing chores from an infinite store of them, always ready for such opportune occasions: 'The bath needs a clean, the floor has to be polished, the fridge could do with a wash-out, and I need more firewood for the copper.'

Advancing narrow-eyed to the thumb, she pushed up her plotting mouth and imposed more anxiety upon the errant pair as she consulted her mental arsenal of penalties. Then the almost-jubilant salvo: 'And you can forget Superman for the rest of the week, and no matinee this Saturday.' Her cold, merciless spirit conveyed: *So there, put that in your pipe and smoke it!*

In all her battles with her brother, Annie triumphed only once. During another dispute, she bounded breathlessly up the back steps to the safe temple of the kitchen. Herbie's navigation of the backyard with its flotsam of kids, billycarts, scooters and leaping dog afforded her a vital rest. As she leaned, panting, on the table, her nose detected sardines. Herbie's loathing of fish, matched only by Annie's repulsion of oysters, begged exploitation.

Villainy urged: *Do it!* She pressed her hand into the dish of smelly, oily fish and waited in trembling expectancy beside the door, ears alert for the scuff of ascending footfalls. This Napoleon was about to meet his Waterloo!

Most obligingly, in ran Herbie – *Splat!* He stumbled away gagging, desperately seeking soap and water. His wicked sister stood there grinning victoriously until jolted by a spasm of panic at the thought of reprisal. She searched for precious Mother to offer her assistance, even if that meant chopping disgusting liver or tripe. There beside Margo, Annie welcomed the colander of pea pods, but with every sense alert to Herbie's approach, she was forced to snatch it up to follow whenever her protector strayed. Ironically, Annie began to resent her unsettling, self-imposed exile. *One of life's little trials.*

With Jack's return, Margo melted into smiling serenity and did not burden him with a report of brat crimes – a fine tribute to her sense of forgiveness, or compassion for her work-weary husband. Subdued now, Herbie and Annie attended their chores without a single haughty glance, but always after that Annie kept the memory of her persecutor's revolted fishy face close to her heart, and it warmed her immensely. *One of life's little compensations.*

Another summer came and with it the incident which brought an end to the shameful fighting. Brother and sister were skylarking down in the river. Herbie was bailing out the flat-bottomed rowing boat (ingeniously called The Flattie), and Annie paddled alongside in their leaking, home-made tin canoe. They both laughed as Herb began dumped the bailed water into the canoe, hastening its submergence, but in the sinking, it rolled over, and the edge of the tin struck Annie's leg.

Upon reaching the wharf they both gasped, shocked by the sight of the blood running down. Herbie, much distressed, lost no time in getting his sister up the series of stone steps, and along the garden path to the back door of the house. There Annie waited, bleeding profusely, while he ran indoors to tell their mother.

Although shocked, Margo quickly dissembled. Her calm voice assured, 'It won't look so bad once I wash the blood off,' and she hastened inside for the necessities. As always, her words and manner provided comfort. Herbie sat with Annie on the step, both of them staring, fascinated with the red oozing.

In a moment, Margo returned with old sheeting to tear into bandages and a bowl of water with drops of antiseptic turning it milky. Using a face-cloth, she gently patted the blood from around the wound, but the gash was gaping and needed to be stitched. While Margo bandaged, Herbie ran across the road to their saviour-in-crises neighbour, Miss Gilbert, and again she assisted by phoning for a taxi.

Dr Sweeny stitched the wound and told Margo to bring Annie back in ten days to have them snipped out. It had been a big ordeal for the girl and, in an empathetic way, also for her brother. Indeed, for both of them, it was an initiation of the reality and stress of pain.

But good came out of it. Annie felt a heightened love for her brother and, appreciating his solicitude, she placed him a notch higher in her estimation and no longer wanted to fight with him. But the most blessed thing of all was that Herbie no longer called her Frecks.

~

10   The Farm

Nana and Grandpa Hughs owned a small farm on the New South Wales South Coast. It was relatively primitive, with no electricity or running water. The rustic setting possessed painted-picture charm, reminiscent of something Constable might have depicted, complete with the contrast of white on the buildings and home fences, and a dab here and there of red.

The farm consisted of eighty acres of bushland, some paddocks and some tea-tree scrub. Over the paddock across from the homestead and against tall gums, stood the holiday cottage; Ruby and Otto Hughs let it to various families at Christmas and Easter. The homestead and the cottage were situated on level elevated ground, the land sweeping in a gentle grassed declivity to the water where there was a jetty with a rowing boat moored alongside.

About one-third of the property was bordered by salt water in an elongated crescent, or bight, with tall Saltwater Oaks flourishing along the shore. There was no necessity for fences by the water, but the other boundaries were fully enclosed by sturdy bush posts and barbed wire.

During the quiet seasons, some of Jack's children often spent a week or so there and, when he and Margo also could get away, they all stayed in that rustic holiday cottage. They went from the bright illumination of electric lights to the soft glow of lamps and candlelight, and every one of them took great pleasure in the holiday and the novel change of routine. That little waterside farm was their Arcadia.

Herb and Annie, one hot season, were recruited to assist their grandparents in the tedious task of raking away the leaves from under the boundary fences to save them from a threatening, but still distant, bushfire near Wandandian. The shrill of cicadas in the thick bush seemed to pierce their eardrums and they all marvelled at the sudden contrast which followed the synchronised cessation of the noise.

The bright plumage of noisy lorikeets lifted all eyes to the sun, vermilion through the haze, and everyone became more aware of the smell of burning eucalyptus drifting heavily in the air. Herb and Annie had always liked that aromatic incense, but now they wished instead for the earthy scent of rain thrashing the parched ground.

Stocky Grandpa, with runnels of sweat scribbling tracks in the dust on his forehead, peered at the distant cloud of smoke and said, 'Well, we've done all we can, so let's go home.' On the way back to the homestead, they threw firewood onto the cart, and Bess, the draught horse, pulled it steadily along, the cartwheels crunching up the sticks and brown leaves on the track as they all walked wearily behind. The great cauliflower clouds mounting the horizon did not send rain to thrash the earth that day, but mercifully for the Hughs, a change of wind direction sent the fire danger elsewhere.

Visitors had no difficulty in locating the property. The first entrance, a white wooden gate in sentinels of white posts bordered by post-and-rail fences, was conspicuous against the background of eucalypts and the understorey of native bush.

From this main gate, the track threaded through tall gums and native undergrowth – a haven for kangaroos and wallabies. The wheel furrows straightened and emerged from the bush to traverse the open paddock with the old homestead westward to the right, and the holiday cottage farther over to the east. Beyond all, was the vista of the beautiful sparkling bay which, nevertheless, frowned grey sometimes and blasted cold Southerlies over the farm.

One year, the holiday cottage was leased to a well-to-do family from Sydney's North Shore area. Bored with their usual expensive holiday destinations, the parents wished to give their children a novel change – the simple life embracing nature.

Paul and Annie were staying at the farm and, excited and curious, left the homestead with their grandparents and strolled across the green expanse of the paddock to welcome the newly arrived visitors. The sleek black Buick appeared shining and grand, yet somewhat incongruous parked there against the provincial weatherboard cottage with its wooden stumps, latticed verandas and corrugated iron roof.

In the family of four, there was a girl aged fifteen who immediately became enthralled with the place. Her smile was bright, and she spoke with an "I-like-you" inflection, emanating an aura of natural gregariousness. 'Oh gosh Mummy, this is super – just s*uper!*' she exclaimed. '*Oh,* and look at the *pony!* Isn't it just the *darlingest?*'

Old Bess, with her big hoofs, large rump and frequently rising tail, was as far from "pony" as a wrestler from a jockey. Paul and Annie grinned at each other with amused astonishment. The girl's name was Penelope, (not Penny-*lope,* as Annie had previously thought and deplored!)

Penelope ran along the three-sided veranda, pausing to lean on the rails and take in the expanse of blue water, starry with sunshine. Everything interested her, and she squinted up through her expensive glasses at the sky of shifting juvenile clouds and then, for a moment, watched their shadows playfully pursuing one another across the paddocks.

The adults became preoccupied talking and looking around at the scenery. For the young boy's benefit, Pauly extended an arm to indicate the entertaining sight of a small flotilla of distant white sails. The boy looked out across the water and nonchalantly replied, 'We keep ours in Bobbin Head.'

Shyly, Annie trailed along after the fascinating, fashionably dressed city girl. Around the veranda, they went and into the kitchen. There, Penelope extolled in sudden raptures the wonder of the wood stove squatting humbly in its alcove. When she noticed Annie, she smiled and exclaimed pleasantly, 'Oh, hello there!'

If hierarchy were to be established, that was the moment, but only a self-conscious grin greeted her – awe had stolen impressionable Annie's tongue. Penelope was replete with enthusiasm. 'Oh, I can't wait to see how this *dearest* cooker works,' she said, moving her hands about in graceful expression. 'Isn't it just the most … most …?' and unable to find a worthy superlative, she released a huge sigh, lifted her shoulders, spread her hands outward and grinned comically.

The girl from North Sydney was curiously elated at the prospect of a fortnight's endurance of privations. She gloried in the *cute* lamps and candles and in the novelty of pure rainwater which came directly from a tank outside the kitchen – *super!* Annie decided that she liked this strange girl, so confident, so "posh", who nevertheless appreciated all the primitivism of her grandparents' holiday cottage – including the ingenious idea of the sticky flypaper hanging from the ceiling!

Try as she would, Annie could not quell her amazement at the girl's elation over all things mundane. She almost expected Penelope to fly into ecstasies when the moment arrived for her to encounter the *divine* pit lavatory out the back near the *super* woodheap by the *darling* leaning trellis of grapes thriving in Bess's *splendid* fertiliser!

Margo later laughed gently and said: 'Oh, God *bless* her!'

11 Jack the Joker

Whether their recreation was spent as holidays at the farm, picnics to Towra Beach or to a spot up the river or, as was more usual, a period of simple leisure-time at home, all members of the Hughs family were orientated towards fishing. Sitting quietly in the boat, they used hand-lines to catch bream and mullet in the river, and when the "tailor-ticing" season arrived, they ventured further into deep waters and dragged vicious-looking tri-pronged hooks on lines behind the launch as it churned along under the stars.

The tailor catch was usually plentiful. Margo often sent a bag of cleaned fish over to Miss Gilbert's, and occasionally the surplus went to neighbour Molly Martin on the east side of their house.

At any time of year, the older Hughs children set down roughly constructed fish traps near the wharf or under the towering cliff and sometimes out by the island of mangrove near the channel, resulting in moderate success.

Even after the tide had ebbed, a hessian bag scooped along the dished-bottom of their netted swimming baths, occasionally caught prawns that were trapped in the pooled water left behind. Many a time, the youngsters, at perfect liberty to expand their resourcefulness, picked out the tiny portions of meat from the small crabs and peri-winkles they had cooked on riverbank campfires. Considering all this, it is fair to state that their diet was well supported by the bounty of the sea.

Jack, Paul and Tony were relaxing in the backyard one warm late afternoon sitting near the low rock wall opposite the chook yard. They were busy detangling fishing lines, and the conversation, quite naturally, was about fish.

One of the boys asked: 'How long do fish live Dad if they don't get caught?'

And the other posed the logical question: 'Do they just keep growing bigger and bigger into giant fish?'

Jack Hughs, an expert when it came to recognising fertile ground for a yarn, became increasingly interested in the subject and proceeded to expound on his hypothesis for the longevity of fish … quite forgetful of his cynical daughter tuned in on the nearby swing.

'You see,' he began, 'some fish are so healthy and clever that no one can ever catch them, so they just keep growing. Next thing you know they have big scaly legs, green slimy arms, and jaws that could snap a man in two!' To his credit, Jack gave full measure to his own particular version of the theory of evolution. The boys gasped and gazed in wonder, seeing clearly the image their dad had conjured. He finished winding one reel and took up another, his creative mind already busy on the next part of the story. Tony initiated it by asking where the dangerous creatures live.

'Well, I wasn't going to tell you this, but seeing you've asked me...' Jack conceded expansively, feeling highly qualified in the essential knowledge concerning all things nautical and monstrous. 'It so happens that the biggest, most ferocious, man-eating monsters in the whole world live right here in Oyster Bay. Right here! And I'll tell you something else.' He paused dramatically and moved his face closer to the awe-struck young boys. 'I've *seen* one!' This confidence was imparted in a reverent whisper, which quite challenged the efficacy of Annie's hearing faculty.

'Have you?' they chimed, and there was an undeniable, most gratifying blend of amazement and admiration in their voices and expressions for their invincible father. 'Fair dinkum, Dad?'

Jack gave a sideways nod of serious affirmation and abandoned the fishing lines. 'Too right!' he said. With slow deliberation, he lit up a cigarette, allowing time for further fabrication. 'Yairs, right down there in the channel, just this side of the mangrove island.'

Annie was sitting there on the swing methodically spitting out mandarin seeds and observing how far they could be projected. She stopped for a moment and thought: Isn't that the spot where they always set the fish traps?

'Aah, come on Dad!' exclaimed Paul. 'You're pulling our legs, aren't ya? 'cause we were there today putting traps down, and we would've seen it!' he reasoned. Yet he shivered at the unthinkable and glanced nervously at Tony for corroboration which was swiftly imparted by much nodding of the head.

Initially, Jack feigned foreboding response but then changed tack for reasons later apparent. 'Well, I dunno about that,' he mused, leaning back against the warm sandstone wall bordering Margo's clothesline area. He stretched out his legs, crossed his ankles and took a long, contemplating draw on the cigarette while the boys waited expectantly for more exciting shocks. Playing for time and inspiration, he projected his lower lip forward, blew a plume of smoke upwards and watched it dissipate as he concentrated on his next sentence.

The plot hatched, Jack sat forward and returned his full attention to owl-eyed Tony and the doubter, Paul. 'See, it was sunny then, wasn't it, and these fellas don't like that. No. They hide over near Oyster Bill's boatshed till the sun goes down, and then out they come to search for food.' But, feeling that mere words did not suffice, he stood his height and formed a half-circle with his arms to indicate the dimensions of the monster's gaping mouthparts.

There followed much pacing about, dramatic flinging of arms and animation of expression, all necessary to relay the profound agitation he was experiencing because of the memory of his mythical near-encounter.

'What an actor!' muttered Annie, sniggering away there on the swing.

He seemed to be on the point of imparting another gem of thought: brows up; eyes focused unseeing on something distant; mouth opening to liberate the new bit of brilliance … but was interrupted by little Josie tugging at his sleeve. 'What is it, love?' he asked, flinging down the cigarette after its glowing end had bitten his nicotine-stained fingers. (No filter-tips then.)

'Mummy thaid tea ith weddy,' she lisped charmingly. Her attention was diverted at that moment by the flapping, hen-mounting rooster in the yard beyond. 'Oh! Oh! Naughty woothta!' she cried, stamping her foot in agitation. She frowned up at her dad, puzzled by his laughter. 'Him alwayth do that! Chop him head off, Daddy!' ordered the sweet little thing.

'Righteo love,' Jack said to humour her. 'Now, you go and tell Mum we'll be there in a minute.' And, still grinning, he crushed the cigarette butt under a boot and packed away his lines. He did not, however, pack away his imaginative train of thought, a process that was coursing ever forward to creative magnificence. Silent and mischievously meditative, he followed the young ones towards the enticing aroma of shepherd's pie being served.

It was nearing summer. As the clear, long day began to relinquish light to the curtaining dusk, Jack reminded the boys that their fish traps were still in the channel awaiting inspection. He offered brief speculation on the sort of fish they might have caught, 'Maybe a big flathead!' A crafty insurance against their possible reneging at the last moment.

'But what about the monsters, Dad?' asked Tony as he collected the table scraps for the chooks – one of his allotted responsibilities for the day. Margo, by this time, was busy in another room and had been spared, or denied, the tale of the monsters. Jack, noting her absence, warned the boys against frightening 'Mum and the girls' with their terrible knowledge. Annie's earlier silent presence and attentive ears had been overlooked, so they felt safely united in their exclusively male secret.

Glancing at the dimming sky, Jack reassured Tony: 'Well, the big blokes won't come out till dark, so you'll have time to check the traps. You and Pauly do your jobs now and then get going. I'll come down soon,' he promised. This shrewd arrangement allowed Mr Stealthy time to slip away unnoticed down the backyard. Off he went past the vegetable gardens and trellises, along the path with its dry-stone wall and down the steps to the wharf and slips where *The Margo* was resting.

A little later when the boys scrambled down the same steps, Jack merged into the shadows. The tide was low and the water pleasantly warm. They lifted the anchor off the wharf, dumped it into the Flattie and climbed in. Paul took the oars, slid them into the rowlocks and, leaning forward, he began rowing.

'We'd better hurry before it gets dark,' he said urgently to Tony who was already glancing around nervously at the still water, and he spoke in a loud and bold voice to quell his anxiety.

The oars quietly, rhythmically plop-plopped through the surface towards the channel and the foreboding dark mangroves beyond, until the boat had reached the small sapling poles sunk into the mud to mark the trap sites. Together the boys pulled up the first trap. It was empty. They dropped it with a loud watery announcement.

'Sssssh!' cautioned Paul. 'Don't make any noise ... just in case.' And all the time the human submarine's periscope ears were nearby, just above the water and beyond their view.

The boys proceeded more quietly to lift the second trap. Suddenly, the bow of the boat lurched up and down in a loud splashing commotion. They abandoned the trap, dropped onto the back seat and hung on. Before recognition had time to preclude alarm, the leviathan roared up out of the briny bay.

'The *fing!*' shrieked Tony as he clung to the reassuring frame of big brother.

Dubious Paul, however, realised there was something very familiar about the "monster". 'Aaw, it's onlyDad!' he declared, with a distinct note of grinning relief in his voice. 'We were gunna whack you with the oars, Dad!' he informed the laughing shape now clambering into the boat. 'And anyhow, we knew all the time it was you!' he exclaimed.

It would be reasonable to assume Jovial Jack would have behaved himself after Margo's castigation that evening. Not so – there was more excitement waiting. Jack had been listening to the wireless, and he relayed to Margo, as though it were a personal triumph, the news that Jimmy Carruthers had become the first Australian to win a world boxing title. 'Well, whata-y'-know! Woo-hoo!' he exclaimed jubilantly and made an air-punching gesture. 'The South African didn't even last three minutes – Carruthers knocked him out with the first punch!'

Margo, not really interested, made some acceptable response and went about her work, but her children's impatient objective was to remove command of the wireless from their news-hungry father and change the station. They didn't want to miss a single shuddering syllable of their favourite programme, 'The Witches Tale'. Jack obligingly sat at the table, content with his bottle of wine and still revelling over Jimmy Carruthers' fantastic win. The kids settled down on the mat in front of the wireless with typical kid-masochism to thrill again at being frightened witless.

The scary stories were always prefaced by Nancy the witch crackling out the same creepy appetiser to ensnare children's ravenous imaginations and lead them into the main course. 'Heh, heh, heh!' she cackled wickedly to her devilish black cat. 'A hunerd 'n 'leven year old I be today, Satan ... yes, sir! a hunerd 'n 'leven year old.' She always elongated the words in an eerie, foreboding drawl: 'And now I be tellin' ye a tale that'll cu-u-rdle y' blood!'

Here, she would pause sufficiently to allow the studio sound effects to increase the fear. That nicely accomplished, she continued on in the following vein: 'It all begins on a night as black as a tomb with a cold wind scre-e-eamin' across the moors. Wolves are a-howlin' and the shutters a-bangin' ...' And then she'd rumble low and ominously in her rattly old voice enticing her listeners into the heart of the story.

As Nancy's tales seeped into the children's brains, they became wholly hypnotised. Every Saturday night, forsaking all else, they sat as close as was possible to the wireless speaker and their actual world ceased to exist as they were carried along the exciting trail of intrigue towards the thrilling fright at the end.

One evening, a particular story portrayed the adventures of a severed hand that terrified children as it crabbed around in the dead of night leaving its trail of blood. It then sprang up with spider agility, turned the doorknob and, finally mounting someone's bed, searched out the neck and strangled the victim. It was real bed-time story stuff, an illogical blending of horror and delight which Jack's kids relished – little chips off the old block of seasoned tomfoolery that they were.

So entirely enthralled were they during that particular story, that no one noticed their father switching out the lights. When the frightening climax was thrust at them – violins screeching, 'cello droning, cymbals attacking each other – Jack clamped his big cold hand on the back of Annie's neck. The explosion of shrieks this produced woke the baby and almost catapulted Margo from the bedroom to investigate, angrily snapping on the lights as she advanced.

Jack Hughs was in serious trouble, a development that enlivened his children with renewed happiness. Margo thumped him. 'When will you ever grow up?' she scorned. *Whack!* 'You're just a big kid!' *Whack-whack!*

Jack, as always, affected innocence. 'What did *I* do?' This earned him a few more thumps. Laughter had stolen his strength: 'By gee, the mozzies are bad tonight!' he managed between bouts of body-shaking hilarity.

'Oh, you!' Margo scoffed. 'Scaring them like that! They'll all have nightmares'.

'But I was only making it more realistic for them,' he explained in weak defence.

'Realistic, my foot! You were scaring the living daylights out of them. Now get to bed, you big overgrown kid!' And Jack, a helpless puppet to Laughter, allowed his gentle little dove to propel him towards the conjugal nest – exultant "dovelets" following.

'Help me, kids!' he entreated as he allowed their mother to push him onto the bed, and he wrapped his arms around his head in mock protection. 'Y'see what I suffer from this wild woman?' That scored him another thump. 'Aw, knock it off, woman!' At last, he surrendered. 'Ah, you're a hard woman at times, Sweet-one,' he groaned, puffing with the effort of recovery.

'Yes,' answered Margo, scooping up the whinging baby. She was trying to exert stern wifely authority but could not hide the treacherous mirth rising in her own voice. 'And I can be a lot harder, too, and you'll find out for yourself if you turn the lights out again next time.'

And it came to pass that on the following Saturday night the children settled down in front of the wireless again to listen to The Witches Tale ... in total darkness!

12   Adding On

Eventually, Margo and Jack had saved enough money to begin the "add-ons". Grandad Carrington, years before, had built his own house and was glad to come at weekends to help his son-in-law. Naturally, they began with the digging and bricklaying. After school, Paul and Annie played in the spaces among the piers, and when the bearers were in place, they started leaping across from one to another, just as they did with their beds – although making foot contact with narrow bearers required balance and sharp concentration.

When Margo saw them engaged in this activity, she cried out in alarm for them to stop at once. After beckoning the children indoors, she related the story of her maternal grandmother who, when a child, had been doing precisely the same thing and had fallen and severely injured her leg. Great Grandmother, then aged about five, had disobeyed her father's warning to stay off the bearers and, too afraid to tell her parents about the fall, she lay in bed enduring hours of pain.

Providence was not protecting the child that night – a downpour flooded the creek that separated the house from the road. Her parents, frantic upon discovery of her fracture, were unable to get help. Days passed, and when the torrent eased, and the depth subsided enough for her father to cross, he carried her to the nearest horse and buggy, and finally, medical aid. But it was too late – the leg had become gangrenous and had to be amputated. The brave, dark-haired little girl from Werris Creek grew up and became a tailor, later to marry and bear five children. One of them, Alice, became Margo's mother.

After two bedrooms and a kitchenette were added to the Hughs' house, a carpenter affixed the cupboards and bench. The electrician wired up several power points and the plumber installed a shiny stainless-steel sink. Margo had always washed-up in a large enamel dish on the table and drained everything on a tray. Back then, every drop of water for the kitchen had to be carried from the laundry, so she gratefully welcomed the tap and sink in her new kitchenette. Even so, there was no *hot* water – it still was necessary to use the electric jug, or the kettle if the wood stove was alight, for every dishwashing.

The kitchenette brought ease and pleasure to Margo. In past summers, she had cooked on two camp-style "metho stoves" but now took delight in the new electric stove. Yet in colder weather, she remained loyal to her old green and cream *Bega*, economical while wood was plentiful, and a reliable backup during blackouts. Jack often declared that the fuel stove was the heart of the house – a warm heart in winter. He savoured the incense of the she-oak needles and eucalyptus leaves on first lighting and often went outside to enjoy the sight of the rising chimney smoke, sometimes white and puffing, other times bluish against the tall gums.

The kitchen was an enticing place. During winter the cooking space at the back of the stove was regularly given over to a pot of soup or stew smelling deliciously of beef, rabbit or less often, poultry, with vegetables and herbs. There, they simmered gently, waiting for the dumplings to be dropped in. The kettles sang to each other, an assurance that all was well with the house's heart, and often from the oven there drifted the delightful aroma of a cake or a batch of biscuits.

As the children grew up, there were many material things they went without but they were a well-fed bunch. Much of their food was homegrown, all of it home-cooked, a significant proportion of the protein being obtained from the beloved river.

Time moved on, and as the Hughs kids watched one another's progress through all the gradations of growth, they also followed the evolution of their house. Asbestosis (as before mentioned) was not generally known about then and Jack, like many others, was using fibro sheeting to line the new rooms. He tackled the front bedroom first.

Cutting the last sheet to size, he asked Annie to draw a treasure map to hide behind the lining; he wanted the sketch to depict land on the other side of the river. 'In a hundred years someone will find it and search for the treasure,' he prophesied. The map was drawn; he rolled it up and placed it in on one of the noggings and nailed up the fibro.

Before lining the other bedroom, Jack used the space as a storage area for his numerous bottles of ginger beer brewed in the laundry's large copper when lemons were plentiful. Each bottle was corked tightly in optimistic defence against the growing pressure of the brew. Despite this, it became quite usual for the family's slumber to be interrupted by the metallic bang of wine cork missiles striking the unlined tin roof. Eventually, Jack lined the room and put up a ceiling, and that place became his and Margo's.

Relative to the times, the Hughs had made steady progress in their small part of the world. The house, which had started life as a simple dwelling with only one bedroom, a single power point and no kitchen tap, had expanded over the years to become a modest, comfortable home with three bedrooms, two verandas and all of it newly painted. Green – naturally.

13 The Wireless

Jack worked in the city where he worked as a chef, as did his father before him. Every day Jack walked, cycled or took the bus to Como railway station then boarded a train for the journey to Central. From there he took a tram or walked along Pitt Street to the restaurant.

It became the children's habit, whenever Margo took them in the train to the city, to watch out for "Dad's sign". It was painted in large lettering on the rear of a building not far from Central, so positioned to offer train travellers time for contemplation. The kids called it Dad's sign because their father had expressed a great appreciation of its message: *What you eat today walks and talks tomorrow.* Both parents had been brought up on fresh, plain, healthful food and Jack encouraged his children to think about the message on the wall and endeavour to live by it.

That was not difficult. As soon as the famished tribe entered the house after school, Margo handed out nutritious snacks: the end crusts of fresh bread with various spreads; chocolate milkshakes, or lemon drinks when the fruit was in season; and sometimes breakfast biscuits spread with honey. It was something they looked forward to after being out all day. In perfect contentment, they then settled down with their snacks in front of the wireless to relax and enjoy the serials before going out to play.

"Wire*less*" seemed to be a contradiction in terms – it had *many* wires. It also was the heartbeat of the house (this status shared only with the fuel stove), and the family revered its particular set. Apart from the launch, for many years the polished wood cabinet-style wireless was the Hughs' most valuable possession (Margo's treadle sewing machine, a close second), the wireless' initial value equating to several weeks' wages then. It remained thus prized until Jack bought their first electric refrigerator, but wherever it hovered on their domestic gauge of economic importance, the wireless remained a vital part of family life.

All had their favourite programmes, and there were plenty of stations providing variety: music, song, drama, news, quiz shows, comedy, and for children, exciting afternoon serials. It seemed unfair that hard-working Jack could not avail himself of the wireless' entertainment as often as desired, but he always made a concerted effort to be home in time for any fights relayed live from the Sydney Stadium.

Of vital interest on one occasion, was the forthcoming battle between the favourite and much publicised American boxer Freddy Dawson and Australia's Vic Patrick. Everyone – neighbour, grocery man, baker and milkman – was talking about the fight during the weeks leading up to the great night. Jack Hughs of course, made many speculations regarding the possible outcome of the match and everyone at his house became aware that only his death or the failure of the wireless would prevent him from hearing the broadcast.

To preclude the possibility of the latter misfortune, Jack, professing absolute confidence in the technical competence of the repairman, arranged for the set to be completely overhauled a fortnight before the fight so that all he then had to do was to remain in good health and be home early on the special night.

His children waved him off to work that morning with the last of his oft-repeated warnings resounding in their heads: they were not to lay a finger on the precious wireless; definitely, they were to abstain from turning any of the small brown knobs, and even from leaning against the polished wooden cabinet.

Margo was relieved after she had sent at least half of her liabilities off to school for the day. Diligently she strove to keep the others away from the wireless and turned it off to lessen its attraction which, with all the recent interest, had become like a magnet to metal filings. However, with the afternoon hours slowly and hazardously wearing away, she decided to turn the set on and have it warmed up and running smoothly for Jack's homecoming.

But the sacrosanct wireless would not respond! The children learnt of the disaster when they arrived home from school and found their mum fiddling with the knobs and apparently very upset. Her usually smooth forehead was creased with worry, and she answered an emphatic *'No!'* in a distracted manner to all requests.

It was evident when she stood and straightened her back, that she had been on her knees for some time, and it was equally apparent that the hitherto wondrous talking cabinet was not speaking that day.

Maternal compassion stepped in then and saved the brood from starvation. Margo set about with a sort of silent, frowning automation mixing cocoa and sugar into hot milk to accompany the Anzac biscuits she had baked earlier. And then her attention flew back to the sulking wireless.

'One of the little ones must have fiddled with it this morning ... somehow,' she muttered in her distress, 'and oh, today of all days!' She gave the cabinet another shake. Nothing happened, so she decided the next best thing to do was to have all her children fed, bathed and in bed before the breadwinner arrived home.

This, she attended to and, warning them of the folly of shenanigans, advised an instant departure into the deepest slumber and closed their door. But boring old sleep was the last thing on their active minds. Confined to safe quarters, they read comics, sprang from bed to bed, their ghost shapes *woo-wooing* under floating white sheets ... and it was all such riotous fun that they almost forgot World War III was imminent.

Pauly had been posted *lookout* by the window. 'Here he comes!' he shrilled in sudden drama and a deep hush at once descended over the chaos of the room. But Pauly was suddenly struck by a spasm of lunacy, and before anyone could intervene, he leapt from the window and ran out past the gate towards his unsuspecting father.

'The wireless doesn't work, Dad!' he announced in a loud, important voice. Margo, also keeping an eye on the front gate, hurried out, grasped the young herald by the back of his striped pyjamas and ushered him swiftly into the house and the bedroom. Jack's pleasure, built up over many weeks, vanished instantly, to be replaced by an understandable display of almost incandescent fury.

Young ears listened at the door, at intervals eyes stared around at one another and mouths gasped at Jack's explosion of swear words and blasphemy. Annie opened the door a little and peeked out. Her mother was serving the master's dinner.

'No, Jack, the kiddies didn't go near it,' she said with smooth aplomb and lowered coils of spaghetti onto the plate. Jack gave up tinkering with the back of the wireless and began pacing with the restless energy of a caged lion, angrily raising his arms to vindictive Fate and exclaiming in a voice of agonised incredulity the absolute irony of it all.

'I can't believe it!' he almost shouted. 'The one night *I* want to listen to thebastard of a thing it doesn't bloody-well work!' After a long and colourful denunciation of the repairman with whom he had entrusted the overhauling of the precious "bastard of a thing" and whose fault, therefore, the disaster obviously must be, he gave the perfidious cabinet a sudden kick.

Margo shot him a quick, sideways glance of alarm and went on spooning the hot mince over the spaghetti. 'Try not to get too upset about it, Jack,' she said, hoping to mitigate his rage and endeavouring to employ calmness to cover her own nervousness. 'There'll be other fights,' she added in a last attempt to pacify him.

But her words of solace were met with blazing-eyed, hostile resistance. Her husband was on that high plateau of unappeasable anger from which only the restoration of the wireless' fickle soul, or the passing of merciful time, or the immediate extermination of the repairman could bring him down.

'T' hell with *other* bloody fights!' he exploded, '*This* fight – Freddy DawsonandVic Patrick. *This's* the one I've been looking forward to for *bloody weeks!*' he reminded her needlessly. With a sudden heart-stopping bound to the capricious wireless and with a violent excess of energy, he lifted the whole thing up and crashed it back down onto the floor.

'Oh, for heavens' sake!' Margo exclaimed in a spasm of fright and appalled disapproval, '*that* won't do any good!' She knew not to suggest that he go over to Martins' place to hear the broadcast, for it was one of his principles never to prevail upon others for anything and being fiercely independent, the proud man now had to suffer the unfair consequences. It was all too much for him, and his eyes flashed in absolute rage.

'Bah!' he roared. Resorting to his usual radical method of dealing with such situations, he grabbed the wireless again. With a strength the kids, peeping boggle-eyed from the bedroom, did not know he possessed, he shoved the large cabinet across the kitchen floor where it slid out the back door and landed with a crash ... and they stared mutely at one another as the glass panel smashed into shards on the concrete porch.

When the last tinkle had faded into silence, the children closed the door with careful stealth and crept into bed where they remained statue-still, listening intently for the expected sounds of another assault on the wireless and probably its complete obliteration.

How worrying it was for them! Their concern for the wireless carried a selfish aspect – it was the reliable broadcaster of *Hop Harrigan, Superman, Biggles, Yes What* and *The Witch's Tales*. As they listened for more drama in the kitchen, Annie imagined her mother glaring at her father and shaking her head. After a short interval, voices could again be heard, Jack's querying and Margo's defensive in the answer. Finally, she reminded him that his dinner was getting cold.

There was a protracted period of silence, which prompted the children to look at one another in wonder. When the suspense and curiosity could no longer be endured, they crept back to the door and opened it an eye width. Jack was sitting at the table, head in hands, the spaghetti and mince untouched before him.

The wireless, its front mutilated, had been retrieved and Margo was staring at it most attentively. Then, obeying a queer little impulse, she rose from her chair, pressed the plug into the power point and switched it on. Oh! Miracles *do* happen! The wireless worked! Jack turned his head in jubilant astonishment and beamed at his genius wife. The chair scraped back noisily, and in one stride he was bent before the set, turning the knob to set it to the correct station in plenty of time for the fight.

Relief, happiness and gratitude were at once in evidence in the room and a possible sense of shame on Jack Hughs' part for the fury he had unleashed, advertised there before him now for all to see in the damage inflicted upon the set – its former aesthetic qualities undoubtedly consigned to memory.

With the wireless working faultlessly, he drew Margo into his arms and hugged her closely for a long time, trying to atone for his actions and the general upset. The spies at the door knew the war was over; knew it was safe at last to run out and stare appalled at the injured wireless; to kiss both parents goodnight and then perhaps read a few more comics before their mum came in to put the light out.

14 Starlings

There were starlings nesting beneath the eaves of the house. 'Starlings bring lice,' Jack reminded Margo one morning and began contriving a way to eradicate them. Immediately after breakfast he went into the shed and carried out a wooden fruit box, hammer and nails, and his expression was eager and determined as he removed its base in readiness for a wire-netting replacement.

'What's Dad doing, Herbie?' asked Annie, carrying her bride doll down the back steps.

'Making a trap,' he mumbled and reminded her again, as he was now a teenager, to call him Herb.

'What for?' she persisted, forgetting to acknowledge the reminder.

'To trap the starlings,' he told her. 'And its *Herb* now,' he added, to help it sink in.

'Okie-Dokie,' Annie said. 'And when I'm thirteen you have to call me Ann*ette*.' She sat companionably next to him, and he immediately moved up a step, disdainfully distancing himself from Princess Elizabeth in her flowing bridal finery. 'He doesn't expect them to just walk into it, does he?' Annie asked.

''Course not dill-brain, but he'll catch 'em. Probably use breadcrumbs, and then kill 'em.'

'*Kill* them!' his sister cried, even though she knew that would be the logical result.

'Well, what else would he do?'

'Yeah, I know … but anyhow' (a shrug of unconcern) 'he won't catch 'em. Birds are clever. They won't fall for the breadcrumbs trick.'

'Wanta bet?'

There were two things relating to mental stimulation that Herbie – *Herb* – and Annie particularly delighted in: debating, otherwise known as arguing, and betting upon the outcome of some activity.

They began thinking about what they could wager. Herb confidently, and somewhat uninterestedly, offered his tattered old Phantom comic and much-dented skull ring. Annie's catapult seemed a safe risk. Margo had declared war on it after her daughter accidentally shot her on the bottom a week before and she had been trying to find it ever since … but Annie saw no reason to share that incriminating bit of information with Herb.

Jack's hammering ceased. He looked pleased and satisfied as he surveyed the newly fashioned trap. Propping up one end using a stick with a string attached, he tossed the string ball up over the back-veranda windowsill. Then, regretfully complicit Margo at the back door handed down some breadcrumbs which Jack scattered under the trap. Herb paused to grin back at Annie – he was right about the breadcrumbs.

'Now you kids come in here,' Jack ordered as he bounded up the steps.

They waited, quiet as mice. The white crumbs soon attracted the starling's attention. Fluttering down, they peered around guardedly for predators and hastened under the box to feed. Jack pulled the string – SLAM! Three little birds crashed about their prison in absolute panic; indisputable proof that man is smarter than a bird.

At once Annie's heart filled with worry for the starlings' future, which didn't seem at all lengthy, and the appalled query sprang from her trembling mouth. '*Now* what happens to them?' Before Herb could answer, Jack hurled the birds down hard onto the concrete, and mercifully, they knew no more.

Herb nodded at them dispassionately and shrugged. **'That's** what happens!'

Annie broke into tears. 'That's cruel!' she wailed, staring down rainy-eyed at the three feathery forms and then up at the avid face of their executioner. 'That's *so* cruel, Dad!'

Jack flicked a glance at her. 'No, love, they didn't know what hit them,' he muttered absently, sparing a full two seconds of compassion to lessen a young girl's anguish as enthusiastically, victoriously, he reset the trap. It occurred to Annie then, noting Herb's keen expression, that men and boys all seem to have rock-hard hearts.

The death rate of starlings quickly increased. They needed burying. A sudden, novel notion checked the flow of tears. 'Herbie, – *Herb,* – we could give them a funeral, and you could be Father McKinley. What a beaut idea!' Annie exclaimed. She was almost happy again!

Herb pulled his features into a withering sneer: '*Dooon't* be stupid,' he scorned. Remembering their bet and casting new maturity momentarily aside, he went off to retrieve the catapult from where he knew it was hidden – behind the picture of the Blessed Virgin Mary, the recently appointed guardian of homemade weaponry.

Thus rebuffed, Annie knew she had no choice but to conduct the funeral alone … while her father continued his murdering. A funeral is a weighty responsibility. It fell upon the young sufferer to provide the services of grave-digger, priest and floral bearer. And so, using this activity to lessen her grief, she sat Princess Elizabeth on the garbage bin lid and went under the house. Soon there were nine tiny graves, decorated with flowers and marked by twig crosses, lined up at the base of the chimney.

However, after burying and praying over sixteen suicidal starlings, whose intelligence Annie now rated as infinitesimal, the reality of her father's words at breakfast struck. Lice! How gruesomely awful it would be, she realised, to suffer the onslaught of filthy bird-lice crawling down the walls into the house – most specifically into her bed! Reliable imagination augmented this most disturbing realisation and depicted the white wall turning dark; a terrifying shadow moving soundlessly, inexorably downwards.

Annie's concern for the birds' welfare vanished. It had been a waste of time and a tedious, fiddly task making all those little crosses. The floor bearers had twice cruelly descended to whack her unprotected skull – as though blows from a mallet. And nipping fleas, waiting impatiently for Thumper's warm blood, condescended to feast upon some of hers.

Inspecting the bumps on her daughter's head, sympathetic Margo suggested the practicality of a mass grave – a most agreeable alternative. So, Jack took time off from his bird-slaying to dig a trench in the garden into which he intended later to empty the lavatory pan and then plant some bean seeds. It mattered not to Annie now where the birds were buried. Her reliable olfactory sense had been aroused by the whiff of the caraway-seed cake

Margo had removed from the oven, and her stomach was experiencing the first debilitating signs of malnourishment.

The children gathered around to receive the warm, fragrant slices of cake. Margo smiled amusedly at her now dry-eyed daughter, and then at Jack. 'Marvellous how quickly the young heart recovers from grief, dear,' she remarked.

15 The Accident

The postman's whistle shrilled one morning as he poked a letter into the Hughs' post box. Annie ran out to retrieve the letter and then took it indoors to her mother. Margo's face grew serious as she opened out the page. 'It's from Nana Hughs. Oh! There's been an accident!'

'Not Grandpa? Or Uncle Charlie?' asked Annie urgently before her mum could finish what she was about to say.

Margo read on: 'No ... no, a bus and ... and a log truck ... oh dear *God!*'

'*What* Mum?'

She finished reading and without speaking, handed Annie the letter.

What Annie read remained with her for a very long time.

Her grandmother's letter, dated 18th April 1951, began: 'Dear Margo and Jack. You probably heard on the wireless about the bus accident down here yesterday. We can hardly believe it! It was horrific!'

'Dad, Charlie and I were actually travelling behind the bus after shopping at Nowra and were on our way home. It was a Parlour Coach, *Aussie Tours* from Sydney and full of tourists. We

114

lost sight of the bus when we stopped for petrol at Falls Creek and later turned off the highway, so we forgot about it. But we'll never forget it now. This is what the *Nowra News* headlined: It says "Six die in tourist smash near Nowra".

'Here are the main parts from that front-page report. "Three Huge Logs Shoot Through Bus. Five passengers and the driver of a tourist bus were killed yesterday when the bus collided with a semi-trailer jinker, laden with three giant logs, near Wandandian, 18 miles from Nowra … (The logs) weighing up to 4 tons each were forced through the cabin of the bus instantly crushing five of the passengers to death."

'It says that one of the women was decapitated.' Nana wrote, 'and there's a list of names and addresses of the dead and injured, and then more details. Apparently, the bus swerved across the road and went head-on into the cabin of the semi-trailer. It says here, "The logs plunged through the door and windows of the bus and emerged through the windows on the other side. The driver and passengers in the first three seats were killed instantly."'

'There follows heart-rending details regarding the dead and dying (which you may be able to imagine)' wrote Nana. 'And then there's something about the lack of hospitalisation at Nowra, so the poor people had to be taken the thirty or so miles to Berry. (Something should be done about Nowra's old hospital. Otto and I have been saying that for years!) There is a sad bit here from one of the passengers who said that there wasn't any panicking because the survivors of the seventeen passengers were just too shocked, even to speak. Poor blighters!'

And as if to show that life still goes on the same for everyone else, Nana added a postscript. 'By the way, Annie left her two-storey wooden pencil case here last time so we'll bring it with us at Christmas. Hope you are all well, Love from Mum.'

The details of this incredible bus and semi-trailer accident remained in people's minds and on their lips for a long time afterwards. Six decades since, it is still sorrowfully remembered by some older people, who were then young adults when it happened, and by others who were mere impressionable children.

16 Bedtime stories

Saturday to the Hughs children (if homework was completed), meant fun: rowing, swimming in the summer, playing various games or merely idling the morning away taking pleasure in just doing nothing – and being good – for exemplary behaviour was rewarded with a shilling for the matinee at the Como Pictures.

They cherished Sundays too, once the obligatory attendance of morning Mass was behind them. The weekly ritual, so symbolic of the Roman Catholic religion, was strictly enforced, not so much by their parents but by the interrogating brothers and nuns under whose authority they were educated. Mr and Mrs Hughs no longer attended Mass. Margo pleaded exemption owing to domestic and maternal duties, and Jack had descended into heathen-hood. Annie thought her dad was shameful because he had no respect for prayers and often found ways to alter the wording. For example: "Hail Mary full of grace …" became "full of *rice*", and "mourning and weeping in this valley of tears" became "valley of *queers*."

Margo proclaimed to her children that if their father ever crossed the hallowed threshold, the Church roof would fall in. But *they* had to go. Their reluctant participation in the hour of Latin and religious rhetoric was punctuated by genuflecting, sitting, standing and staring with affected attentiveness at their Sunday

Missals. They lined up at the altar rail to receive Holy Communion and then, seated again, tongue-stroked the host, which usually stubbornly adhered to the roof of the mouth for the remainder of the hour.

Sunday Mass attendance was further enforced by the prospect of having to confess the mortal sin, had they defaulted, to a thunder-faced priest, or of being transported after death directly to hell to burn for Eternity. Annie, one day, was suddenly struck by the significance of that term. She pondered, appalled, upon her own estimation that eternity was more than a million, million, million years, a circle of time without end. Having recently burnt her finger on the stove, Annie multiplied the degree of her suffering to suit her body size. After the force of that clumsy calculation hit her, she tried earnestly to be pure. However, this proved to be a great trial to her.

Once Mass was over – duty done, liberty gained – the Hughs kids enjoyed their Sundays, primarily as their father was home and invariably engaged in some interesting activity. As well, Margo usually baked a cake, for relatives sometimes visited. Often, when the sky was "picnic sunny", the family set off for a cruise on the river, breathing in the evocative smells of petrol and salt water as they boarded the launch. *The Margo* put-putted over the gorgeous green water, speared with depth-seeking sunrays, to some secluded picnic spot. Nothing less than a sanctuary devoid of human footprints suited Jack Hughs.

There came a day in August when a roaming wind visited Oyster Bay Road, and its playful sweeping gusts inspired Jack to take up again his seasonal zeal for kites. He was able to fashion a kite in less than half an hour with nothing but sticks, string, brown paper or newspaper and with strips of rag to give weight and colour to the tail. When the flour-and-water paste was dry, he carried the kite outdoors for its maiden flight.

The chattering entourage followed, eager for hours of running to and fro in the teasing wind; the kite, soaring, plunging and hovering. Jack's commands could be heard: 'Reel it in, reel it in!' Or 'Give it more string … let it climb.' Finally, he blasphemed and shouted: 'Watch out for the power lines – here, give us that *bloody* thing!'

And so, with Jack's aviation energies expended, the children all knew there would be no more kite-flying until he had forgotten that the last one had ended its aeronautical displays with a crash. It was stuck irretrievably on Miss Gilbert's tin roof, directly opposite the Hughs' house. A short time later at her gate, the friendly neighbour mentioned to Margo and Annie that she had been quite startled by the noise of possums dropping cones again from the pines which sprawled over her roof. Annie's guilt heard a hinted reproof, and she cringed and affected a sudden interest in ants.

Margo believed the comment was innocently incidental to the conversation, and so did not volunteer unnecessary enlightenment. Miss Gilbert, however, was genuinely unaware of the trespasser up there, but its fluttering tail (Margo provided the rags, so bore *some* complicity) remained a reproachful reminder to those of the Hughs mob who were troubled by conscience.

On Sunday nights, if the broadcast of the Caltex Theatre Playhouse was unsuitable or uninteresting, Jack always turned off the wireless to then happily embark upon a session of his favourite game of logic. After stating the category: animal, vegetable or mineral, of his chosen subject, he instructed his children to ask no more than twenty questions to track down its identity. Jack strictly confined his answers to *yes* or *no*.

Sometimes, if Margo was not using the table for ironing, Jack set up the Bobs on it to keep the older ones entertained. The Bob set comprised a wooden row of small stable-like cubicles, each with a number painted on the facade, and two arms reaching along the table edges to prevent the balls from straying. The older children took turns with the cue to shoot the balls home and tally their score.

Margo put a premium on the value of reading bedtime stories or reciting nursery rhymes to the smaller children. Many a night, they lay snug in their beds listening and watching every expression of her face as the contours and texture of the dear features moved permanently into their hearts and souls. While absorbing every nuance of voice inflection, which aided their speech development, they learnt the meaning of fantasy and how to separate it from reality.

Thus, Margo again related their favourite stories. She was never permitted to shorten the narration nor alter specific terms (Goosy Gander took the old man by the left leg – *left*, mind – and threw him down the stairs) but she sensitively used laughter to nullify brutal aspects of some of the tales. One example was the sad plight of abandoned children, *Hansel and Gretel*, dumped in the dark woods finally to stumble upon the witch's cottage. Old witchy rated Hansel as somewhat scrawny and shoved him into the fattening cage while Gretel toiled in the kitchen. Cannibalism, too big a word anyway for the Hughs children, was never alluded to.

Another favourite was *Little Red Riding Hood*. This little girl might have been sight-impaired; she could not detect the subtle differences between the wolf's features and those of her grandmother ... whom she visited every day.

Margo used contrasting treble and bass voices and delivered the drama with emphasis: *'Oh Grandmama, what big eyes you have!* All the better to SEE you with! *Oh, Grandmama, what big teeth you have!* All the better to EAT you with!'...

The ending was rather gruesome. In keeping with children's demand for satisfying conclusions to their bedtime stories, this one certainly complied. Papa barged in wielding an axe and slaughtered the wolf right there in Grandmama's bed – in full view of his gentle, impressionable little daughter. Nice, soothing, sleepy-bye story!

The children loved those tales and never grew tired of hearing them. The stories served as preparatory, for having survived all the horror and violence the kids were sufficiently desensitised to withstand Jack's bedtime stories. Eagerly they looked forward to blackouts when soft candlelight inspired him to settle back and spin a few yarns before sending them off to bed to dream sweetly.

Whenever Jack was too weary to spend time with his tribe or when he was working the late shift at the restaurant, Margo would sit on one of the beds and read to them from *Uncle Arthur's Bedtime Stories*. Each tale carried a moral lesson and provided a character-building principle for the young to absorb as they grew dreamy-eyed watching her lovely face. The stories were always gentle, mellow and sleep-inducing, but they could never compete with Jack's thrillers. Naturally, the kids preferred his, even though Herb and Annie knew that much of the narration was contrived along the way.

One night, Jack told the yarn about the scar on his right leg. He had always maintained with a particular element of pride that it was the result of his having been shot during the war. Annie suspected that he would have preferred a greater mutilation than that small scar to crow about and it occurred to her that an army kitchen would have been a reasonably protected place to work in. She reasoned that if her father had been shot while cooking for all the soldiers, it must not have been safe anywhere!

Margo always emitted a sardonic little laugh and rolled her eyes whenever Jack related stories about his war wound, relegating his accounts to the mental repository for such colloquialisms as tomfoolery, flapdoodle and poppycock. Defensively, Annie wondered how her mum would like to get a bullet in the leg and have someone laugh about it.

But understanding dawned one day when Jack was explaining to young Tony that a snake had bitten him there, and he indulged in a great deal of theatrics relating to how he had nearly died in excruciating agony. It struck Herb and his sister that there was a major flaw in their father's narrative, and they protested. However, undeterred by juvenile mirthful scoffing, he assumed a tone of gravity befitting the traumatic memory and continued.

Tony stared in rapt attention at Superman who, encouraged by the naive adoration, suddenly pretended to retrieve from lazy memory a giant boa constrictor. He claimed that it had savagely bitten his leg while crushing his bones in a vice grip from which he had miraculously extricated his cruelly mangled body.

At this rapturous juncture, Margo walked into the kitchen carrying Clivey. 'Ba-*loney!*' she exclaimed, and a sea of blue eyes turned her way. She bent to Jack's ear and deposited a timely reminder of the mythical bullet and, straightening up she lifted an eyebrow, pursed her lips and bestowed upon him a most amused and challenging glance and awaited his response.

Unperturbed, Jack cunningly amended the blunder by marvelling over the amazing coincidence that the snake had bitten him on the very scar of his war wound. He shook his head. 'You wouldn't read about it!' he exclaimed in sham astonishment. His presence of mind and capacity for swift creativity was remarkable, second only to his acting, but those who were around him long enough eventually became sceptical about all hisamazing coincidences.

'So, it was just a snake bite,' Annie muttered to Herb while their father carried on with the kind of talk Margo called twaddle. This was a great disappointment to Annie; she felt selfishly let down by his leg not being machine-gunned. She hadbragged about it to her friends, her indulgent exaggeration kindly elevating Jack Hughs to a pedestal of significance in the hero hierarchy. Understandably, Annie gave little credence to her dad's other yarns after that and thought that he ought to have listened more closely to Margo's advice: 'If you're going to be a fibber you need a very good memory.'

Snakes had always fascinated Pauly. Jack decided to exploit the boy's eager credulity and to give him the benefit of his expansive knowledge on the subject. Naturally, he focused on the incredibly ferocious snakes that proliferated only at Oyster Bay because of their taste for oysters, which empowered them with blood-hungry savagery, especially at night.

Tony, most eager to hear more ophidian yarns, was struggling determinedly to fight off the unsporting sleep, which progressively stole strength from his eyelids. But the others were wide-awake and intent upon learning about (or sniggering at) all the terrible ways in which snakes bedevilled human beings.

At times, Herb and Annie exchanged knowing grins over the boys' heads in response to Jack's fanciful inconsistencies, but their young brothers stared mesmerised at the animated face of the story-teller. The more colourful the variants He-of-the-Trophy Scardreamed up to reveal about reptiles, the larger and rounder his younger sons' unblinking eyes became, glazed with the exquisite fascination of fear and horror.

Once complete darkness had descended, all the kids, except older and fearless Herb, became reluctant to navigate the passage of peril towards the outdoor lavatory. It was a long creepy trek down the path between the shed and the overhanging trellis of climbing roses wherein lurked all manner of prehensile creatures. The area behind the shed was always ominously black, and the children imagined an embodiment of something big and terrifying waiting, poised to lunge at them before they could cover the last five feet to the dubious sanctuary of the primitive little building.

To save her children from their fearful imaginings and to obviate the deferring of kitchen chores to accompany them and wait for them all, Margo placed a bucket in the laundry and, noticing Pauly fidgeting, told him to go and use it. Jack leaned towards Herb then and whispered something, and they exchanged conspiratorial grins.

Naturally, being of inquisitive mien, Annie's curiosity was hugely stimulated. She strained every faculty to learn the design of their plot, but Margo sabotaged her eavesdropping by inquiring if she'd had her nightly wash. 'Yes Mum,' came the impatient untruth. Margo glanced briefly at Annie's freckled face (cleansed most happily earlier by a juicy crescent of watermelon) and frowning doubtfully, told her to put on her nightwear in readiness for bed.

The yearning to follow Jack and Herb outside and the duty to obey watchful Margo were competing for supremacy. The girl was chaffing under the restraining influence inflicted by the tedious nightly preparation for boring bed, and she yearned to know what exciting mischief her father and brother were up to. Annie loitered as long as dared until Margo's glare and her dangerously raised hand relieved her of the anguish of indecision.

Shortly, being at last pyjama-clad, the naughty girl joined the others listening again to the snake stories; a reprieve from the banishment to liberty-depriving bed.

After further embellishing a few of the more wanting aspects of his yarn, Jack's voice became lost in a cavernous yawn, which he emphasised with an exaggerated wail. He began stretching and rubbing his eyes, as if desperate for sleep, and he said to Paul: 'Well, off to bed now, Pauly and have sweet dreams.'

What, after *that*? thought Margo as she washed out the billycan for the morning milkman. ObedientPauly dawdled off wearily to his bed and climbed in. One yelp later, he streaked back to the kitchen, almost knocking over the chair he had so recently vacated and, grabbing Margo's skirt, he hid behind her.

'There's a big snake in my bed, Dad!' he gasped.

Annie, too, jumped behind Margo. It did seem very strange to the girl, however, that the hitherto protective mother-of-six did not panic and consign them all to the table top. Annie also noticed, how nonchalantly her mum ignored the imminent potential slithering of the alleged reptile into her children's precious midst and how she pushed up her mouth and sent her steady glare-darts across to sparkle-eyed Dad!

His response to Pauly's announcement, it was noted, had been an unconvincing display of sham fright and correspondingly Margo wore that oft-used expression which the kids knew meant:

127

'Ooh, I ought to dong you!' But she said merely: 'Oh, for heaven's sake, Jack, how could you?' and raised the billycan threateningly.

Jack was applying a magnificent effort to confine a burst of mirth to his throat. 'Me?' he asked, face struggling, voice wobbling. 'What'd *I* do?' His features conveyed that same innocent surprise his children always adopted whenever their mother accused them of committing some transgression they had not the slightest intention of owning up to.

Margo sent Herb to retrieve the boa constrictor from Paul's bed. She had seen Jack with it earlier but was too preoccupied to ask what he was doing at that hour with a piece of garden hose. Pauly laughed when he met the imposter, and the joy of complete relief escalated in one heartbeat into excited playfulness as Jack chased him with the "snake". In fact, so cavalier had the boy become, that he laughingly dismissed the absurd idea of having been frightened in favour of a *just pretending* admission.

When all the playfulness was spent, and the sighing of wide yawns had begun, Margo herded them all off to bed. Pauly's heroic charade vanished with his swiftly revised contemplation of the scary episode, and he asked his mum if he could sleep in her bed from now on. Margo fixed an ironical glance upon King Fabler, whose face suddenly clouded at the prospect of little knees, pointed elbows and razor-blade toenails all night separating him from the comfort of his cuddly queen. With a wry grin Margo said: 'Well, you asked for it!'

All threats of soap, water and toothbrush, Annie assumed, had slipped safely into oblivion. Her cautious feet soft-treaded towards the haven of a warm bed, but before escape to it could be managed, she was faced most startlingly with the error of that careless assumption.

Margo's sudden grasp halted her step. She observed her daughter with a reproachful eye, studying with alarming intensity her dirty feet. Her searching eyes then glared at the grubby arms. Not a word did Margo utter. She whacked the disobedient girl hard across the bottom. Annie's two hands flew there in case her mother decided that inflicting physical punishment was an enjoyable, therapeutic pastime. Her mouth corners began tugging downwards, and her moist-eyes looked up in shock and guilt.

'Don't – tell – fibs!' Margo said, and Annie turned her head to stare accusingly across at the sanctimonious King of Fibs, who sank back in his throne and shook his head slowly, sadly in a manner conveying feigned self-righteous disapproval of her. 'Now,' Margo ordered, 'get into that laundry (which also was the bathroom) and have a jolly good wash and clean those teeth!' She handed Annie a dish of salt to use, for they were out of toothpaste again. (The Hughs family was an absolute marvel of resourcefulness owing to its lack of affluence.)

Later that dark night Annie awoke with her heart banging. She was certain that a burglar was prowling around the creaking kitchen. She flew into her parents' room and scrambled into bed with her mum and their valiant protector – still deep in his didgeridoo snoring. After a moment Margo went out to the kitchen and put on the light to allay Annie's fears, explaining sleepily that houses often creak, but it becomes apparent only at night when there are no other sounds. And back to bed, went Annie.

The next night the girl's drama-inclined imagination challenged the validity of that explanation. She was convinced there was a determined intruder and in the morning, she again whinged. Margo patiently demonstrated the efficacy of the door locks and told her fantasy-prone girl that, because of recent cold nights, the windows were kept closed, the arm-bars further securing them. Finally, fed up with Annie's obsession, she returned her attention to rescuing the saucepan of porridge, erupting now like volcanic lava.

Being Saturday, Jack was home. He listened and observed while he ate his omelette and knew there would be no peace until stronger proof dispelled the notion that a burglar could get into the house. After pondering, he startled Margo with his radical plan to sprinkle flour over the kitchen floor that night when everyone was in bed, thus providing irrefutable proof in the morning that no prowler had been creeping around.

But of course, Jack, whose powers of imagination shaded even his daughter's, could not allow such a ripe opportunity for an absolute peach of a practical joke to evade harvest. The next morning (her sole concern in life was still the kitchen floor), Annie leapt out of bed to investigate. She saw *hu-u-uge* shoeprints!

The explanation should have been obvious: After Margo had gone to bed that previous night, mischievous Jack had busied himself sprinkling flour over the lino … and imprinting exaggerated shapes in sinister, purposeful steps from the back door. He directed them straight to the "kiddie's room" (well he would, wouldn't he!) where all night Annie had slumbered trustingly.

At first sighting, she squawked and ran into her parents' room. 'I told you! I *told* you!' she yelled in a tone wavering between triumph and alarm – loud enough to wake the entire family. Margo sighed and cast a highly suspicious glare upon Jack, slowly emerging from the peaceful slumber of the innocent. She muttered something meant only for errant husband's ears, climbed out of bed and went sleepily forth to investigate.

'Oh, for heavens' sake!' she exclaimed at the kitchen door. Returning to the bedroom, she grasped the incriminating sandshoes and held them up for Annie to see their floury soles. She leaned over the bed and gave the now grinning joker a good whack on the shoulder … and urged the gleeful girl to do the same.

17 Grandma Carrington

Annie Hughs' maternal grandparents owned an elegant cabinet style wireless. The timber veneer gleamed with the frequent polishing, and there was always a velvet runner with an elegantly framed family photograph gracing the top – Grandma was particular about such things. Indeed, she inspired admiration in many ways, but perhaps the most fantastic thing about her was the fact that she had borne eight daughters and three sons.

A particular attribute of Grandma's was her deep, resonant voice. To Annie and her siblings, the familiar sound of her pleasant, unusual voice was synonymous with holidays, love, discipline, fairness, politeness, understanding and wisdom. And there were other less easily defined qualities, such as the comfort of her bright enquiry: 'Who'd like a cup of tea?' or 'Dinner's nearly ready'. She was always guiding, instructing: 'Walk a mile in another's shoes', she often said, and there were many more impressions stimulated by her moral influence which all seemed to belong to the unique voice.

It is understandable that Grandma Carrington often spoke with an air of command, a characteristic that evolved as the family grew. She occasionally became snappy with her strong-minded teenagers, yet it was a transitory irritability, and her mild natural manner soon returned.

To Annie's ear, there was always something novel and endearing in the way Grandma spoke to Margo, calling her *Marg*. It was a reminder to the girl that her mother's name was Margo and not merely Mum! This sometimes kept her mind occupied trying to imagine the old days when Margo was Grandma's little girl – Margie.

It was a natural enough progression to picture Margie as a plump, freckled, *good* little cutie with brown hair falling in waves about her gentle blue eyes. But then reality obtruded and excised the "good" when Margo laughingly admitted that Grandma said she was a 'bugger of a kid'. (It seems Margo's innate refinement might have come solely from her English-bred father!) No doubt Grandma merely meant to convey that Margie possessed determined, wilful tendencies; traits providing emotional strength, obviously required in a family of eleven children.

The Carringtons moved around several times during Margo's growing years. At Auburn, they ran a small poultry farm, which helped financially in the raising of the "crowd" (Grandma's term) of their children. Young Margo was Grandad's "off-sider", and it was her responsibility to collect the eggs, renew the straw in the nesting boxes, clean and replenish the water tubs and generally to keep the yards clean. Grandad maintained the sheds and yards and raked up the manure for his vegetable gardens. He also took care of the killing and the preparing of fattened, past-laying hens for the table. Margo always ran indoors and blocked her ears when this grisly event was about to occur.

As well as owning chooks, the family ran a few goats, which provided milk and cleaned up all the weeds around the place. But one day the rogue of the goat tribe got into the home-yard and trotted over to a pile of rubbish where Margo had accidentally dropped her rag doll, and the curious goat somehow managed to eat the toy. Sometime after that, her milk dried up, and the family then ate the goat. It tasted almost the same as lamb, Margo recollected years afterwards.

Sometimes, when Margo's blue eyes looked back into the past, a dear memory of some incident relating to her tribe of sisters and brothers, brought a sudden little laugh to her lips. At one time, she revealed that she had always been plump and because of an earlier injury to her right foot, somewhat slow and clumsy in her gait.

One balmy afternoon, she was wistfully watching her petite young sister Enid prancing around the lawn, pirouetting, balancing an arabesque and floating her arms about as if performing in Swan Lake. Margo's interest began to wane – but then Enid's foot landed ungraciously on an upturned rake, which threw up its handle and smacked her in the face, sending the dancer sprawling.

Margo burst into shrills of laughter, and her legs buckled throwing her onto the grass. This earned her "a sound belting" from Grandma for her apparent lack of sympathy. Margo lamented years later that although she had felt sorry for Enid, she was cursed with a nuisance trait of translating such incidences into humour. This always leapt in first and got her into trouble with Grandma.

Rhonda, the eldest of the eleven, took piano lessons and later taught those of her sisters who had a wish to learn, one of whom was Margo. Annie yearned to be able to play the piano, but she knew that obtaining and housing such an instrument was unfeasible for the Hughs family. Her parents had neither the money for a piano and tuition to justify it nor the space in their crowded house to accommodate so large an instrument.

About this time, a sudden moment of insight prompted Annie to wonder at the cost of her father's weekly bottles of wine, his beer and the packets of cigarettes. Margo dismissed the curious speculations regarding his "treats" as irrelevant and steered the subject back to other less incriminating reasons for their not buying a piano. She deliberated upon a compromise: an instrument of compactness and portability – a flute perhaps? But that did not solve the problem of tuition fees. Later, when the subject dared assert itself again in Jack's presence he suggested a harmonica, and of course, Mr Funny then progressed – or *re*gressed – to a comb covered in tissue paper!

Margo decided at least to teach her daughter the musical theory she had learnt years before. To assist Annie's education, she painted four octaves of a piano keyboard on the underside of her old Glory Box lid, which had come adrift from the box. She taught the sol-fa scale by humming the notes while guiding the young fingers over the white "keys".

'The black keys are for later,' Margo explained.

Thus, Annie learnt the finger-to-key pattern of a little French song. Whenever she could lay her eager hands upon the smooth ivory of a real piano, such as the Carrington's Broadwood or the Beale at school, she would practice her favourite piece until dormant sensitivity awoke and delivered the timely reminder – *you're driving everyone batty!*

It is a coincidence that Annie's grandmothers were both afflicted by deafness. A natural and compensating recourse, understandably, was to seek contentment and entertainment in books. Every night Grandma Carrington read for a while before she settled down to sleep. One day while visiting Margo, she handed Annie a book. The purpose of the gift was to instil a little culture into the tomboy child.

Grandma's generosity, however, was received without a shred of enthusiasm. Book-reading loomed large on Annie's list of unpleasant duties because it represented an annoying restriction of her freedom. And there was no escape; she knew that her grandmother would later enquire about her progress and want an opinion. Annie saw stretched before her the sentence of weeks of suffering no fewer than half a dozen pages a day. The book's volume alone (compared with comics) deterred any inclination towards even opening the hard, dull- brown cover and it was rendered more uninspiring by the absence of illustrations.

Being well-acquainted with the occasional conflict with mutinous children, Grandma ignored the apparent lack of interest and informed her granddaughter that it was an excellent story. She affirmed that the author was highly skilled and assured Annie that images would soon form in her mind. And so, encouraged by Margo and submitting to a resigned, trapped feeling, the girl flopped onto her bed and opened the book, wishing instead to be down in the river with Herbie trying out his new flippers, snorkel and goggles in the glassy high tide.

The book was entitled *Dusty*, written by Frank Dalby Davison. It related the story of a bushman's devotion to his loyal dog and their struggle to survive. From the first few pages, the realisation of what Grandma was trying to convey became clear to Annie. A new door had opened to her, and an exciting world beckoned.

For a while afterwards, she wanted to do nothing but read about Tom and his faithful dog, and Margo had to prise her, verbally, off her bed to help with the chores. It amazed Annie how quickly the last page was reached. So wholly entertaining had it been, that rather than close the book her fingers sought the first page again. The young convert gleaned more details from the second reading and a greater appreciation of the author's writing-craft. Books almost completely replaced comics after that.

Occasionally, Margo sent her daughter down to the red phone box outside the post office to ring Grandma and ask, for instance, if she and Grandad were coming to their Christmas dinner or perhaps to the bonfire, or merely to relay some message. But often the reason for the phone call was to inform Grandma about her latest school library book.

Annie always experienced a feeling of maturity as she dropped the two pennies into the slot and dialled Grandma's number. There was a short interval: brr-brr, brr-brr, brr-brr, during which time her eyes fixed an unseeing gaze upon the mottled red and green paintwork of the walls, but only seeing Grandma wiping her hands on a tea towel and walking briskly towards the black telephone in the hallway.

And then along the wire, all the way from her house at Marrickville, Grandma's unique voice, velvety and contralto, would tingle against Annie's ear: 'LB2152 ... Hello?'

18 Daisy

When reflecting upon her father's awful responsibility to rid the house of starlings, Annie realised how merciful he had been in killing them so quickly. It brought to her young mind the universal truth that most men are brave, hardy and well-equipped to take care of such dreadful things. She acknowledged that neither she nor her mum could have slammed the little creatures down to their deaths as her dad had done. Moreover, to Annie, it felt reassuring to be able to cringe indoors without feeling cowardly whenever there was a noise at night, while intrepid Dad and Herb went out to investigate.

'Men are such heroes!' she mused one wild and windy night, and snuggled down contentedly in her warm bed with a new book, while her father took the torch and went outside to investigate some noise.

Annie recovered from her grief over the starling incident, although she did not always rally so quickly from that sort of upset. There was an occasion sometime later when Daisy, an elderly neighbour, gave the family some kittens. She was one of their more distant neighbours in terms both of location and the Hughs' limited knowledge of her. She lived in a small fibro house situated about halfway between Annie's house and Ruthie Collins' place. It was known only that Daisy was from Inverness, Scotland

and that her husband had died shortly after the family had arrived in Australia, around 1930.

Understandably, Daisy welcomed company and conversation. Annie was walking home after visiting Ruthie one afternoon when the thick provincial accent caught her as she neared the gate: 'Halloo there, lassie!' Daisy beckoned the child up to the garden steps for a glass of "Fifty-fifty" cordial and some of her homemade shortbread.

During that visit, Annie learnt that Daisy had a daughter and two sons, but that her "bairns" were all fledged from the nest and scattered. The young girl did not appreciate the full extent of the woman's loneliness and at the time. At the time, under a stinging hot sun, her sole thought was that a glass of chilled, sweet orange-and-lemon cordial and a couple of shortbread biscuits sounded *sooo* good. Shortly afterwards, they were sitting and chatting in the shade of a loquat tree, enjoying the refreshments and laughing at the antics of four kittens climbing over their reclining tabby mother.

Presently, after a contemplative moment, shrewd-eyed Daisy told Annie that she would have to get rid of the kittens, for the old cat was now too weary to care for them. This greatly concerned the child, as it was meant to do, and wily old Daisy quickly responded with opportunistic-laced empathy: 'Ah lass, I'm sorry t' grieve ye, I am ... I'll be verra sad to see the wee kitties

go, I will, an' there's nought ol' Daisy wouldna do for 'em', so ...
so here's a wee bit of an idea.'

She moved closer and applied more confidentiality of tone.
'Do y' no think y' could tote 'em home with y', lass? I had a mind
t' sell 'em, I did, but ...' (A solemn pause here to emphasise a
great sacrifice in the making) '... but I'll let y' have 'em *free!'* she
announced expansively and shook her head as if marvelling at her
own magnificence. 'Ah lassie, they'll give y' lots o' fun an all ...
an' y'll be rid of y' varmin. The mice'll *fight* the rats t'get oot the
door. I'll bet m' boots on it!'

The poem Annie was learning at school, Robert
Browning's *The Pied Piper of Hamelin,* came instantly to mind
and her mouth opened to dispel the offensive notion that the
Hughs' house was infested, but Daisy continued talking. 'Y' willna
be sorry, lass,' she promised, beaming at her. To further her cause,
she handed Annie a kitten, the most appealing of them all for its
large, fascinating eyes.

Naive gratitude had rendered persuasion unnecessary.
Fondling the kitten, sipping cordial and munching shortbread,
Annie felt elated. She rejoiced over Daisy's generous and
sacrificial offer and marvelled at her own fabulous good luck –
free kittens! The benevolent lady sat back in the wicker chair,
hands locked behind her grey head, and with an air of satisfied
finality, declared: 'So that's *that*, then lass. The wee kitties are

yourn, an' their poor auld mother'll thank ye for takin' 'em away from the sore, stretched old titties.' Annie's surprised eyes left the kittens for Daisy's. 'Oh aye, lass, (nodding) she will that, she *will* that.'

The adoption business successfully concluded, the relieved lady now felt inclined towards further conversation, prompted at that moment by her neighbour heaving dish-water out onto the front path. 'For *shame* – dishwater oot the door!' Daisy tut-tutted, shook her head and gleefully embarked upon a brief gossip session. With pleasurable avidity kindling her features she set about criticising the woman … who she loved as "me ain sister", but who was "as deaf as a post" … (and did not merit Daisy's loyalty).

The bent old neighbour had retreated and closed the door firmly behind her. Still, a lowering of the Scottish voice was deemed necessary to reduce the immense risk of harsh words transcending the kookaburras' maniacal laughter and the yawning distance of two front yards, offending the afflicted ears of the absent neighbour. Young as she was, Annie could not help but smile and wonder at this comically unnecessary precaution.

Daisy leaned forward in her chair: 'I wouldna share a cuppa tay with her, lass, not for all of the auld Scoteland – she's that durrty! And yet, she's a big-hearted auld woman … a'though she hasna the sense of a beetle, and wears a dress ootside-in when it needs a wash.' She squawked happily at the girl's surprised laugh: 'Oh aye lass, she does that! She does that!' and nodded a vigorous, merry-eyed affirmation of her comment.

'An' *more* I'll tell y' lassie. She scratches the back of that mangy ol' dog of hern, an' then – mits straight into the flour for scones!' Daisy squawked and shot her hands in the air and gave a shake of the head, expressing dismay and disapproval. 'Oh, I tell y' lass, it's true her hands are always cleaner *after* the scones than before.'

And then, with a wrinkle-nosed expression of distaste, another headshake, and her chin and voice lowering: 'I canna eat from her table, lassie, never I can … she's that *durrty!*'

Annie carried away an uncontrollable grin and a cardboard box of furry life, reflecting on how perfect it was that there were *four* kittens: one each for Paul, Tony, Josie and herself, and she began to consider cute names. At the same time, the kittens' weighty restlessness was becoming a burden. She was glad to be nearly home and enjoyed the expectation of everyone's rapture upon the first darling sight of them. Her mother, she believed, would be besotted with the gorgeous little creatures – but Mother was as far removed from "besotted" as a mother could possibly be!

The reason for her worried frown and lack of excitement was beyond Annie's understanding until given the reminder that there were a lot of humans to feed in the Hughs family. Margo explained that the four kittens would quickly grow into large cats. 'And these will all have kittens of their own,' she added. Belatedly, she subjected them to a swift inspection and amended: '*Two* of these will so we could end up being swamped with cats!'

Jack always asserted that cats and airborne lead were good company. When he came home from work, Margo showed him the litter, which she had soft-heartedly fed with warm milk while the children all doted (except Herb who was now too manly for such juvenile sentimentality).

Under a veil of gentle assurances, Margo implied that the kittens could go to another family, but told her sorrowful brood that she regretted depriving them of 'the little dears.' Jack and Margo exchanged looks of particular meaning here. Jack, serious and thoughtful, nodded sagely and told the children that he knew of someone who would probably take them. The next morning, they were gone.

Later that day, sorrowed by Annie's futile searching, Herb hesitantly revealed that their dad had hoisted the kittens over the cliff in a rock-weighted bag. To Annie, this atrocity seemed too horrible to accept, but she knew that Herb never lied, and the inflexion of sadness in his voice lent credence to the words.

Emotional strength was now expected of her. She, too, was weathering the trials of growing up: had recovered recently after standing her weight upon a live mouse in her gumboot (which brother, this time?), had survived bird-executions, chook-beheadings, and had finally accepted that little Peggy was in dog heaven. It seemed reasonable therefore to expect a higher insulation against shock, grief and fear. This being so, Annie determined that she would *not* go running down to peer over the cliff at the expected dreadful sight. She did *not* require proof.

She *did*, however! As soon as the tide receded, impatient feet scampered down the backyard, and frightened eyespeered over the foreboding cliff. With a heart-banging shock, the girl shrank away from the edge … from the awful reality of the wet bag wedged between the rocks.

Back in the house, her fists pummelled with bruising intent, but Jack's only response was his usual stolid: 'Gee, the mozzies are bad today!'

Margo, shaking her head scornfully and tut-tutting at him, rocked Annie in her arms until the jerky sobs dwindled to a sniffle. 'No one wanted them after all, pet,' she half-fibbed against the fair hair. '… and Dad made certain they died very quickly. They didn't suffer, pet,' she said, kissing the top of her daughter's head.

Annie did not wholly accept this last assurance and in her limited child-vocabulary, wanted to question her mum's ability to acquire that knowledge. Margo anticipated by quickly steering her thoughts towards a different turn of the subject: 'and in the future, if anyone offers kittens or puppies – or *anything* – you're *not* to take them, understand? Thumper is enough for us to care for.'

Annie regretted that they had not merely taken the kittens back to Daisy, but Margo explained that Daisy's term "get rid of them" meant drowning, and she added in a sad tone that it would be a hard thing to impose upon an elderly lady. Hence it became yet another unpleasant task for stalwart Jack to deal with and after thinking that over, Annie understood.

19 Cracker Night

When evaluating the major occasions that brought an expectant pleasure to the Hughs' year, bonfire night was second only to Christmas. In the decade after the Second World War, Empire Day, commemorative of Queen Victoria's birthday, was still observed on the 24th May, but the lapse of time gradually faded its original significance, and a lesser title became more relevant to Australian children – "Cracker Night".

In the Sydney area of New South Wales, the late autumn evenings were not yet too cold for families to remain outdoors enjoying their fireworks and bonfires. Mothers still kept infants rugged up though, and at a safe distance from exploding bungers and mal-launched skyrockets.

The construction of bonfire pyramids usually began in early May, and by cracker night the piles of debris had grown proportionately. Margo and Jack always welcomed the opportunity of an annual clean up and gathered all the old tree-pruning, fruit crates, newspapers and various items of combustible material to supplement their stack.

In earlier years when the family was small, the bonfire was erected, and crackers let off somewhere between the chook yard and the outdoor lavatory. However, as the family increased, and after consideration was given to the egg supply for the following week and to any possible occupant of the little separate building, it seemed wiser and kinder to establish it elsewhere. Margo chose a safe site farther down the backyard, an area where Jack, who had a talent for masonry, was constructing rock walls and pathways.

During the weeks leading up to Empire Day, the children thought nothing of squandering their precious pennies and shillings on crackers. Every pocket-money day Mr Gumm, the grocer, handed fireworks over the counter into acquisitive little Hughs hands. Once home, the crackers were laid out with reverent carefulness on someone's bed, and inspected and admired before being stashed away with others in the sizeable pickled onion jars Jack brought home from the restaurant.

There were tall, heaven-bound rockets, strings of bungers, and dumpy little packets of Roman candles promising starry displays of gorgeous colour. And there were colourfully wrapped discs of Catherine wheels, which Jack would tack onto a post where they'd be free to burst into symmetrical sprays and swirls. Meanwhile, the exciting sight, smell and feel of the cache of fireworks filled the kids with a heightened sensation of delight and happiness.

The Hughs children were well infected with the expectancy of cracker night. They could hardly wait for it to arrive and willed away the time, as children do. Each vanquished day was a triumph for it brought them one step closer to their special night. It was a bonus then that all school children were given a half-day holiday and their going home at lunchtime emphasised the day's uniqueness and fuelled the escalating excitement. The daylight hours of those Empire Days seemed endless. As the afternoon crept into the past, the impatient kids became convinced, in effect, that the earth had slowed in its revolutions and that a most unsporting time-warp had intervened, preventing darkness from ever descending.

The teasing twilight of Cracker Night finally arrived each year. Allotted chores were attended with negligent haste and food was quickly scoffed down. Indeed, so very impatient and excited were they that none of the Hughs kids knew after that meal what it was they had eaten … and their blue eyes kept returning to the indigo sky beyond the window.

At last liberated, the children's eager hands grabbed the jars of crackers, and they filed out after their father into the crisp night air of autumn. With restless excitement, they gazed around at the orange glow of other backyard fires. The smell of gunpowder from the early-lit crackers was already in the air, and the children craned their necks to follow the skyrockets whooshing splendidly into the smoky black firmament, trails of sparks drawing gasps of delight from everyone.

Jack lit the bonfire, and the family watched the flames grow, faces glowing red with the reflection. All about them, on the hills and across the flats which flanked the Oyster Bay roads, other fires could be seen. Skyrockets streaked up into the infinite expanse of velvety blackness. Explosions stabbed the air with staccato rapidity, some close by, others muted by distance – short, dull, popping sounds – and everywhere the smell of Cracker Night grew stronger.

Sometimes, when the fire was almost spent, Margo threw potatoes into the glowing coals to cook slowly. Later, when they could be handled, she buttered them … and no doubt a smear of charcoal was swallowed as the family feasted, (for there was no aluminium foil then). Oh, it was such fun when you were five to stand close to your mum and wave a sputtering sparkler. Later when ten, it was so exciting to toss penny bungers out into the darkness, and when you were a brave and mischievous thirteen, to throw double bungers at one another ... and best of all, near your surprised dad!

As the evening progressed to this reckless stage, Margo usually announced that she must take the baby indoors – there was always a baby. Her departure often coincided with the opening of the Jumping Jacks packets. Annie never managed to acquire Margo's good sense and was often caught leaping about shrieking hysterically as the insane, concertinaed thing jumped erratically with each explosion – usually in her direction.

And when laughing Paul lit a Jumping Jack right behind his sister on the back steps, it appeared to chase her up into the kitchen, and her feet barely felt the floor as the devil repeatedly exploded around her legs. Young brother was in big trouble that evening – but for violating the sanctity of the kitchen or for the threat to sister's sanity? Annie never knew.

Jack, one year, had to work late on Cracker Night and Margo had insufficient rubbish to justify a bonfire, so she took her children to the Community Hall 'Do'. There she bought cakes and cordial for them, drank tea from a glass cup and enjoyed the convivial company of other women. After an interminable delay, the men prised themselves from the magnetism of their jocular conversations and headed for the paddock opposite the Hall to light the bonfire pile. It had grown immense with all the donations of flammable material and now wore the crowning addition of a scarecrow staring down at them all in an attitude of Joan of Arc martyrdom.

Margo's children watched from the roadside, joining in enthusiastically with excited exclamations. To them, it was the most enchanting of nights, even more so than the night before Christmas because the hands on the clock became irrelevant. They were not ushered early to bed as on Christmas Eve (lest they should observe rotund Santa attempting to squeeze down their narrow chimney) and were allowed to participate well into the night.

But there came a year when Jack was too weary, and Margo for some reason was unable to attend the local Do. Disinclined to allow her children to go unchaperoned, she suggested a small fire in the backyard, and so there they set off their crackers.

Later, Margo went out to the road concerned about the rapidly growing illumination in the direction of the paddock, exclaiming as she went that it seemed too close to be coming from the community bonfire. Jack, following, suddenly stood unnaturally still and then ran off along the road. 'It's not the bonfire,' he shouted back, 'it's Mrs Gracely's house!'

He bounded away, silhouetted against the trees against the brilliant amber light, which climbed higher by the second. The three older kids hurried out to the front gate and with the heart-thumping fear and fascination of horror, watched the broadening glare and listened with painful envy to the distant, excited shouts and the nearing clang of the fire engine. Oh, how they longed to run after their father that terrible, thrilling night!

There arose a loud commotion. People came running down the road shouting to one another and desperate to see what was causing the towering glow. Annie moved forward to run with them, but Margo gripped her arm: '*No!*' she almost squawked, and Annie could feel her mother's sudden shaking. They stood there gaping at the retreating figures. Someone called out that Mrs

Gracely was still in the house. Margo groaned: 'Oooh! I feel sick.' She hurried back into the yard and leaned over the garden.

A reluctant and restless wait ensued, and when at last Jack came home he sat wearily with his elbows on the table and combed rough, blackened fingers through his hair. 'Poor old lady ... poor old lady' was all he could say.

Margo stared at him. 'What is it? Is she burnt?' Her voice wobbled out the rapid words.

Jack shook his head and flung out a hand, seeking in that gesture to give expression to the horror he had witnessed and began pacing back and forth and glancing around in a strange, disoriented way. In a throaty voice betraying raw shock he told white-faced Margo: 'They couldn't get her out! She was clawing at the window and–' His eyes looked around at his kids and fell into a stunned silence. And then, recovering a little, he went on to describe the fire's ferocity and the incredible speed of its destruction.

Deeply affected, Jack sought to sublimate his horror into vigorous, arm-flinging criticism, deploring the fact that the old weatherboard cottage had been enshrouded in vines and dead shrubs and that no one had cared enough to make the place safer for Mrs Gracely. Then he turned his wrath inwards: '*I* should've done something for her ... cleared away the vines atleast,' he said in an anguished tone of self-recrimination. 'I could've done that.'

Margo wept without restraint. Later she lamented in tremulous tones, 'If only I'd visited sometimes.' She found her handkerchief. 'Only yesterday I intended taking some eggs, but … just didn't!' It had been one of those friendly, caring impulses that had lost its impetus when urgent domestic matters arose. 'She must have been so lonely, Jack,' cried Margo. 'I should have stopped longer to talk at her gate – she was often there, waiting I suppose, for someone to talk to, and I was always too busy to talk for long…' Margo's last words trailed off as Jack drew her into the comforting circle of his arms – united in their sadness and regret.

A sombre hush fell. The stunned children were sent off to bed. The awful day was over. The magnificent moon moved in its arc across the smoky sky – a moon Mrs Gracely would never again see – and another morning dawned.

The clacker of kookaburras and the warm autumn sunshine should have given a happy lift to the new day, but all thoughts, immediately upon waking, returned to the horror of Mrs Gracely's death. And the acrid smell hanging sickeningly in the air chased away the possibility that it had been a terrible dream.

Later that morning, Billy Meadows called in smilingly pleased with his discovery of a sizeable burnt tin of coins and medals. Jack pounced on him. 'Where'd you get that from?'

Billy, who was slightly afraid of Mr Hughs, stammered: 'In-in-in the ashes,' and he pointed unnecessarily towards the Gracely property.

Jack examined the stolen goods and shoved the heavy tin back at Billy. 'Well get back home then y' shonky little swine, and give the tin – and the money – to your father and tell him where you found it.'

Billy recovered from his initial fright and, aware of his audience, thrust out his jaw. 'Finders keepers!' he said insolently, his glittering eyes glaring back challengingly at the threatening Mr Hughs.

'Geez he's brave!' murmured Paul with reluctant admiration. He expected him to receive a swift clout.

Jack pointed an angry finger at the rebellious face and growled, 'You get home now, y' cheeky lout.' Billy finally placed prudence above pride, yet compromised by sauntering off casually, although his feet wanted to run ... and the alarmed kids wished they would before their father exploded.

That afternoon while Jack was at work, two detectives came to the house inquiring about the money. They had heard of it from several people to whom Billy had bragged and now wanted the Hughs' account of it. The children told what they knew, and the detectives tipped their hats to Margo and drove off towards the Meadows house.

When Jack came home that night, he and Margo began discussing the matter again. Annie looked up from her homework when she heard her dad say '– and wouldn't you know it'd be thieving bloody Billy Meadows?'

Margo nodded in reluctant agreement. However, she was endowed with a compassionate gentleness and always strove to find something uplifting about an individual regardless of identity or fault. 'Well, he's still a child, Jack, even though he's big.' she replied, 'He'll learn from this.'

Jack let out a cynical snort of laughter. 'Learn? *Him?*' He shook his head and made a sour grimace of exasperation. And then, with a sudden motion, he turned in his chair and focused intense blue eyes upon the younger ones sitting there quietly so they would not miss anything. 'Well, you kids had better learn from it anyway and never do what that bugger does. He's a bad egg so keep away from him. Right?' And vigorously they nodded their wise old heads.

During the following days, a rumour spread from mouths to ears that the house fire had been deliberately lit. Local louts, as devoid of intelligence as the stones they threw at windows, had been overheard planning some invidious prank 'to shake up the old prune.' These rumours gave rise to much anger, scorn and contempt, but nothing eventuated.

Farther afield angry citizens proclaimed that crackers should be banned – a few letterboxes had been bombed. Others spoke out on behalf of traumatised animals, and asthmatics voiced many condemning words regarding the smoke problem from the sheer number of fires. There were reports in the Sydney papers of how the city and suburbs were illuminated by the glow of countless blazes; reports of burns and larrikin vandalism; criticism of louts who adopted the attitude that the freedom to throw crackers was a licence for atrocities. The "fun" seekers roamed the streets on Empire Night looking for mischief and found it everywhere.

On the evening after the fire, Jack sat back in his chair, unfolded the *Sydney Morning Herald* and glanced over the large pages. It was his habit to read selected items aloud so that Margo, busy in her kitchen work, could offer a response.

'It says here, "Sydney Empire Day celebrations closed last night with one of the most brilliant and noisy fireworks displays seen for years."' He lowered the paper and looked at Margo. 'Well, that's ironic, isn't it? – when you think of what happened *here.*' Pensively, Margo at the stove swayed her head expressing incredulity and regret, and her stirring slowed.

Herbie looked over Jack's shoulder and read aloud another headline: '"Bonfire Blaze for Empire Night Revels".' He saw a photograph of four children, some wearing beanies, girls with

157

fingers in ears, a boy handling a large bunger about to be lit, and a smaller boy leaning towards it, eager to help. In the background, a bonfire blazed. 'They look just like us!' he exclaimed.

Margo came over to the paper and nodded her agreement. 'Yeeees – they do too! But let's hope they never know the horror you kiddies have been exposed to,' she said. They all fell into preoccupation then, each according to age and maturity, dealing as well as possible with the raw memory of Mrs Gracely's terrible death.

A few days later, Herb, Paul and Annie went along to Billy's place bursting with curiosity to know if he had really "copped it", that is to say, the strap, wielded by an angry paternal hand. There he was on his haunches at the front of the house scrubbing mould away from the base of the south fibro wall and smelling overpoweringly of bleach.

Billy's self-disgust was influenced by annoyance and regret for the lost opportunity. He told the kids that he was in serious trouble with his parents. Indeed, for some further time, he was to become the object of a mixture of curiosity and dismay and the recipient of disdain from his siblings. The punishment imposed proved relatively severe: more jobs, no pocket money and no Saturday matinee for a period of time to be determined by his ability genuinely to repent and to repair the damage inflicted on his family's hitherto good reputation.

158

Billy did exhibit a smidgen of regret, however. 'I should've sold 'em to Butch when I had the chance!' was all he had to say regarding the booty from the house fire, and went on scrubbing more furiously than before.

The tall stone chimney stood for many years after the fire; a constant symbol of reproach to all who had mocked, shunned, or just neglected the old lady. Eventually, it was pulled down, and there remained only a few regenerated fruit trees to remind that someone, for many years, had lived there.

Time passes. Things change. Memories fade … Years later Annie went back to the place which had featured so dramatically in her childhood. There, she found a children's playground where once had stood the old woman's cottage. A magnificent Norfolk Island pine towered over the ghost of the gateway … the triumphal maturation of the little pine Mrs Gracely had decorated each Christmas to give pleasure to passing children.

20 The River

Always, after the terrible night of the house fire, the children tended to walk slowly, almost reverently, past the site of the burnt cottage. Gradually, as the area was cleared leaving only the brick chimney, they became used to it and began to notice that the absence of the house revealed a full north-east view of the river.

The Hughs had an excellent south view. The back veranda overlooked the domestic foreground: a mulberry tree with its skin-staining fruit and broad, almost heart-shaped leaves for shoeboxes of silkworms; clucking hens dust-bathing; and fruit trees, ablaze with colour in springtime. Farther to the middle-distance amid the freckled gums, the river glinted enticingly, and the steady, rhythmic sound of frequent passing launches rose, clearly amplified by the broad body of water.

The older children sometimes regarded their part of the river – their bay – as a massive kind of living body. They took notice of tidal activity and became adept at judging the speed at which the river flooded in and then drained out of the bay. There was always an impatient yearning to swim or to take out the Flattie, which they were permitted to use provided that they did not lose the oars or row locks.

The heavy rowlocks had the exasperating habit of clinging to the withdrawn oars, then to drop into the water and deep receptive mud a split-second before hands could grab them, seldom retrievable. The kids were not entirely negligent, though – they never lost the oars.

But there were times when Herb had to take over to row frantically before the tide retreated and left them stranded at The Point. Whenever that race was lost, they had no choice but to tether the Flattie at the jetty and scuff their feet remorsefully homeward along the gravel road; anxious minds speculating upon their father's reaction to their carelessness.

Occasionally, when evenings were warm, and the sky was displaying a blaze of almost imperceptibly changing colours, the Hughs family would sit well back from the high cliff at the end of the block to watch the panorama and listen to mullet slapping and splashing in the tranquil water below. Invariably, the late crows winging overhead contributed to Mother Nature's Serenade in a plaintive, descending lament: *ca-a-ark, a-a-ark, ou-er* on their return to the bushland beyond.

The river was a playground, as were the backyard, the vacant eastward block and the dirt road, and it provided food and recreation, smelt salty and muddy in turn and often sparkled in the sun as though filled with the bright reflection of a starry galaxy. Conversely, in dull weather it lay gloomy, sombre and grey; the colour of the drab, woollen army blankets on the children's beds.

On breezy days, the water lapped out a gentle rhythm against the stone-walled wharf and the rocks beneath the cliffs, and at Christmas the tide swelled voluminously, completely covering the whole area and becoming as glass. On calm days whenever a launch went by, the first wave from its wake would ripple over the surface and gently rock the nearby anchored boats. Upon reaching the waterfront, a familiar sound would grow, *shlurp, shlurp, shlurp* as water slapped against the stone wall. One by one, the subsequent waves would quieten as the *put-put-put* died in the distance and then the stage would be restored to the birds until another launch went by.

Sometimes, looking down from the cliff, dozens of large orange jelly-blubbers could be seen, some, a foot in diameter. When those creatures were visiting, swimmers kept careful watch, for the slightest touch of the tentacles produced a painful rash. There was nothing to fear from above, however, except nesting magpies in the spring.

Jack and Margo always gave their kids wide latitude to roam. One favourite spot, aptly named Divers Rock, was situated farther along from their own netted baths and closer to the mouth of the bay. Herb and several of the neighbourhood children enjoyed swimming there during the Christmas tides. Annie did too when she eventually learnt.

At Divers Rock, the water was deeper, for the channel ran past, and there was a prominence, which lent itself to diving, the reason for the rock's attraction. Herb and Annie realised one day how dangerous it was to swim in that place when they spotted the fins of two sharks slowly slicing through the water over near Oyster Bill's lease on the other side of the river. After that, while one of them swam the other watched for the sharks. However, they did not worry Margo or Jack with the knowledge of that little bit of inconvenience.

Oyster Bay was a rewarding place for the angler, as the sharks well knew. Usually, Jack and Herb caught all the fish required, although occasionally Margo bought mullet or bream from the cheery fisherman, Mr Hale, who walked bare-footed from door to door with his basket of sea-treasure.

The Hughs never bought oysters though, which was hardly surprising living where they did with their own waterfront, or water *back* as it happened to be. Jack was the only person in the family who ate them as no one else could bear the sight of them, much less the taste, and you could not live at Oyster Bay and not have at least *tasted* one.

Jack often took Annie along with him when he was collecting oysters. Her small child- frame was able to squeeze into the low caves where all the well-matured ones were hidden, larger than others because adults could not reach them.

The process became easier to do with practice: a chipping around the edges of the top shell to separate it from the base which was stuck to the rock; an invading prise and a scrape with the knife and the oyster would slop into Jack's billycan. Then an advance to the next one. Annie usually had to lie on her back to do this. Although muddy and wet, comfort was never vital for she had won her father's admiration and found her niche – an expert oyster gatherer. How exalting!

Margo chopped up chives to mix with the oysters, vinegar, salt and pepper for Jack's enjoyment. Sometimes, he just swallowed them whole. One day, the girl fell prey to the inevitable when Jack said, 'Come on Annie, *you* try one.' What a horrible idea! she thought. An oyster, in her estimation, was aesthetically revolting: a mollusc of slime, odour, and unappealing colour and, unless it contained a pearl, wholly devoid of a single redeeming feature. Although she could not describe an oyster as such, she certainly felt the repugnance – even before tasting one!

On one particular excursion, Jack had been heaping praise upon Annie for her ability to wriggle in under the most claustrophobic of protruding rocks – a daunting challenge which, because of the cavity's low ceiling, had produced some beauties. 'She never baulked at it, either!' he exclaimed to Margo. (She would have trodden *embers* for him!)

Jack believed that Annie's taste in food was the same as his own and was certain of her immediate conversion. 'Just try one!' he insisted. Nothing at that moment could be more alien to his daughter's inclination. On the other hand, Annie considered it a sad, retrograde step to forfeit his recently expressed pride in her by refusing "the dratted thing", so to please and win more approval, she drew on her meagre store of courage and agreed to suffer just *one*.

Her pleased father chose a big fat cream-greyish abomination which he proclaimed to be the best of the lot and after further persuasion, and a self-reminder that the sacrifice was unlikely to prove fatal, Annie shut her eyes, opened her submissive mouth … and received the oyster. Plump and cold, it slithered around filling her mouth, prompting an impulse to retch; to return it onto her dad's shirt. But in checking that urge, the oyster slipped down, and her stomach heaved.

It was the same reaction most kids experienced after swallowing castor oil (that dreaded good-for-you, evil-smelling elixir of *the good old days*) but, with the aid of a glass of water to chase away the initial taste, it stayed down. Margo's empathy turned her eyes away while Annie groped in the dresser for the forbidden tin of condensed milk (always available for babe-bribery) and it took a good long swig before the girl and her taste buds recovered.

Unsurprisingly, that first oyster was Annie's last. Pondering later, she lamented sourly that she might have lived at Coffs Harbour where bananas grew, or Mildura, with its vineyards of grapes, or the Apple-Isle, Tasmania. 'No!' she scoffed, 'fate has plonked me in the middle of Oyster Bay where things that taste disgusting grow on muddy rocks. *What a heavy cross I carry!*' she moaned theatrically.

Most of the time, the Hughs children loved Oyster Bay, chiefly because of the water. Climbing in and out of the mangroves kept them entertained, too. Even during winter many neighbourhood kids rowed boats or paddled canoes and spent many hours on the warmed, pleasantly iron-smelling rocks and the riverbank. They built cubby houses and constructed rough campfires on which to cook small crabs and pipis, and they competed with one another by throwing stones far out into the bay, adeptly skipping them over the water's surface.

Herb could skip his six or seven times, every throw. He taught Paul and Annie to choose broad flat stones, to bend to the right as they pelted them and showed them how to aim the throw close to the water's surface applying plenty of force to the action. A good, patient teacher, he soon had them skipping the stones reasonably well.

Mid-summer nights became special events for the Hughs family. When it was too hot to sleep, they sat on the boulders at the end of the block and watched the enormous golden moon creep up behind the silhouetted trees and gradually turn silver as it appeared to rise and become smaller. As soon as it was far enough over the river, it sent its reflection to sway gently in the water, imbuing the feeling of unreality – it was all so strangely beautiful.

On starry nights when the moon was on the wane, they again gazed heavenward. There was no street light nearby to spoil the galactic splendour. Lying there with her kin on that wide flat rock, Annie felt that the rolling movement of the planet was almost palpable and that sensation evoked in her a compelling link with Heaven.

By day, when the tide had left exposed a vast expanse of black mud, no one saw beauty there ... but how silken the glorious mud felt – like junket or thick cream! On steamy, hot days when the children were impatient for the tide to come back in, deep enough for swimming, they compromised by plodding through the calf-deep mud to reach the channel. Crabs frantically scurried into holes at their advance, and there in the warmer shallow water, carefree bodies stretched out, supremely happy.

Sometimes they slopped around in the thick mud and threw it at one another – as the kids at Thredbo would hurl snowballs – but they had to remember to avert their faces while laughing, or receive a mouthful. Although the kids loved the river, all agreed that the malodorous mud tasted vile. Margo declared it took three hot soapy baths over three days to remove the smell of mud from her children's bodies completely.

The Hughs kids learnt to swim in their part of the river, although to Annie it seemed an impossible dream. Patient Herbie repeatedly demonstrated what to do. She would try it – and sink! Billy Meadows and Ruthie Collins often attempted to teach her, but she always came up spluttering and gasping, complaining and self-deprecating, hating the whole business of learning to swim. Eventually, all volunteers gave up, realising their efforts were wasted.

Annie's closest encounter with drowning occurred when Jack took the family in the launch for a picnic farther up the Woronora River. Ruthie was with them that day, and while the girls jumped and frolicked around in the water, Jack and Margo settled down with the little ones on the narrow stretch of warm sand to watch.

There were unforeseen potholes in that part of the river and Annie was the casualty. Her head surfaced briefly, arms thrashing, throat choking, eyes glimpsing laughing Ruthie – who was unaware that these "antics" were Annie's desperate attempts to stay alive. Going under again, growing weaker by the moment and coming up for the third time, the struggling child saw her father running, lifting his legs high to move faster through the water to reach her in time. *Oh, hurry Dad… hurry!*

Annie knew that for as long as she lived and retained the faculty of recall, the blissful feel of those strong arms lifting her clear of the water in one mighty swoop, and the accompanying sensation of weightlessness, would remain in the treasure-bed of her heart. The struggle was over. Exhausted, she melted limply against her father's thumping chest, a unique feeling enveloping her of just-in-time deliverance. Annie's hero carried her to shore where her distraught, white-faced mother waited with a towel ... and then Superman discovered that his desperately needed cigarettes were in his soggy pocket!

The belief that swimming was an accomplishment unattainable to her became well entrenched in Annie's mind. She saw her future as one in which she was condemned to suffer the humiliation of carting the cork float around whenever toying with the absurd idea of immersing herself in deep water. The kids had been saving corks and depositing them into a small hessian bag to be sewn up once there were enough to provide buoyancy.

Jack was their chief resource for this project. He brought home all the discarded wine bottle corks from the restaurant and further supported their project at significant personal and monetary cost by drinking port most evenings. He had a helpful attitude towards his children's invention – and disdain for wet cigarettes. No doubt, this helped to keep them well supplied with corks. Jack once allowed curious Annie and Herbie to taste his port and it struck the girl then that her father was making a noble sacrifice for their rough floatation device … and all this because of her inability to achieve what other children her age seemed to master with relative ease.

One afternoon she was sauntering along Collins's jetty while Ruthie and her dog, Blacky, were enjoying a noisy, splashing time near the riverbank. Margo had exacted a promise from her daughter to stay out of the water because she was worried about her nasty cold, and so Annie's activities were confined to a walk along the jetty, which reached out to where Ruthie's father kept his boat moored.

The planks felt warm under the girl's feet and, strolling along, she squinted up at the screeching cockatoos flying across the white sunlight, and it struck her that they sounded exactly the same as squeaking gates that needed oiling. That was when her feet strayed. Down into the depths she plunged and came up spluttering and frantically thrashing limbs, believing *The End* had come – again.

More struggling followed and then, buoyancy! Her thrashing body was moving towards Ruthie. Moving? She was *swimming!* Ruthie, wildly excited, kept exclaiming: 'See? I told you. It's easy, isn't it? Good on ya, Annie! Ooh, good on you!' she cried out with genuine exultation.

Down the dusty road Annie's feet scampered, mind elated by the joyful news; tongue impatient to relay the good tidings to the trusting one who had forbidden her to get wet. Clouds had hidden the sun and a chilly wind whipped up. She raced down the side path of the house calling out: 'Mum! Mum!' as though she had just found a ten-pound note.

Margo came hurrying out and saw her all sopping wet and coughing again. 'Oh no!' she said worriedly. '*Annette*, I told you not to get wet!' But abruptly she stopped scolding. She could see that her girl was wildly excited about something.

Fighting against the fits of coughing, the small, happily drenched girl forced out the words: 'Mum! ... I – can – swim ... I can **swim!**

21 Nana and Grandpa Hughs

Jack and Margo's children regularly looked forward to holidays at the farm – always an adventure. Everyday chores, which their grandparents considered mundane, were exciting to the young "townies". Of these activities, Grandpa Hugh's milking of Biddy was the first and most entertaining of the morning.

Leaning on the cow-bail gate to watch, the curious kids learnt that every daily performance was the same: the beloved, leather-smelling brown cow trotted in with head forward to her breakfast of chaff. Grandpa sat low on his box seat, and the white enamel bucket began to sing to the frothy, rhythmical pings. Minnie, the cat, waited at a distance shrewdly calculated to avoid a stray hoof and yet to receive the creamy squirt which always found its open target – perfect aim betraying much practice. This was followed by the flash of her pink tongue comically licking the residue from around her mouth, equally well-practised.

Two dogs presided at the farm and kept foxes away from the fowl yard. The male blue-heeler was long ago named Banjo. Younger, ladylike Trixy was a cross-bred border collie with a shiny coat of starkly contrasting black and white.

It was one of Nana Hughs' pleasures to stand on the back veranda and sing *April Showers* so thatBanjo on the flagstones would lift his nose to the sky and howl along with her in absolute importance and happiness, if not harmony until her laughter prematurely ended the song. Only then would he lie down and rest his nose on mottled paws, satisfied he had done justice to the *secondo* of the duet.

Grandmother Ruby Hughs enjoyed the provincial milieu of country village life. A sociable person, she had many women friends who often visited for afternoon tea. On the morning of a visit day, Ruby always set about with enthusiastic industry baking biscuits, scones or cakes in her wood-burning stove in readiness for her friends. She was happy in this task, and in the expectation of snippets of fresh village news, or further instalments upon the old.

'It's *news*, not gossip!' indignant Nana stressed to counter Grandpa's tease.

However, when her grandchildren were staying she thought it wise to caution them: 'If anyone asks you questions about the family, just say, "I don't know"'. Though perhaps somewhat obsessive, this was a legacy of earlier years when they had lived in Sydney, and she had developed an abhorrence of gossip. After that, Nana diligently sought to protect the private affairs of the family from idle curiosity which, she believed, sometimes grew into too many confidential slips of tongues too close to ears that were too trusted.

Nana laughingly recounted an incident that occurred when Jack was a small boy. Near their house dwelt an intolerable "stickybeak" of a woman, whose seemingly dull life was brightened only by the extraction from unwary children of information regarding their parents. Nana warned little Jackie against answering any of her questions, but the child was very young and unacquainted with the wily ways of certain adults, and he confused this concept with school lessons. He thought the woman, who had cunningly waylaid him at her gate, was giving him some sort of quiz, as his teacher often did.

Arriving home, he told his mother about the "nice lady". Suspiciously, Nana enquired, 'And did she ask you a lot of questions?'

Jackie's face lit up with pride. 'Yes, she did,' he said, 'and I knew *all* the answers!' Nana declared that it was enough to make a saint swear.

Nana Hughs however, almost never swore, the singular known exception being in response to something that happened on a frigid and blustery day. Nana's laundry facility was situated outdoors, entirely without shelter. For hours, she had slaved away coaxing the wood copper to boil up all the towels, sheets, pillowslips and tablecloths, and then she had to rinse everything by hand in the old wooden wash tub.

At last, struggling against the icy wind and suffering frequent slaps in the face from the washing, she succeeded in pegging it all up on the long line. The wash was indeed a lovely white sight but still dripping, even though Nana's hands had wrung each article into a hard screw. The only chance of its drying was left to the caprice of the malevolent south wind which seemed mischievously intent on challenging the strength of the wooden dolly pegs.

Nana pushed up the prop to give height to the line – job done at last! With crinkled hands, wet hair, an ache in her back and a yearning for teapot and fireside, she turned to approach that reward when the unthinkable happened! The prop suddenly shot out alongside her, and she spun round to behold the heart-breaking sight of the washing lying in the dirt, the clothesline in two pieces.

Grandpa, at that disastrous moment, appeared around the corner of the house with a wheelbarrow of firewood, just in time to hear his saintly wife exclaim with loud, un-Nana -like vehemence: 'Damn, blast and *bugger it*!' It was fortunate for her appreciative relatives that he did, for devout Catholic Nana would never have told them that most delightful story … and they loved her all the more for her human fallibility.

Nana commented one day that many people do not fully appreciate their hearing faculty until they are denied it. In later years, her own difficulty became more noticeable and more

175

debilitating, and it was quite usual to see her leaning, frowning, with her better ear towards the speaker. Sometimes Grandpa took shameful advantage of that. He uttered funny comments in a voice he judged to be just below the threshold of Nana 's hearing, and which would have landed him in strife had his judgement defaulted.

Jack's younger brother, Charlie, owned a collection of gramophone records, one of which featured a woman whose voluptuous figure consigned all others to the category of "skinny, underfed boys". This *femme fatale* had attracted the salacious attention of a Casanova of Chinese descent who asked, using his peculiar grammar, 'Where *are you being* all my life, baby doll?'

She scowled at him as though he were a fat cockroach inviting instant foot-compression and replied to suit: '*Getting lost, you little oriental creep!*'

This ineloquent command embedded itself into Grandpa's subconscious, there to bide its time for the right moment – which presented itself quite unexpectedly one warm evening.

Several of the grandchildren were sitting on the front veranda reading *Blinky Bill* and playing dominos after enjoying Nana's honey-and-lemon pancakes and drinking Grandpa's explosive ginger beer. Consequently, the kids were all struggling against the increasing urge to "tread on frogs" (their grandmother's delicate alternative term to whatever idiomatic clock-stoppers the boys might come out with) or suffer the indignity of being chased outdoors to shake their rude selves.

The discussion turned to the CSIRO's newest assault upon the rabbit population, which resulted in widespread myxomatosis, a cruel sentence – death preceded by blindness and starvation. It was catastrophic for the rabbits, and also bad news for the family, for everyone enjoyed the rabbit casseroles Nana prepared whenever Uncle Charlie's traps were successful.

The whining mosquitoes had become savage. Nana, who could not hear the needle-thin warning, slapped several to death as they stung her and took a few swipes at others which proved to be a nanosecond faster than her usually lethal swatting. Irritated, she rose from her chair intent on fetching the *Citronella*. In a tentative move to step past Grandpa, who was engrossed in conversation with Uncle Charlie, she voiced a bossy command to move his big "plates of meat".

With his mind still tethered to the rabbit plague, Grandpa absently drew in his feet and Nana went past. But rabbits had not wholly occupied his mind. Belatedly, out came the cherished phrase: 'Aah, getting lost you little oriental creep!' This made him a brave man indeed, for Nana would have whacked him had she heard.

Nana used to grasp at basic terms and fill in the missing words to make some sense of what had been said, often with hilarious results. Similarly, this time she had caught some of Grandpa's words and stopped to think for a moment.

Grandpa worried suddenly that Nana's hearing had improved, but she continued on into the house and he relaxed again. It bothered her though, and she kept trying to work out what he had said. With citronella in hand, she returned frowning to the veranda and curiously asked Grandpa: 'What was that you were muttering about – losing an ornamental creeper?'

Over the years Nana's hearing ability continued to weaken, and everyone learnt to speak louder, to gain her attention first and to pronounce words clearly. Gardening became a pleasurable activity and necessary escape. It solaced her; afforded a welcome respite from the mental fatigue of listening to speech and deciphering; from the wearying concentration involved in lip-reading – in short, from the constant straining to hear. Annie tried hard to help her grandmother to hear what was going on around her, and she felt a pang of sadness one evening on the veranda when Nana was the only one of the gathered family who could not hear the haunting call of the mopoke.

Books and the colourful *Saturday Evening Post* magazine provided particular comfort to Nana and a simple expedient towards blessed silence. Grandpa never imposed conversation upon her after she had taken up her book and settled back contentedly in her cushiony cane chair with her feet raised upon the old velvet footstool. Grandpa, with his newspaper, understood that her hearing faculty and brain needed a recuperative rest.

Philosopher Christian Bovee wrote: "To cultivate a garden is to walk with God". Grandmother Ruby Hughs' life was closely aligned with this beautiful belief. In the fragrant, coloured midst of her personal kingdom, she spent many happy hours devotedly tending her beloved flowers.

Not a single day passed by without her careful inspection of each new bloom, a check to see if the bulbs had pushed through the soil, the insertion of a stake alongside a carnation bent by the wind, or a light cultivation of the earth with her work-worn old scratcher. Sometimes Nana could be heard humming contentedly or talking to the flowers in desultory fashion as she tidied up the beds, planted new seedlings, clipped away dead rose heads and composted the weeds.

Anyone approaching the homestead first viewed Nana's cottage garden from the paddock. A picket gate opened onto an earthen pathway bordered on both sides by everything that sight, tactility and a keen sense of smell could desire.

In the midst of the gorgeous spires, clusters, rosettes and sprays a visitor would delight in encountering tall Ruby Hughs in a longish dress and apron. She always wore a large straw hat, under the back of which could be seen white braids arranged in the figure eight style and pinned neatly into place. Her dresses were usually long-sleeved, and she was seldom hatless, for she had a horror of skin cancer. Her father-in-law had lost much of his nose tissue to melanoma, and soon after, his life. To Nana, outdoors was synonymous with hat – even on a dull day.

There was inspirational self-sufficiency on that small farm. Otto Hughs kept a well-stocked vegetable garden, and it was in this Eden his grandchildren first saw asparagus growing – naked spears piercing up through the hilled soil. Grandpa Hughs stored his marvellous potatoes in a "clamp", a small earthen hill hollowed and lined with bracken to protect the potatoes and topped with a "chimney" space for air. The potatoes kept well for many months. As before mentioned, Uncle Charlie trapped rabbits, Grandpa caught plenty of fish and milked the cow and Nana made butter with the cream.

For most of the year, an attractive display of plaited garlic and onions hung on the back veranda. As well, Nana preserved a number of the tomatoes and the fruit they grew. Her walk-in pantry with a tiny window at the western end was a delight to enter. It had the appearance and pleasant smell of a small shop and was neatly stocked with bottles and jars of pickles, sauces, jams and attractive dessert fruits all lined up on the shelves with white labels precisely positioned. It was all so neatly arranged that Annie, who had a penchant for symmetry, felt that to disturb the regimented rows would be tantamount to vandalism.

While gazing around the pantry one morning, Annie noticed among the jars of jam some filled glasses sealed with white glued-on paper "lids". Their sides were adorned with what appeared to be commercial lettering, which apparently could not be removed, and every one of them wore a Nana-style label adhering to the side, but not entirely covering the lettering. There was about a dozen of those glasses, and the girl assumed they comprised a set. The intrigue of what lay underneath the labels presented an exciting challenge to her, and she studied the exposed fragments of letters until deciding that they were: U-L-V-A.

Presently Grandpa, in his holey old work cardigan came in to inform Annie of newly hatched chickens. Despite her excitement over that, as they walked towards the broody coop she quickly asked him about the glasses.

'What does Ulva on them mean, Grandpa? ... and where did Nana get them?'

'Well ... your Uncle Charlie brought them home,' he answered casually, quite ignoring the first question. 'He got them ... ah, somewhere in – in Huskisson.' He became smilingly meditative, and it struck Annie then, glancing up sideways at him, how very much alike her grandpa and dad were.

By the time they had admired the six tweeting creatures, had survived the pecks of maternal hostility and were returning to the house, Grandpa's creative pondering had contrived a satisfactory response to the intriguing question. 'Those letters –' he began. 'I think they stand for 'United Lovers of Vineyard Agriculture.' His left elbow moved in little jerks as he spoke (one of his dear oddities which always accompanied a joke). The acronym (for The United Licensed Victuallers Association) appeared to have required an intensive claim upon Grandpa's concentration, but once expressed he nodded his head decisively and treated himself to a self-congratulatory chuckle.

Nana had overheard and understood. She gave his arm a chiding smack. 'Oh Otto!' she scoffed somewhat amusedly and offered no argument or alternative. After that, whenever noticing those special glasses filled with jam, lemon butter or tomato relish, Annie would wonder again what the letters under the labels really stood for.

Grandpa loved wine, especially his own made from the purple Isabella grapes – the vine enshrouded the walkway leading from the back door to the vegetable garden. He also brewed his flatulence-inducing ginger beer while the lemons were plentiful. The children were always fascinated as they watched the "plant" (yeast mixture) erupt in its jar to form a mushroom-shaped cloud. This phenomenon occurred whenever the gas had built up sufficient force to escape from beneath the sediment of ginger, and of the sugar with which it was regularly fed.

Grandpa always stored the bottled ginger beer in Nana's sacred pantry. She scoffed and tut-tutted as he irreverently shoved aside her crocks, pots and pans and the set of scales with its weights of different sizes, to make space for all his bottles. But Nana was of tenacious stock. As soon as her husband became busy at the wood-heap, she bustled in, crowded the ginger beer into a corner and rearranged her collection of biscuit trays, cake tins and pie dishes, all waiting their turn to be used for her excellent cooking.

Nana Ruby Hughs was locally famous for her baking, especially for her blackberry tarts with their pastry lattice adornment. But there was *one* culinary task that she had never mastered – the poaching of an egg. The underside usually turned out nicely opaque, the middle, plumply domed, but the top remained raw. Despondently, Annie stared at the transparent albumin, and a message of rebellion rushed from her brain to stomach. Nana always scoffed and scorned and, remarking on her grandchild's diminutive frame, predicted dwarfism.

In Annie's estimation, a raw egg was as evil an enemy as an oyster. Nevertheless, to please her nana and thereby escape some of the grandmotherly tyranny, she ate a small portion of the cooked part and the toast from under it but left the rest. Nana tut-tutted, muttered something about her 'picking like a sparrow', shook her head disapprovingly and transferred the reject to Banjo waiting expectantly at the back door. It was almost as though he and the girl were conspirators.

Grandparents Hughs often took pleasure in their small, teasing disputes. One afternoon Nana enquired of Beloved if he was *ever* going to fix the weather vane. She had already asked him several times that week.

Grandpa's mind had been pleasurably focused upon a vital rendezvous with smooth water and gullible fish. He frowned hard at his wife. 'I said I'd fix it when I'm good and ready Ruby, so why are you making such a big hullabaloo about it?'

Unfazed by this show of irritation, Nana repaid him with a flash of her wit. 'Because it's well-known Otto, that the squeaky gate gets the oil.'

Grandpa lifted his eyebrows, nodded and grinned in amused approval of her riposte. 'Well,' he said, throwing in a nugget from his own coffer of witticisms, 'it is also a fact, I'll have you know Mrs Hughs, that the nail that sticks up gets hit on the head!' He grinned again and eyed her challengingly to see if she could top that one.

But Nana good-naturedly flapped her tea towel at him. 'Oh, go away!' she laughed and went into the kitchen.

And it came to pass that by evening the four arms of the weathervane were once more indicating the correct points of the compass, and the tin rooster's head was again erect and watching over the farm. Nana too had been busy. She had fried the freshly caught flathead, transformed some of Grandpa's potatoes into chips and, using the succulent blackberries Herb, Paul and Annie had collected, baked a large tart for dessert.

All was well again on the farm.

22   Uncle Charlie

'Look up there!' cried Tony one day while three of the Hughs children were holidaying at the farm. Under a ceiling of violet-blue, a flock of Ibis were riding a thermal, floating in an effortless orbit high above the corn paddock. The birds appeared to be spying on the little group who were sampling the golden produce. Annie, Paul and Tony did not know they were Ibis until Uncle Charlie, shading his eyes, gazed upwards and then informed them. The children thought it was handy having their uncle right there sometimes – and sometimes *not*.

Uncle Charlie was a practical joker, and Nana often grumbled about his pranks, iterating that he sprang things on her. She called him a larrikin, complaining that she never knew what he was going to do next. However, an indulgent smile often belied the severity of her protestations, evincing a certain maternal pleasure drawn from the shenanigans of her favourite son.

An example of Uncle Charlie's amusements was brought to notice one afternoon after he had taken off his putrid old gym boots. Sitting on the back step, he observed a squadron of buzzing blowflies, no doubt attracted by the carrion smell. He regarded the odour as too good a resource to be denied at least a moment's contemplation.

Later, while Nana was in the bathroom, he stealthily slid the cadaverous boots underneath her bed. Presently, she emerged with her white plaits hanging over her dressing gown and entered the bedroom.

She halted a moment. The odour had made an immediate assault upon her nostrils, raising the suspicion that Charlie had hung another dead flying fox in the pear tree (the usual deterrent to marauding, fruit-loving creatures). She went to the window and breathed the night air. It was fresh, crisp and heavy with the scent of the eau de Cologne mint thriving near the tank stand. The fragrance betrayed the recent foot pressure of the cat.

'Well, it must be something *inside* the room', she muttered and worried that a rat had died in the wall lining, or worse, a possum above the ceiling. Then her imagination descended to a mouse's corpse decomposing under the wardrobe, so she bent her aching back and creaking knee joints to investigate. 'And I may as well look under the bed while I'm down here,' she sighed, even though she had swept there that day. So up went the bedspread and there were the boots!

Irish-born Ruby Hughs' tendency towards veiled amusement at her son's antics was now extinct. Her annoyance was such that she hurried those long dead, malodorous gym boots onto the front veranda and with all her might hurled them out across the garden, over the paddock and well into the bush. And good she was at hurling things. Despite lately aching joints, Ruby, a strong country-woman accustomed to hard work, was still very active.

Larrikin Charlie lamented that he'd had difficulty in finding his boots the next morning, although his nose might have guided him in their direction, and he was most unpopular with his mother for several days after that.

Uncle Charlie eventually transcribed another of his escapades into his niece's bad books as well. Jack and the two eldest kids went with him in the rowing boat up the river to check some rabbit traps they had set, and to shoot a few wild ducks.

Misery stole Annie's sunshine when discovering all this intended barbarity. She sat morosely on the back seat with Herb as the boat plopped along through the quiet water, and whispered a hasty prayer to St Francis of Assisi. She entreated him to ensure the traps would be empty and that the ducks would all fly off at the noise she intended making. Her warning, she knew, would have to be condensed into the first burst of shouting, before her father could silence her.

They tied the boat to a stump and began to walk along the bank. Annie emitted a loud shout, and something moved in the treetops. Uncle Charlie, who hated crows because of their assaults on lambs, fired his rifle and a feathery creature fell to the ground. It was a kookaburra!

Annie was unaffected by Uncle Charlie's sad regret for his mistake, and her anger gave way to a tearful attack. She could barely wait to get back to the farm to inform Nana of her son's wicked act of murder. She hoped that his adult status would not grant him impunity and that he would be severely reprimanded and dealt a good clip under the ear. From this prospect, Annie derived much anticipatory pleasure. Furthermore, it would please her immensely if Nana banished His Worshipful to bed without his evening meal.

As soon as the boat drew alongside the jetty, the girl leapt out. Anger lent wings of Mercury to her feet as they sped her up the grassy hill, across the paddock, through the gateway of Nana's flower garden, around the back and into the kitchen. 'Nana, Uncle Charlie shot a kookaburra dead!' she gasped, and in rapid catches of breath, told her all about it.

By the time Jack, Charlie and Herb arrived at the house, preconditioned Nana was thoroughly hostile. She bristled as she demanded: 'What's this I hear about you shooting a kookaburra?' Her eyes bored accusatively into "larrikin's" face, intuition and experience unreservedly identifying the culprit.

'It wasn't a kookaburra,' Charlie said. He looked to Jack for support and received it, and Herb's head-swaying tacitly backed them up. Annie was shocked to realise they would actually lie to Nana. Things looked grim now, for that made three against one.

Annie fought on. 'They're telling fibs, Nana. It *was* a kookaburra,' she insisted and proceeded to describe the bird and its last fluttering as it lay dying in the grass at their feet.

Nana glared at them, 'What was it then?' she asked suspiciously, imperiously and the girl moved to her grandmother's side and stared with penetrating intensity at their eyes to ascertain what sort of story they would concoct. Naturally, it had all been worked out before reaching the house – the immediacy and unanimity of the answer: 'A cockatoo!' betraying conspiracy.

Nana raised her eyebrows and cast upon them a most sceptical look; a look she might have used in the past for naughty little boys telling absurd big fibs. Annie immediately rejected their contrived answer – she knew a kookaburra when she saw one. 'It *was*, Nana', she persisted.

Although Uncle Charlie felt a personal invincibility, his affected innocence was poorly delivered. 'Yeah, like, that's what it was all right,' he said and evil-eyed his nuisance niece as a pest to be swatted. Resuming the feeble facade, Charlie turned to his mother. 'We'll go back and get it if you like,' he offered, confident under his halo and entirely counting on the improbability that he would actually have to do so. Moreover, there was always the speculation to exploit that a scavenging fox, which had no qualms about interfering with the scene of the atrocity, had carried off the iconic bird to its den of hungry progeny.

Jack nodded then and introduced a jot of his ornithological knowledge into the deception: 'Sulphur-crested cockatoo – farmer's foe,' he said, and Herb's silence further cemented this most annoying rampart of male solidarity. Even so, the men were quite aware of the dilemma Nana faced. She deliberated a moment, realising the serious consequence of the injuring or killing of an Australian emblem. And, conscious of Annie's tendency to talk and to challenge any act of persecution, she made her reluctant, gender-betraying decision, turned to her granddaughter and said, 'Well, if they're all so certain it was a-a sulph— a cockatoo, then it musthave been, Annie. Now stop worrying about it.'

Annie was astonished. Stop worrying? The injustice had doubled! Even Nana had switched allegiance, and that now made *four* against one. The supplicating little unit of humanity was on her own, or to use Charlie's regular nautical metaphor: completely "up the creek". 'No, Nana,' she wailed. 'It *was* a kookaburra, it was. You've gotta believe me!'

Nana had no option but to shake her grey head, cast aside conflicting feelings of anger, sadness and sympathy, and summon an illusion of conviction to assert: 'No, it was a cockatoo, just as they said.' (Later, Annie was pleased to learn of the stern lecture the errant sons received.) 'Now how about you go outside and

191

play,' Nana suggested, naturally fed up with the lot of them. She hesitated for a moment, looked at Annie very thoughtfully, opened her mouth, closed it again, and turned back to her bread-making, subduing the unwise impulse to warn the child against telling anyone. Red rag, indeed!

Out in the yard, Annie stared in a state of shock. They had got away with it and Nana, her only possible ally, had sided with them. It amplified her isolation and put her at a complete loss to know how to make her grandmother believe that her youngest son, although a mortal immune from sinning and apparently now canonised, had, in fact, shot a kookaburra.

She sat on the chopping block to stew about it all and warned the despotic pet magpie, Adolf, which aloofly strutted around the yard all day pecking any visitors who called, that he had better watch out or he may end up being another dead cockatoo!

Presently, Saint Charlie emerged into the sunshine. With a sudden movement, he drew up his trouser leg and inspected something that was stuck to his skin.

'Geez! A bloody leech!' he exclaimed and snatching at the parasite, pelted it onto the ground and then examined the red spot where it had been dining on his sanctified blood.

The unwitting host then grabbed a rock from the garden border and dropped it onto the swollen leech. Bright blood splattered over him and onto the dirt. 'Ah gawd, look at that!' he said, disgusted by all the mess and the theft of his most precious of body fluids.

Annie felt the sweet thrill of revenge. 'Seeerves you right!' she sneered explosively, satisfied now that at last some measure of justice had been dealt on behalf of the poor dead bird.

As well as being a practical jester, Charlie, like Jack, enjoyed telling jokes. It was impossible for the children to understand their nonsensical little stories though, and Annie and Paul shared the smug conviction that grown-up's jokes could never compete with "knock-knocks". Nevertheless, they enjoyed the sight and sound of the adults throwing back their heads and laughing helplessly.

Some of these adult jokes were tediously long, often involving an Englishman, an Irishman and a Scotsman. Others were strangely short, but all seemed to gain in coarseness – usually in parallel proportion to the descending level in the wine bottle. This left Annie staring at her uncle and father in absolute perplexity, and it occurred to her to wonder if Nana had dropped them on their heads when they were little.

Even Margo, on one occasion ironing with her back to Annie, put her head down. Her plump, shaking shoulders betrayed a struggle to repress laughter, and she was reluctant to turn her face when an explanation was sought. The girl regarded this as discriminatory, and being the most interested outsider of this unfair adult conspiracy, she knew they were not going to grant admittance. She decided to show these infantile grown-ups what joke-telling was all about and spoke up in a challenging tone: **'Knock-knock!'**

'Ah struth!' sighed Jack. 'Not again! Righto – who's there?'

Pleased with his compliance, Annie replied, 'Isabel,' and waited, grinning expectantly.

Her father sat back in his chair, sighed, and made his voice sound sooo bored: 'Isabel who?'

The young joker's voice rose with tinkling laughter as she delivered her screamingly funny punch line: 'Is-a-bell necessary on a bike?'

There were groans and hands-to-heads gestures from the two men, and much lifting of eyes. Jack said, 'Aah, come on Annie! You call *that* a joke? ...Well, I don't get it.' His face changed to a frowning expression, and his voice ascended to a queer treble: 'It's a bit stupid if you ask me, and not even one little tiny bit funny.' The comical mockery had his daughter staring at him in bewilderment, and she looked to her mother for an explanation.

Margo bent to the child's ear and whispered, 'He's just pretending to be you.'

Annie was amazed. 'But *I* don'tsound like that and pull stupid faces … do I?' she asked.

Jack's grinning mouth emitted a consolatory chuckle. He assured her the knock-knock was a "bottler", and to placate Margo and banish her threatening glare, he enquired whether there were anymore of them. (There were dozens!)

Uncle Charlie, however, shook his head woefully and said, 'Gawd, stone the crows like … your old man's a glutton for punishment, isn't he Annie?'

23 Christmas

Oyster Bay was buzzing with all things Christmassy. As always, greedy, predatory commercialism chased Christmas in and inflicted financial worry upon parents. And before tight post-war budgets could fully recover, it scuttled off to prepare for the promotion of Easter, or more specifically, of chocolate – a mean exploitation of two beautiful events.

But the Hughs children knew nothing of the mercenary aspect and eagerly looked forward to Christmas. Increasingly, as it drew near, an air of happiness communicated itself wherever they went – to all who entered Gumm's store, for example. There among the balloons, the bonbons and the tantalisingly high horizon of lolly jars, the cheery "Merry Christmas" became the general salutation.

There was plenty to do at the Hughs' house. Contentedly, the chattering children sat cross-legged on the front veranda floor with crepe paper, *Clag* glue and rolls of coloured streamers. There, they busily fashioned paper chains and lanterns with which to brighten the house and hang on the tree. Margo wrote greetings in Christmas cards in readiness for posting, and she intended, once Jack was home and after everyone's feet were safely in bed, to spruce-up the kitchen lino with cheerful red paint, which would dry during the hot night.

Usually, the festive tree, along with bunches of starry Christmas bush and red-and-yellow bells, was obtained from the bushland on the far side of the bay. That beautiful area was thick with apricot-and-grey-barked eucalypts and a concentration of a wide diversity of native flora. No doubt, some mid-century residents of Oyster Bay took it all for granted and perhaps the flower displays were never encountered by the present dwellers of the houses which occupy that same land – known now as Kareela.

Back then, many ideally conical she-oaks grew there. Once selected the children took turns with the wood-pecking tomahawk until the little tree was felled. And then, tethered securely behind Jack's rowing boat, it followed the excited youngsters home.

Just before Christmas, the Hughs' children attended Mass and displayed a conscientious observance of all that was right, proper and wise to promote favour in the eyes of benevolent God, Father Christmas and their parents. It was never easy to refrain from quarrelling; to stand back for the other child; to still the tongue when an uncharitable thought champed to be forcefully expressed.

They did it though and were rewarded with a moderate number of presents. As well, Margo always tied up bundles of treats in bright cellophane. Each one contained the same amount of lollies, nuts and cherries, leaving no reason for squabbles to arise over the size of the share, and she hung the colourful bundles on the Christmas tree somewhat early to provide an incentive for her children to remain amicable towards one another.

Even Thumper always received a Christmas gift. But one year he appeared to have lost his vitality. He seemed past it, too old and weary to care about the juicy lamb bone in his dish. Jack's visiting brother, Charlie, who sometimes was glaringly devoid of sensitivity, looked at Thumper lying there asleep on the mat dreaming about lost youth and the joy of savaging the Sanitary Man, and commented that he was 'over-ripe for a hole in the ground'.

It was insensitive but prophetic. A week later Thumper died. The Hughs had always treasured their pet as an essential part of the family, and now the children shed many tears over the limp little fellow as they caressed his brown-and-white fur for the last time. Jack buried him in the front garden next to Peggy's small bones, and Margo planted another rose bush there.

One year as Christmas approached, Paul, Tony and Annie attended Jimmy Murphy's birthday party. The Murphys lived farther up the road in a fibro "half-house" which nevertheless had the full set of waiting piers. Those brick piers indicated good initial intentions, but over the years of procrastination, or lack of funds, the spaces among them evolved into convenient dumping places for household junk. That various material in turn protected, indeed *nurtured*, the wattles growing up amongst it.

Mrs Murphy affectionately referred to her property as "Rose Park". The name initially was inspired by the two climbing roses, which later went feral and strangled the wooden archway. This saved it from collapsing onto the gate and defacing the sign.

Pragmatic Jack regarded "Our Little Joint" as a suitable and endearing name for his house. Always averse to even the slightest hint of pretention, he snorted his contempt for the label, Rose Park, and declared that the Murphys should have called their place Gunnahaftado. He would never have fired such an uncharitable arrow had the woman possessed a little humility. It was her ridiculous pretence of being what she apparently was not, coupled with her rough treatment of the English language, that irritated him.

By contrast, Margo considered "Rose Park" an elegant name for a property and remarked sadly that it probably compensated Mrs Murphy a little for the disappointment of her husband's failure to finish building the house. Margo averred that Mrs Murphy had many good attributes and reminded cynical Jack: 'Poor grammar does not make a bad person.'

Nevertheless, Margo Hughs cared very much about grammar and was diligent in correcting her children whenever they became lazy and said *me* instead of *my*,or when they pronounced the *ing* suffix of certain words as *in* or *ink*. Even Jack, who occasionally swore and blasphemed, would rarely drop his *ings*. But the biggest linguistic sin of all in Margo's view was the utterance of *youse* to pluralise *you*.

Jack, having voiced his opinion of Rose Park, evinced acute annoyance when Margo disagreed with him. A scowl warned what was coming, so she shrewdly pre-empted by bestowing a sweet smile. 'It's not every woman who has a clever hubby like you,' she quipped, kissing the top of his head and moved deftly away from his chair before loving arms could grab her – and before the milk boiled over leaving a smelly mess on the stove.

However, Margo's compassionate view of Mrs Murphy did not soften Jack's attitude, and he declared that the woman was a 'peanut-brained illiterate'. This remark was typical of the exaggerated distortion Jack applied to anyone he disliked. When he painted someone black it was jet, ebony or tar. He had no time for the forgiving milky shades of grey. Consequently, it was difficult, almost impossible, for him to concede Margo's well-timed counter-comment:

'Well, I've never heard her swear or blaspheme, you know Jack. Not even once.'

One sunny morning, Mrs Murphy encountered Jack Hughs raking over the area between his fence and the road – the children's extended playground. With well-practised capability,

200

she steered the one-sided conversation towards the subject of her superior relatives, whom she had not seen in "munce" and who were soon to honour her with a visit.

'Yairs, very well-orf they are, a very effluent fambly, very 'igh in society y'know. They been to Cambra even!' she marvelled. Before Jack, raking the ground, could grab at a reasonable pretext to escape the roadside ambush, Mrs Murphy launched another subject, easing it smoothly into the narrative by expressing her genuine admiration of his small fry playing with a beach ball.

'Lovely buncha kiddies you got there, Mr Yooz,' she said. ''Course, I only got the two chil'ren … can't never 'ave no more now y' know after me trouble 'avin' Jimmy,' she said prosaically, as though discussing the rising price of tea … but straying onto very sacred ground. Jack Hughs never spoke of such things.

At this alarming moment, Jack, foreseeing the revelation of some horrible gynaecological mystery, grabbed the ball, which had fortuitously landed at his feet, bid the woman a curt goodbye and hastily navigated the kids through the gate and himself to safe harbour. There in the kitchen, he relayed the conversation, including the masterpiece of troubled negatives, to Margo … who, as always, was sympathetic. And Mrs Murphy, not in the least offended by the abrupt severance and pleased that her proud

201

disclosures had been spread a little farther, waddled complacently back to Rose Park.

Against maternal advice, Annie took her baby doll, Poppy, to Jimmy Murphy's birthday party. Sometime during the late afternoon, she dawdled home with her brothers and, feeling sick from all the cream cakes devoured, entirely forgot about Poppy.

Margo suggested fetching the doll the following day, but the next morning Jimmy's mother called in with something in a paper bag. Margo invited her onto the veranda, and after the brief greetings, Mrs Murphy withdrew Poppy's burnt head from the bag.

'There's only the 'ead left,' she said bluntly, giving Margo and Annie the kind benefit of her prodigious powers of observation. Shocked Annie flopped down onto the doorstep and wept.

'I dunno 'ow to tell y' this,' the woman continued darkly and her gaze, as always, darted everywhere but on Margo's concerned face. 'Y'see, Jimmy didn't 'preciate 'avin' the doll at the party. Chucked it in the 'cinerator, 'e did! ... the little ba– little devil. I'll dong 'im, I will,' she lied. And when belated family allegiance prodded her conscience she spouted the usual defensive philosophy: 'Ah well, I s'pose boys will be boys.'

Margo was incensed. How detestable, that oft-used attempt to waive punishment for the mischief of boys who deserve to suffer in parallel measure to the offence! Had Annie and Josie emptied their chamber pot over the recalcitrant brat, Jimmy, Mrs Murphy would hardly have tut-tutted and exclaimed: 'Oh well, girls will be girls!'

Mrs Murphy at least had the grace to be embarrassed by the incident, however, and after a few apologetic words to Margo, she stepped down onto the path. 'I'm real sorry, deary,' she mumbled, nodding to Annie.

The wounded girl, deeming manners exempt here, withheld the obligatory 'thank you', turned her head away and cringed from the parting pat on her shoulder. She was relieved when the gate clicked shut, and Mrs Murphy carried her stout-self homeward. 'Bummy old bag!' She muttered sinfully.

Poppy was dead! The only substantial component of the otherwise calico doll was now a monochrome lump of moulded clay. The sorry sight earnt Annie many comforting words and hugs from her mum that day. Later, Margo gazed intently at the doll's head. Her gentle fingers felt the contours of curls, eyes, nose and mouth and, becoming meditative, she placed the head on the mantelpiece between the tea canister and the bill-spike. Later, to provide some consolation, she handed the bereaved girl an early Christmas present, a book titled *Little Women* and written by Louisa May Alcott, and told her to rest on her bed and read for a while.

But Annie continued to feel significantly upset by the destruction of her beloved doll, and after reading a page twice and knowing not what her eyes had seen, she closed the book and surrendered to the comforting pleasure of conjuring perverse images to satisfy her lust for revenge. Remarkably innovative schemes came parading across the ceiling, methods of decapitating Jimmy Murphy. Methods, however, which died soon after their inception, thereby saving Annie from being institutionalised.

Clearly, there was nothing to be gained in retaliation, the unhappy girl realised, therefore brooding proved futile. 'Just get over it,' her inner self dictated, and at once brought to mind something Sister Clare had quoted, a gem from Mahatma Gandhi: "The weak can never forgive. Forgiveness is the attribute of the strong". It was indeed a noble principle, but not applicable to Annie Hughs at that particular moment, for she dearly wanted Jimmy Murphy hanged, drawn and quartered.

24 The Gift

The children had been counting the days until Christmas and were down to the final three. Margo was always the last one to bed. Hence Annie was unaware that during the quiet first hours of the children'sslumber her mother was carefully painting the doll's head and sewing up a calico body. Happy with the result and looking forward to Annie's Christmas day delight, Margo dressed the new Poppy in some of the pretty clothes she had knitted for her last baby and then hid the doll in her wardrobe.

Sometimes, Margo placed a piece of cake and bottle of port on the table for Santa (always coinciding with Jack's late shift). In the morning, there was the evidence of the drawn-out chair, plate of crumbs and smeary glass to chase away any doubts the little ones might have had about Santa's visit. Just knowing that the red and white Revered Presence had actually sat at their table lent an ambience of magic to the festive morning.

Every year, generous Nana Hughs baked for Jack and Margo a fruitcake, large and rich with concentric rings of almonds embedded into the glossy brown surface. Margo admired the carefully arranged pattern and remarked to Annie that it would be a shame to cover the cake with icing; it would show a disregard for Nana's efforts and be hurtful to her. This being so, the icing sugar and almond essence remained inside the dresser, and the sprig of fake holly found itself temporarily at centre-stage. Nana's cake was a blessing, one big task Margo could delete from all the extra chores, routines and rituals linked with busy Christmas time.

Jack's other brother Owen, and his sister Eva shared a house at Hurstville, and Nana Hughs always stayed there on her visits away from the South Coast farm. Her daughter and son usually accompanied her when she visited Jack and his family on Christmas Eve. That year, the year of Poppy's resurrection, Eva, alighting from a taxi, carried in a bag of presents.

Despite the children's care in thanking her fondly for the gifts and for the trouble of getting them there by train and taxi, Eva remained adamant that they must not be opened until morning. But that was a whole afternoon and night away! How could they endure until then? All they were able to do in the meantime was shake, sniff and feel the mysterious gifts through the brightly coloured, securely string-tied wrappings. At least, that revealed to Annie that hers was solid and tinny.

Many things ran through her brain that night, hard things which rattled, considerably shrinking the sphere of possibilities, and how difficult it was to fall asleep! Annie wished she could switch off her mind, stop it from going around endlessly with, 'What could it be?'

As with all optimistic humans, Annie was easily led onto her preferred path. In the sudden conviction that the wrapper concealed the cash register money box lately displayed in Gumm's window, her will and desire united and modified the rattle to suit the money drawer. Smiling satisfaction was free then to melt into unrelated drifts of thought, and at last, merciful oblivion.

The rooster, having escaped the chopping block, crowed at the first hint of grey dawn. Upon waking, it took Annie a mere moment to connect the *something good awaits* sensation with the actuality of the event. In the Hughs house, it was always the duty and delight of the first-awake child to rouse the others: 'It's Christmas Day! Come on – Santa's been!'

They bumped their sleepy way towards the tree and presents. Annie's first action that year was to attack the gift that had kept her awake for so long. Her fingers tore away the red wrapper in a frenzy akin to starvation meeting food … but it is so hard when you are a child to feel delighted and grateful when you are *not*! There in the middle of the shredded paper was a tambourine, perhaps the last thing Annie would choose. However, not a complete ingrate, she did spare a thought for Aunty Eva's kindness and felt ashamed of her first reaction. But as so much intense focus had been placed upon that particular item, the disappointment was deservedly proportionate.

This was cast aside and forgotten though when her astonished eyes rested on Poppy sitting there under the decorated she-oak tree. Amazed Annie scooped her up, and the sudden rise of emotion propelled her into Margo's arms, there to cry with love, happiness and gratitude. She finally realised what devoted activities her mum had been engaged upon during those late nights before Christmas.

Later that week the children sat down obediently to write notes of delight to generous Aunt Eva. Annie knew her fibbing sentiments would have to be added to the growing list of sins for next confession, for in the act of impulsive expediency she had bestowed her gift upon joyful Tony. However, as might have been predicted, Jack's vociferous complaint about 'that noisy, bloody tin-can thing' saw the crashing tambourine plucked swiftly from Tony's energetic hands and restored to Annie's.

Later that summer there was a charity drive collecting food, clothing, toys, books, and furniture ... anything at all for an unfortunate family from hilly Caravan Head, whose house had been destroyed by fire and who was now staying in the community hall awaiting rental accommodation. What to give? Margo instructed her children to see what they could spare, but to ensure the donation was in a reasonably good condition so that it would be gladly received.

Gradually the fruit box on the front veranda gained a few deposits. Cunning Opportunity urged Annie to dispose of the tambourine, but Guilt overruled, ordering her to donate one of her dolls. Annie looked fondly at her music box, won at a chocolate wheel event. She thought carefully, winding the key and gazing wistfully at the tiny ballerina moving in jerky circuits to a tinkling few bars of Beethoven's *Fur Elise* ... and her heart softened.

It is a valid truism, as Margo often claimed, there are varying degrees of good in everyone. Annie thought about her own impending generosity, and it warmed her with that self-caressing feeling which sometimes accompanies noble intentions. There happened to be a girl in the family who had lost everything. Annie imagined the child stowing treasures into the tiny drawers of the music box, or cuddling one of the surrendered dolls, drawing comfort from them as she lay fretting on a stretcher-bed in the big dark Community Hall. Annie's imaginings were always dramatic.

However, although not usually given to caprice, by bedtime, she had begun to doubt the wisdom of the intended sacrifice. That night her prayers by-passed God and went post-haste to Our Lady. In Annie's fancy, Mother Mary assured her that the bestowal of a gift which exacted personal forfeiture would carry greater value and move her closer to heaven ... and she certainly wanted to go there – but not just yet! Sleep came quickly to Annie then and carried her off to the subliminal world happy in the belief that the right Divine answer was on its way – a telegram from heaven.

Morning came. Decision made. It was collection day. After breakfast, Margo set about finding some string to secure the box with later, and she told Paul and Tony to gather any further contributions. Paul hesitated with his set of metal warships and Margo cast a soft glance on him. 'Don't give away anything you'd rather keep, dear.'

Her generous-natured son shook his blond head and said, 'Nah – I'm too big for these now,' and into the box went both boys' old treasures, each one deposited slowly with a last reconsidering look to accompany it into the box. While Annie …? while she tossed in her "bummy" tambourine! However, after an hour of increased self-loathing, she gently lowered her music box and reclaimed Aunty Eva's unloved gift. It seemed they were stuck with each other, Annie and the tambourine!

***

In listing memorable Christmases, no one could speak for Paul, but had his life not been cut short by cancer, there may have been some exceptional Christmases in store for him. However, the Hughs were left with a beautiful memory of an ear-to-ear grin on the face of a taller Paul on his fourteenth birthday when he found a shining new bicycle waiting for him in the lounge room. His beloved blue eyes sparkled beneath that blond hair, in the absolute zenith of happiness.

25 Rusty and the Neighbours

Not long after Thumper died, providence kindly arranged for a stray, rusty-coloured dog to wander into Oyster Bay. Annie Hughs immediately claimed him, her brilliant light-globe moment fixing upon him the name Rusty. She fed him well, and he grew in strength and proportion – and into her heart. Therefore, it was disappointing when it appeared that he had been loitering near the fowl yard. Annie's subsequent, covert investigation revealed a gap under the fence which would nicely accommodate his suspected poaching shape.

A few days later, the worried girl discovered a feather trail that led her across the vacant bushy block next door, and there she found Rusty chomping into one of the best layers. This was serious! If her father found out, he would give him "a dose of lead", his usual radical method of dealing with wayward creatures. Annie buried the hen's remains and filled in the gap under the wire netting. She felt unhappily furtive deceiving her parents, but the need to save Rusty from execution overrode her tyrannous conscience.

Shortly after that, Margo noticed the absence of a few hens and Jack instantly blamed 'that good-for-nothing-useless-mongrel, Rusty'. IndignantAnnie's desperate bluffing attempt to convince her myopic dad that it might have been dingoes, foxes, wolves or Tasmanian tigers raiding the yard at night, fell flat. Jack turned his eyes upon her in amused contempt. 'Don't they teach you *anything* at school?' which Annie thought was a peculiar and irrelevant thing to say, just then.

Jack glanced across at Margo feeding Clivey his porridge and nodded several times – a non-negotiable decision in the making. 'Well there won't be any more missing from now on,' he announced resolutely. Margo's gentle face grew sombre. Her blue eyes sent a mute appeal to her unreceptive husband, while the forgotten spoonful of porridge hovered in transit, Clivey leaning forward, his little mouth wide open and comically attempting to receive it.

It was Sunday, and the children were being urged to hurry for Mass. Herb was exempt that day. His duty to check the fish traps and cycle to the shop for Jack's cigarettes and the Sunday paper took priority. Margo issued the usual instructions regarding manners and road safety. She warned snuffling Tony, 'Use your hanky this time, dear, not your sleeve', and with a sceptical glance, reminded them all to place their sixpences on the plate when it was presented. Maternal trust was in short supply on Sundays, the walk to the church taking the kids with their brief opulence, most temptingly past the grocery shop and its treasury of lollies.

When they returned, Rusty did not hurtle out as was usual, to bark and leap all over their Sunday clothes. Annie looked in all the prominent places and attempted to interrogate Herb, but he was impatient to head off into the bush with hunter-keenness in his early-teen heart. He had recently acquired a *B-B* air rifle, and there were a few scores to be settled with egg-stealing snakes and goannas. And so, Annie walked on down past the vegetable gardens and fruit trees, then descended the stone steps to the wharf, returning slowly in thoughtful abstraction.

Margo was busy clearing up after Jack's breakfast. He relished omelettes, and that worrying fact did nothing to favour Rusty's future ... or the longevity of certain reptiles. 'No, I don't know *where* he is,' she told the sad-faced girl and glanced quickly at Jack. Conscious of Annie's analytical scrutiny, Margo averted her eyes and began wiping a dishcloth over the table. 'Dogs wander off sometimes to find mates,' she said to the green-and-white check baize. It was a valid possibility Annie conceded, but having discerned sorrow in her mother's tone, her anxiety increased.

Jack, seated on his throne – the large chair with arms – shook out the newspaper, glanced at the photograph of Prime Minister Menzies and began reading. After a moment, he turned the page and looked over at glum Annie. 'Rusty's probably in Timbuktu by now, love ... having fun with his new girlfriend,' he said.

Tony glanced up from his comic to enlighten his father: 'But Rusty couldn't walk *that* far.' Every geographically literate child knew that Timbuktu was out past Woop Woop beyond the

Black Stump in the Never Never. 'It'd take him a hundred years, Dad!' he exclaimed with the satisfied air of having corrected a glaring misconception.

Jack laughed at that lightning calculation and continued teasing Annie. 'Or he might've slipped over the cliff chasing those Tasmanian tigers.' He could not resist another chuckle. The serious girl stared at him coldly, nascent suspicion stirring, and Margo shook her head and tut-tutted when he added: 'I thought I saw a dodo the other day scratching around your cubbyhouse!' He flicked an assessing glance at his daughter, chuckled again and returned to his paper.

Unwilling to allow her worries to be dismissed as of no account, Annie remained silent. She sensed that, although her dad seemed innocent, the playfulness in his manner suggested some new mischief. She fired thought-arrows at him, cursing the newspaper, which shielded him from her ferocious scowling.

Margo had nothing more to say. Her mouth compressed into a hard line as she went over to the stove, and her daughter wondered: 'Perhaps Mum's not sad at all; perhaps the baby's kicking, or her back's aching again making her tired and cranky'. Annie's child-mind interpreted the silence as indifference. How wrong she was! How Margo's heart ached for her that long ago day!

The morning was heating up. The gravel road led Annie down the hill and along towards the shops, all the while calling for Rusty. She paused outside the Post Office to talk to white-haired Mr Quinn resting on a bench. He lived a simple and sedentary life in his nearby quaint cottage yet still enjoyed the sociability of the Oyster Bay populace. His kind hazel eyes had not noticed Rusty about, but Hope reached out to Annie when the God-like baritone assured: 'Don't worry, he'll come home when he's hungry,' and the gentle fatherly smile seemed to impart divine knowledge and a firm belief that it would indeed be so.

Everyone liked Mr Quinn. At the last Christmas Do, Annie's gaze lingered on Santa's face, an embryo notion stirring into life. Despite the red cap and cotton-wool beard there was a familiarity about those merry hazel eyes. This kind-hearted octogenarian was widely respected and casually regarded as the patriarch of the community. Whenever Annie sought to conjure an image of God, Mr Quinn came into her mind. Sometimes in dreams, God, Mr Quinn and Santa were interchangeable, but she always wished Santa did not have to share alphabet letters with Satan!

Presently, along came local bully, Big-head '*I-don't-need-no-book-learnin*,' Butch, a surly, rotund thirteen-year-old whose achromatic landscape of a mind regarded all other earthlings with a contemptuous arrogance. He had never been overburdened with the niceties of manners, charm or concern for others and gleefully, had just heard about Rusty.

'Betcha he got run over ... bloody *squashed!*' he said with cruel delight. A horrible squelch sound spluttered from his loose wet lips, and avidly he watched as the mental pain of that image distorted Annie's features.

She yearned to screech out: 'Ah, drop dead you *basket!*' But the size of the brute and his menacing expression prompted her to suppress the urge. Besides, some respect had to be shown for her having received Holy Communion at Mass an hour before. Strangely oblivious to her state of grace, he took aggressive steps forward and stood with his bare feet apart, arms folded, barring the way. Annie turned and ran towards the shortcut across Nancarrow's paddock. She halted abruptly, for there, earning his daily banquet of meadow clover and rye, the Friesian bull was trying to impose piggyback antics upon a restless cow.

What a dilemma! Should she risk the possible charge of a disgruntled bull or the foul mouth and shoving paws of the bully? (who so badly needed to be bashed up, she scorned, and she wished the local boys would do the right thing and see to it *soon.*) As Kipling wrote: "The strength of the wolf is in the pack." The bully's pack of underlings was not in attendance that day, and so she chose the latter jeopardy.

With renewed fleet-footedness Annie took a long way around, widely skirting Big-head Butch, and headed along Oyster Bay Road. She halted in response to the cheery 'Hello-ello!' from Mr Birtles, Jack's fishing mate. The wiry, grandfatherly neighbour was leaning on his gate, as was his custom, watching the passing parade of Oyster Bay life. It was a good time for Annie to stop and rest under the shady bough of Mr Birtle's unwitting protection.

'Real runny-honey weather, this!' was his preliminary as the girl stepped up onto the bank of the earthen pathway. There, the sun-yellow calliopsis swayed and nodded at her as she approached the gate, and a fleeting thought registered to pick some of them for her mum – once her huffing and puffing had calmed.

When asked about Rusty, Mr Birtles moved his head with a slow, thoughtful 'Nooo,' yet his tone conveyed hope. 'But he might be behind the butcher's y'know.' He thought a moment, 'I s'pose you've looked at the park?' and then offered solemn, frowning advice, 'Dogs need to be tied up, y' know. They need discipline'. Lastly, his kind words of solace, 'All dogs go walkabout, Annie love, but they usually come home again.'

His features settled back into the cheerful mien most habitual to him. Always more disposed to talk about fish than of anything else, he was skilful in the art of merging almost any topic, however obliquely, with fishing. In fact, so adroitly did he change gear, the shift was hardly felt. 'Dogs love to roam about … just like fish do,' he said with satisfaction. Had Annie been smarter, she might have escaped when his pleased nods warned of narrative looming.

Too late! The transition accomplished, he became animated in his description of the whopper he had recently caught. It was last week's yarn, but now the veined and calloused hands underwent greater separation, and he gesticulated comically, recounting the battle he had fought to land the flathead. It was gigantic now, for as every angler knows, the growth of any extraordinary fish does not cease at death.

Quite recovered after her escape from Butch, Annie became restless and moved to go. The forgotten calliopsis and Mr Birtles waved her off, and he reminded her again to tell her dad about the phenomenal fish.

After another disappointing survey of the backyard, Annie returned to the road and scuffed despondently along to the Martins' house, separated from the Hughs' by the vacant block. Son Ned, on the front step, had a new cigarette stuck to his lower lip and was pocketing the tobacco pouch and digging out the matches. He swayed his head in response to the Rusty question and echoed Jack's casual comment: 'Probably found a girlfriend' – this universal conclusion fair testimony to the awesome power of females.

Annie continued the rounds of the neighbours receiving the same grim answer. Ruthie and a friend Robyn with Spotty, her Dalmatian, offered to help. Ruthie herself owned a romping black hound named Blacky, which always bounded after her father's motorbike whenever he conveyed his pillion passenger – his wife – to the beer garden of the hotel.

Billy Meadows tagged along, shadowed as always by Snowy, his almost-fossil albino hybrid of no-one-knew-what. (Great expenditure of thought preceded the naming of kids' dogs.) Thus, magnificently supported by six extra eyes, they sauntered on down the last hill to The Point. Anyone glancing near curtains or looking up from weeds and flowers might have thought the little procession a quaintly merry affair. They could not know that the heaviest of hearts dwelt amongst them and that the children would find no sign of Rusty at The Point to bring relief.

Ruthie, with her grand capacity for wisdom, passed on a snippet of dog-knowledge. She was sure Rusty had been stolen and, in effect, explained that his value lay in the diversity of the many breeds that comprised his being. This superior evaluation of Annie's mixed variety of dog at least had the merit of neutralising Jack's oft-used and insulting description.

'Never mind, Annie, we'll find him,' Ruthie said with the air of a grown-up and deftly swerving from her earlier dog-thief theory. Annie always took notice of wise, confident, senior Ruthie who now inspired some hope. Her heart fluttered with pride, imagination depicting valuable Rusty resplendent in blue ribbons, the wall by her bed adorned with pendants from the Royal Easter Show, his photograph pushing Frank Sinatra off the front page of the *Daily Telegraph* … his chook-culling but a minor blot belonging to the forgiven, fast-receding past.

Whenever Ruthie's parents were going to the pub, Mrs Collins would hang on tightly to her husband as their old motorbike stuttered over the corrugated road. Occasionally she would release one hand briefly to wave back at the panting dog. 'Go home Blacky, you bloomin' wretch!' was the usual command. It was then Ruthie's responsibility to drag the big, resisting fellow back to the house and tie him up. Annie was always glad her own mother never visited the beer garden.

The Hughs children, applying simple logic, assumed the beer garden was where grew the beer-flavouring hops. Jack had already explained to them (the subject dear to his heart) about the yeast, malt and hops that constituted the ambrosial fluid for which temples were erected universally. These sacred edifices were identified by odour, a rumbling of male voices and the curious term "BarBar" on the female-excluding swinging doors. Jack did not use the word bar, but *pub,* and so Annie assumed that "barbar" meant "women keep out!" – a most superfluous warning to the gentler human who preferred teapot, scones and bird-song among the flowers.

The sun mounted high. The trees' shadows shrank and told the group it was lunchtime. With the search exhausted, there was no recourse but to head homeward. Ruthie and Billy turned into their yards with the usual parting 'hooroo'. Robyn and Spotty reached their gates and dispiritedly, Annie dawdled home. The aroma of roast beef lingered at the back door, but her heart sent her onward down the yard, there in solitude to ponder Rusty's fate.

Peering over the precipitous cliff, and remembering the sack of kittens, it was easy for her to imagine a violent slamming of flesh upon the jagged rocks. Staring at the seeping tide claiming them, a sinister influence began to pervade her awareness, a growing disorientation, a dominant force which glassed eyes and drew a body downwards with malevolent incitement. This weird phenomenon frightened Annie and sent her hurrying away from the cliff edge before the long beckoning drop wholly mesmerised and drew her down.

In the full blue summer sky, streaked here and there with a light white brush, a cloud of galahs gave momentary pink and grey contrast, wheeled, swerved and moved on. The lassitude of the summery noon added weights to the weary girl's feet as she started back towards the house. The thought of the Sunday roast still held no appeal even though the search had occupied her all morning. She pictured Margo in her apron serving the dinner by now, glancing out the door, wondering why her daughter had not returned in time to set the table.

On her way back, the sight of a small patch of newly dug earth jumped up and stopped Annie. It was an island in the sea of seed-heavy grasses, the more apparent because of the yellow clay, indicative of depth, now spread on top. Staring horrified at the grave-shaped plot, she dared form the words: 'Did Dad shoot him while we were at Mass thismorning?'

Margo's frequent warnings against jumping to conclusions required the generosity of allowing the benefit of the doubt, but anxiety, having progressed to suspicion, now soured to an ugly conviction. Rusty *was* there, and his murderer was not going to get the benefit of the doubt from Annie!

Anger and nimble feet bore her to the house. In the kitchen, she confronted her father. He was Innocence personified, knew nothing about the grave, did not have a clue! Eventually, however, he wearied of his charade and with a dismissive wave of his arm professed to have upended the lavatory pan there. 'What a whopper'! scoffed Annie. She knew how selective he was. Every spent garden became the repository for the contents of any pan that had been filled too early for the sanitary day, and he always dumped the goods where the exhausted soil would be replenished.

King Fibber's story had transcended the ridiculous and Annie's pride was offended, that he had so little regard for her level of intelligence. This rankled her. She could not stand still. In a state of adrenalin-charged emotion, she fast-treaded back and forth on the lino, verbally attacking him with the tenacity of a peewee harassing a hawk. The words flowed, barely able to keep up with the thoughts which inspired them – a dangerous self-indulgence.

'That doesn't make se–, you wouldn't lug a heavy pan all that way– that *long* way down the back to bury it in the ground that's not– that's no good for anything, let alone a garden. *Don't fib, Dad!*' Annie was being outrageously insolent to her omnipotent father but felt helpless to suppress the anger which so forcefully demanded release.

Margo observed with a reproachful eye. 'Mind!' she warned, shaking a finger, for her daughter had indeed crossed the threshold. Jack usually applied leniency to the protests he provoked, drawing a strange delight in teasing, but Annie and her mother both knew that this time a clout was looming.

However, the distance between daughter and father easily exceeded his reach. Daughter drew on the reassuring fact that once ensconced upon his throne with the Sunday paper spread out reverently before him, His Majesty was as difficult to dislodge as a starving tick.

Wily fox Jack adhered to his feeble contrivance with the most benign of expressions, but the finite fragility of his patience began to exert itself. He exhaled vigorously and with an impatient hand, waved the irritating distraction away from him and his sacrosanct newspaper.

'Look,' he said with an unchallengeable air of finality, 'just forget the bloody dog!'

'Forget him? Forget *Rusty!* He might as well tell me to stop breathing!' Annie muttered and sank into a morose silence – expressing anger can be extremely depleting. Gradually her agitation abated. Feeling stunned, and drawing from her father's changed attitude the insulting inference that she should "get lost", Annie drifted to the door, leaving Mr Cranky unchallenged so that his AWOL conscience may eventually skulk back. And so, with a quaking heart, having found no ally in Mum and no confessor in Dad, the heavy-hearted child stomped off down the yard to dig up the awful evidence.

She intended to place her trembling hands upon the earth and scrape it aside until catching only the first painful glimpse of Rusty's fur and then to confront her father again. But Annie's courage was not a commodity of unlimited supply. She squatted paralysed, fearful even of touching the little grave. Eventually, the fear of knowing bowed to the need to know and hesitantly she applied fingers to the task.

In a moment, her hands flew back as though scorched … for there was the beloved rust-coloured fur. A sudden tide of noisy

225

wailing overwhelmed her. When calm finally descended, she replaced the soil and stumbled into the bush for wildflowers.

The little plot sufficiently decorated, she joined hands and sobbed a prayer to St Francis of Assisi, guardian of animals – although he had reneged on his duty to Rusty, it occurred to scornful Annie, and therefore should not be trusted in the future. And yet, how fervently she believed in all things divine and how supplicating became her next prayer for St Francis' protection of Rusty's soul – if soul he had.

When all was done, and the reality of the terrible thing had found a lock-up dwelling place in her brain, she turned away emotionally depleted, yet utterly heart-sore, and wandered back towards the house to begin her next phase of life, meaningless now without Rusty.

Annie's attitude towards her father assumed a conscious distant aspect. Her mind was shocked by what she had seen and in that mire of negative thought there sprouted a thorny resolve never again to speak to him. She derived a child's satisfaction from vengeful, punitive thoughts and, loyalty to Rusty reigning paramount, the earnest decision germinated – 'I'll never forgive Dad. *Never ever!'*

It took two days for Annie's capacity for forgiveness to begin to manifest itself. Punishment had proved difficult to impose. By the time the first day and night of its intended interminable stretch were passed, the softening had begun. Try as she would to stoke the anger by recalling the emotional pain suffered, the natural magnetic pull of affection between a young girl and the father she so loved could not be negated. Gradually, the two Hughs became teasing, joking, loving friends again.

Shortly after her ordeal, remorse stepped over Jack's heart. He bought Annie a wristwatch – time no longer frozen at "a hair past a freckle". It threw her into rhapsodies of tearful gratitude, and after that, she wore her sleeve at half-mast – until candid Ruthie asked her to spell "skite".

Palliative time passed. Rusty gradually retreated behind a few more veils of memory, and eventually, Annie forgot to look in the other direction when walking by his grave on her way for a swim. Moreover, sensitive counselling from Margo enabled the girl to understand the many problems Rusty had imposed upon the family.

He seasonally carried fleas, which proliferated in his under-the-house den. It was his Friday delight, if not tethered, to catapult from his kennel and bark furiously at the Sanitary man (as Thumper used to do) inviting an accident, best not described, which would have had the merit of fertilising the lawn most bountifully. Furthermore, the dog's quest for poultry would have extended to the neighbours' properties, bringing condemnation upon the Hughs.

Until Rusty's death, Jack had not realised the depth of Annie's love for the animal she had looked after with the obsessive attention of a mother, and for this reason, had not appreciated the extent of the pain of parting. He had earlier decided to end Rusty's life when he suspected the thinning fur to be an outbreak of mange, and the incident of the dead hens brought the problem more urgently to attention.

Jack's deception to Annie was to spare, or at least reduce, the anguish. Her consolation: he was skilful with a rifle and merciful. Unsuspecting Rusty, trotting beside Jack towards the back fence, had known no fear and had died before pain could register.

Not long afterwards, a joyful event quickly healed Annie's broken heart. The white-wrapped bundle Jack carried proudly into the house behind Margo's careful step was Peter, another one for Annie to lavish sisterly devotion upon. From her perspective, the timing of little Peter Hughs' arrival could not have been more fortuitous.

26 Playgrounds

With few cars about in the 1940s and early '50s, many children used the gravel roads as play areas. The Hughs' particular stretch of road was ideal, being straight and flat at the front of their house, and ten or more others, before it turned and ascended another short hill.

The primary activity conducted on this flat area was the game of rounders, the prerequisites: enthusiasm, an adequate number of players, bat and ball, and a wooden fruit box for the wicket (whippy). The game was sometimes interrupted by vehicles, for a moment only, although often a dusty moment.

The neighbourhood kids were boisterous with their triumph or protestation, according to the progress of the game, and Margo felt quite at ease being attuned to her own children's whereabouts. Always they would quit when late afternoon descended for there were specific deterrents to a continuation: weariness, extreme hunger and the sudden mutation of the game into the extreme sport of "brandings".

As well, workers tramping over the rounders pitch on their way home from the bus consolidated the players' homing urge. Gradually, the kids strolled off towards food and comics and wireless serials, there to exult or deplore the outcome of the game, some of them wearing the imprint of the branding ball.

One summer afternoon when the worst of the heat had passed, lackadaisical Billy Meadows wearing his natural lop-sided grin, came swaggering down the road and into the Hughs' front yard.

'Wanta bit of a laarf?' Billy asked, brows up, eyes rounded, and face glowing with the promise of fun. From his pocket, he took an old leather wallet his father had discarded and attached a length of string. Paul, Tony and Annie watched expectantly, realising what he was up to.

They were all aware of the comings and goings of the people who lived along Oyster Bay Road and were able to estimate the time of the bus's arrival at the shop and the time it took the subsequent procession of walkers to reach their "rounders pitch" stretch of road. Billy used this knowledge to help him successfully carry out his practical joke.

He placed the wallet near the middle of the gravel road and after sprinkling dirt to hide the trail, took the other end into the bush. The four kids squatted behind a dense clump of bottlebrush and waited for the leader of the after-work exodus to trudge up the hill and approach the wallet.

They were pleased to see it was Jimmy Murphy's jovial father pacing along carrying a brown *Gladstone* work-bag, eyes on the road before him, and mind preoccupied. As he drew near, he stopped abruptly, took the hand from his pocket and reached for the wallet. Billy's timing was perfect. He jerked the string and the wallet shot into the bush, comically, with the scuttling movement of a fleeing mouse, leaving Mr Murphy's face a picture of astonishment.

The rascals' squawks of laughter betrayed them, but they saw that he was enjoying the joke and so out of their lair they came. Mr Murphy, laughing now, gave Billy a congratulatory slap on the back for his amusing trick. The boy knew then that when the joke reached the rest of the Murphy family that evening, they too would have a bit of a "laarf".

That year, after the deceleration of Christmas excitement, the days of the summer holidays seemed boringly long. Paul and Annie, walking home from Mass one morning, decided to take a detour up Green Point Road where there was a shady park with the usual variety of playground equipment, including a "razzle dazzle". The heat, discontent and competition for rides on the carousel soon grew into irritation and argument among the half-dozen children there.

One girl, with a high tangle of dark hair, protuberant brown eyes and beautiful olive skin was exploiting her hefty proportions to gain exclusive possession of the whirling thing. She was spinning it dangerously, making it impossible for any other child to climb aboard.

Angrily, Annie moved forward to correct the injustice but hesitated – the girl was sturdily built and could easily throw her to the ground. Having a particular aversion to pain, she thought it better to use her supposed capacity for wisdom, newly acquired with the passing of another birthday, and to stand back and exercise patience. Annie was considering the merits and shame of this cowardly decision (and wishing larrikin Billy was present) when Paul spoke up, his voice unusually loud and commanding. 'Stop, so we can get on too!'

The big girl did stop, bored with it anyway, and with hands on her hips, she swaggered over. She looked them up and down – in their Sunday clothes, they appeared over-dressed for the park – and exhibited her home-grown weaponry; ten painted claws the Hughs children certainly would not tempt to be deployed.

'Is that freckle-face your sister?' the girl enquired as though Annie were a block of wood, and Paul nodded, innocently unaware of the doubled insult.

Annie stared hate-darts. "Freckles" was an occasional gibe flung at her (and many freckled children) by kids who were just being kids, but it reinforced in her the belief that anything speckled would be persecuted. She began to wonder what on earth was wrong with the big girl. Odd, she was – very strange. Her broad face screwed up into a sneer and without any reason or provocation, her tongue burst into an effusive boast of accomplishments accredited to her talented, older and absent, sister: tap-dancing, singing, piano playing, drawing…

'Oh gawd, that's nothing!' interrupted forthright Paul in a bored tone '*My* sister can climb trees, row a boat and peel an orange in one long peel (Annie *so* appreciated his intelligent appreciation of her!) and she's not scared of crabs or frogs either!' He was becoming quite reckless in his defence of the maligned one whose elbow immediately made subtle contact with his ribs. But he *would* go on. 'She's a bloody good fighter, too!' he asserted in a louder tone.

Annie suffered a peculiar sensation of shrinking. 'Hey, don't tell her that!' she whispered and eyed the bulk as it moved closer. She was too alarmed to reproach Pauly for the swearword he enjoyed using, which obviously produced a *Popeye's* spinach effect on a boy's physical proportions. After all, Big-head Butch, the other local bully, said it all the time!

The big girl's scathing eyes measured Annie. 'Garn! She couldn't knock the skin offa custard.' She turned away and clomped over to the park's grand old gumtree, which for years had protected many scallywags from sunburn. Paul and Annie presumed she was retreating. Before Annie could congratulate herself on the efficacy of her hate-darts, the pugnacious girl snatched up a large stick and began swishing it about, like a samurai with a sword.

At this dangerous juncture, the Hughs kids moved back judiciously to bide their time for a spin on the coveted razzle-dazzle. "Big Girl" approached, and the stick assumed bough dimensions, hovering as it was in threatening proximity to their heads; heads, which had that same morning, received the sacrament of Holy Communion (which should have conferred some protection, Annie mused later).

'Go – home!' the bully ordered as though they were a pair of mangy, skulking dogs.

Pride demanded swift retaliation. Hugely intimidated now, Annie nervously prompted her brother: 'Why should we? She doesn't own the park!' Before Pauly could relay this sound response, Big Girl lunged forward and thrashed the weapon down at their feet. Their wisdom was unsurpassed – they leapt back – and she hurtled into an abusive tirade splattered most startlingly with words beginning with F and the muscle-enhancer B ... an ignoble offence against the Hughs' kids' temporary Sunday purity.

Self-interest being a dominant human motive, the two "shot through like a Bondi tram". When their fleeing feet had slowed to an amble, Annie glanced at her valiant and serious companion. Nearing the refuge of Oyster Bay Road, they dawdled on in silence and after a moment of frowning contemplation, Pauly looked over at his sister and asked, 'You wouldn't tell on me would you Annie ... for saying bloody?' She grinned back at her courageous young brother who had stood up so manfully to risk assault and battery for her unworthy self and assured him that the forbidden "humdinger" of a word would remain their secret.

In such a small place as Oyster Bay, it was always probable that Annie would again encounter the same bully-girl. This worried her for a while until other things gained prominence in her daily life and she forgot about her.

Time passed. Margo, in a sewing mood one day, made red and white check sun frocks for Josie and Annie and sent them off in their new dresses to the shop. Presently, with hard packets of flour, bar soap and *Rinso* cruelly stabbing her leg through the string bag, Annie took cute little Josie's hand, and they hastened across the bitumen to the gravelled road homeward. A sing-song voice followed.

It was the girl Annie so feared. The brown eyes were just as protuberant as before, and the thick dark hair appeared not to have suffered the detangling invasion of a sturdy comb since their last meeting. The girl's olive skin compensated for the anomalies though; it was satiny-beautiful, but now it stretched over a body significantly fatter, and a proportionate increase in spite and belligerence soon became manifest.

'Oh, aren't we sweet in our stupid tablecloth dresses!' she jeered. 'Hey freckle face! I'm talkin' to you. And who's *she?*'

Annie had intended to ignore the girl, for it was well known that she was far from normal, but the tone she had used to add disdain to the pronoun instantly stirred Annie's temper.

'This is my sister, Josie, not *she!*' Annie snapped back, at the same time wondering why she bothered to answer the bully. True to the memory of their previous meeting, Big Girl again picked up a weapon, a stone this time, and drew back her arm. 'You'd better *not!*' Annie warned in a voice she hoped sounded menacing and, grabbing Josie's hand, prepared to hurry away. But could they risk turning their backs? Would she *dare* to throw the stone?

She did dare – it went flying past them. The thrower immediately searched around for another missile. Annie's sudden blazing anger left no time to think about consequences. She grabbed a more substantial stone, verging on the category of rock, and threw it with full force. (Herb had taught his sister to aim accurately when throwing stones, targets usually confined to inanimate objects.)

Annie felt shocked and frightened when she saw blood running down the girl's face, and stared at her as she stumbled away, hand over the eye, howling and shrieking: 'Oooh my eye! Blood! My eye!' And with mounting self-disgust, Annie wondered what further depths of disgrace she was destined to sink.

Grabbing Josie's little hand, she hurried her on towards home. With every step, the worry of what may happen descended upon Annie with rapidly increasing weight. She imagined the girl's parents as larger models of Bully Girl from whom she had inherited or learnt her nasty, aggressive disposition; imagined them stomping through the gateway and banging on the door to complain to Margo and Jack. Eventually, her fearful imaginings progressed to a visit from the police! *'Oh, gawd ... what if I've knocked her eye out?'* Annie exclaimed as they hastened along.

Josie remained quiet the whole time, and when Annie was able to stop thinking about herself, she gave kinder consideration to her little sister's distress. She wondered if Josie felt that she was required to keep it a secret. 'I'll tell Mum now, Jose, so don't you worry about it. And don't worry about that girl. She's not all there, you know, dingbats, not the full quid,' said Annie tapping her temple and, taking a deep breath, went to find Margo and confess the terrible thing she had done.

Naturally, Margo was very much concerned at first, but after thinking it all over, and when some time had elapsed, and their door remained un-battered when the incident had receded sufficiently into the kind past allowing them a modicum of detachment, she relaxed. 'Most things we worry about never do happen, you know,' she said, 'so try not to worry about it. And *learn* from it.'

237

And so, having entirely run out of *brave*, Annie clung leech-like to the hearth of the home, seeking to consign her apprehension to the comforting veils of increasing yesterdays. Eventually, though, it seemed that Margo had been right – nothing happened – and Annie became sufficiently bold to resume her regular excursions to the shop. She never saw Big Girl again, and it comforted her to assume she had recovered. Nevertheless, Annie felt the shame and regret of her notorious act for many years afterwards.

27 When the Rain Came

When Josie turned five, it became Annie's special duty to introduce her to Sister Evangeline in the kindergarten classroom. Big sister held little sister's hand and fussed over her like a hen with a single chicken. Reluctant to leave her, she repeatedly conveyed assurances that her own classroom was 'just over there across the playground'. Annie handed the little girl the small school case Margo had packed with play-lunch and indicated the benches outside. 'We'll sit out there at playtime – in a little while – and eat our lovely cakes together, Jose', Annie promised her.

Josie had not uttered a single word since entering St Mary's school gates and her wide blue eyes, shyly hiding behind blonde curls, stared at the nun's magpie-witch outfit and looked around apprehensively at the other children, the desks and playthings. Sister Evangeline took the little hand from Annie's, and with the bright tone reserved for new, anxious pupils, she said kindly, 'Come along Josephine, and meet your first special friend.'

Upon leaving, Annie paused at the door, suddenly remembering something important. 'Oh Sister, um … Mum said to tell you that Josie sometimes has *bilious* attacks,'

WRONG! Bronchitis was the word.

Sister peered at her, somewhat stunned. 'Well!' she said doubtfully and paused to process the full ramifications of the innocently imposed threat. 'Well, I hope *you're* going to come and clean up the mess, then.'

The school bell demanded immediate departure and Sister Evangeline returned her attention to her chattering charges. After a slight hesitation, Annie proceeded on her frowning way in a state of utter bewilderment. '*What* mess? There was never any mess – just a lot of coughing. Doesn't Sister know anything about children?' she pondered.

When this puzzle was presented to Margo for clarification, she laughed a little aghast, shook her head and groaned, 'Oh, Annie! *Annie!*' and immediately wrote a note for Sister Evangeline, correcting her mentally disorganised elder daughter's blunder. The next day Margo's note brought a broad smile to Sister's sweet face. She folded the paper, slipped it into the side pocket of her black habit and, still smiling, said, 'Thank you, Annie … thank you.'

Thus, a long decade of Catholic education began for "Josepha Mary"(the endearment Jack occasionally bestowed on Josie) without her making the slightest mess and never giving the Hughs family a single moment's fright from the unthinkable threat of her becoming *Sister* Josepha Mary!

Barely had Josie become accustomed to the frantic early morning routine of being herded off to school when it started to rain and another Saint Patrick's Day drifted into the past. And hardly had she begun to enjoy wearing her new tunic and blazer when they had to be covered up with Tony's old raincoat, which was a size too large for her. But worse – her new leather shoes were encased in a pair of ugly goloshes to keep them and Josie's feet dry.

The news on the wireless was focused predominantly on the latest dramatic reports of the Queensland floods, where an area of about 500,000 acres of good pastoral land was drowned. The Hughs children's sympathies were more keenly felt than perhaps they might have been, chiefly owing to their own discomfort – for them at first that was all it was, an inconvenient nuisance. For the Queensland farmers, it meant the severe loss of stock and crops. Besides that, some rural families and townsfolk saw their houses being carried off by the raging, frothing brown rivers where once there had been creeks and roads.

The daily reports of tragedies generated extensive discussion everywhere, and at school all pupils became genuinely empathetic, developing a greater understanding of the plight suffered by the Queenslanders. Self-concern too naturally grew out of this. In class, they prayed that the floods would not come near them, thought a great deal about Noah and big boats, and longed for the wet weather to be over and consigned to the past.

After the eighth day of unceasing rain, Margo became desperate to get the washing dry, especially nappies and uniforms. She had made practical use of everything that lent itself to the support of damp clothes. Essential items, such as underwear and nappies, each took a turn over the oven door and on the line above the stove, but most things hung miserably upon curtain rods, the backs of chairs and on both veranda lines. The maze of damp, hanging washing enveloped everything in gloom, and a claustrophobic atmosphere pervaded the house.

To add to the general hardship, Margo now had to dry the wet wood in the oven before it could be burnt to heat the stove to dry the clothes. The interdependence of the elements of this difficulty is reminiscent of a particular story she often recited to her children:

'An old woman was taking a pig home from the market, but it would not jump over the stile, so she asked a passing dog, "Dog, dog, bite the pig. The pig won't jump over the stile, and I shan't get home tonight." But the dog wouldn't. This pattern progressed through the list of uncooperative animals, objects and elements until a horse came along. "Horse, horse, kick the cow. Cow won't drink the water …" and so on.

"Glad to oblige!" neighed the horse and promptly kicked the cow. Everything then went along very neatly in reverse culminating in the dog's biting of the pig, which took fright and jumped over the stile … and the old woman got home that night.' Martyr Margo was never allowed to make any abridgements to alleviate the tedium of the telling. Her children knew the sequence, and their despotic little brains demanded that every word was relayed in exact order.

On the ninth wet day in their drowning ark on a trembling Ararat, Margo experienced a desperate sinking of her ability to cope with the almost overwhelming problem. The weight of imminent defeat became the catalyst for allowing them all to miss a day of school, provided that they helped to rearrange the furniture without complaint of the work involved. This stipulation drew immediate and vigorous nods of smiling compliance and threw them into yelps of jubilation. Soon, there arose a lot of animated discussion on whose bed was going where.

Oh, what happiness! The children revelled in the passing of the school-bell hour and prepared their exuberant selves to enjoy the day to the absolute limit. Margo several times had to yell at the noisy mob to 'pipe down', and there were moments when she questioned her sanity in not packing them all off to school that day.

The project began with enthusiasm, and the children applied themselves wholeheartedly to the task. Margo superintended the emptying of drawers and the sliding of mattresses off the beds to be relocated. She removed clothes from lowboys and emptied drawers, and everyone helped to push and shove the furniture. They found many articles in the shifting, including the recently lost dummy.

But it was all such fun! No one cared that the roof grumbled monotonously and the road had little rivers running along where the earthen gutters used to be. However, this work of nature always created a bonus for the Hughs kids: the erosion revealed streaks of white clay, very much the consistency of *Plasticine,* and was the precious resource for their clay-dib manufacturing enterprise.

In times past, dozens of small white balls of various imperfections had been turned out to augment the marble supply. From their inception at the roadside "factory", these imitation marbles always progressed in weather-breaks to the top fence-rail, there to sit lined up and waiting to dry when at last the sun shone. But there were no clay-dibs made that day.

'Look at the poor chooks!' Margo exclaimed from the misting window. 'They walk around in the rain rather than stay dry in the shed.' She cooked vegetable scraps to mix with Pollard to warm the 'poor little blighters,' and in hat and coat took the food down to the drenched hens. At lunchtime, it was the family's turn. Margo heated sweet cocoa and cooked egg jaffles and French-fried bread, and then well-fortified, back to work they went.

The rearrangement of the rooms occupied most of the day, and by the end of the afternoon the children were far better acquainted with the real meaning of the word "work". The result, however, was satisfying and justified the effort.

Happiness is so relative. How excited the kids were to have their beds facing a different direction and how sincere, their promises to keep everything in its new tidy arrangement! Joyfully the next morning they welcomed the sun and forgave the neglect. The great smiling orb brightened the cloudless blue sky and glistened upon every surface, warming their hearts and backs as off to the school bus stop they ambled, clutching their absentee notes.

28 Dunnies

Jack's enthusiasm for playing practical jokes, at his family's expense, extended one day to involve the back-yard lavatory. There was a specific individual who trotted down Hughs' side path every Friday morning and loudly cursed the explosive protestations of their third dog Rusty (recently departed). This caller was the Sanitary Man, or as some culture-conscious people preferred to say, *night soil man*.

To Annie's way of thinking the term was a "bung-on" and absurdly inaccurate. This view was duly aired to Margo: 'It should be *morning* soil because that's when we—'

'All right!' Margo snapped and shut her up with a warning glare. She at least paused for a second to consider the logic of the aborted statement, but preoccupied as always with a multiplicity of essential tasks, shook her head dismissively and reminded Annie not to be vulgar. She asserted that ladies do not *think* of such coarse things, much less *say* them.

Margo, still under the residual influence of refined Grandad Carrington and not entirely transmuted into the Hughs' earthiness, cherished high hopes for ladylike qualities in her daughter – attributes Annie considered unnatural and restrictive. And yet, the young girl dearly wished to emulate her mother who was deservedly respected and admired by all in the Oyster Bay community.

The Sanitary Man in his handkerchief cap with its corners knotted would bring a clean pan, black and shining from its tar submergence back at the depot, clamp a lid onto the used one and hoist it to his shoulder. A man had to be strong to carry a full pan. Not surprisingly, many of the workers were robust footballers.

Every Friday morning, He of Herculean strength and desensitised nose would stomp back to the truck parked with its motor idling, shove the burden onto one of the shelves and run off with a clean pan to the next house, his mate taking care of the other side of the road.

Everyone knew when it was a sanitary day (dunnyday to all the kids in the neighbourhood) because the truck could be smelt long before it was sighted. Margo would never risk being caught in the lavatory when the Sanitary Man arrived and took care that none of her children was placed in that predicament. To be discovered there was one of the worst embarrassments she could imagine. There was merit in punctuality, the family was often reminded, and Margo became increasingly annoyed because of the Sanitary Man's tardiness. The Iceman, the garbage man, the Milko, the baker … none of those services mattered much regarding punctuality, but the Sanitary Man had better be on time!

She kept a vigilant surveillance on those mornings, to ensure the humiliation would not befall her and this imposed an annoying inconvenience upon her and much hanging on for some of the children. 'Can you hear the truck?' she would anxiously ask whichever child happened to be out the front, and her expression evinced frustration and irony. 'As sure as I take the risk, that's when the blighter will turn up!' was her prophecy.

On one particular Friday morning, Jack had cycled to the shop for his *Craven A* cigarettes and *The Daily Mirror,* and he noticed the truck in the distance, still making its way along the tarred road towards Oyster Bay. Upon his return, he assured Margo she had time, so she hastened down the yard.

Jack, incapable of resisting the temptation to play a practical joke, waited a moment or so and then put his plan into action. He stomped loudly along the path and knocked on the door with aggressive impatience. 'Sanitary Man here!' he announced in a deepened, gruff voice.

Margo became flustered, as anyone would do, and in a high embarrassed tone called out, 'Oh! Just a minute,' and when she emerged a bright red flush covered her whole face and neck. 'Oh, *you!*' she exclaimed angrily and immediately started thumping Jack. 'You think you're funny, don't you? You silly big fool!' Margo exclaimed and kept on whacking until her indignation began to abate. The children revelled in this spectacle, and Jack became rubbery with laughter, even though the blows he received were leaving red marks.

'Help me, kids!' he pleaded in sham distress. 'This wild woman is trying to beat up y' poor old Dad. You've gotta help me!' Margo's thumps and the children's laughter increased.

As Christmas approached Hercules always placed a card on the seat: "Enjoy your Christmas as best you can but don't forget the Sanitary Man!" Margo usually left a two-shilling coin for him.

The sewerage system was still a luxury of the future for Oyster Bay residents and not yet available to the convent school where the outdoor pan lavatory was even considered normal by some pupils. Annie harboured a particular abhorrence of the daily sight of waste which came from others; by contrast, she knew how nice it was to use Grandma's sewer lavatory at Marrickville.

There, she and her siblings always enjoyed the novelty of pulling the chain of the flash-flush-dunny and watching the gushing water wash the white bowl clean – until they were warned to stop playing with the lavvy chain – or else! It was Annie's dear wish that one day her family would own such a symbol of affluence … and effluence.

Once back home though, the inferiority of the old unlined fibro lavvy did not cause much concern, except for one injudicious time when a bright idea prompted Annie to create more space in the high-tide pan. Fetching a box of matches, she got ready to set fire to the accumulated crumples of newspaper – lavvy paper. Annie was soon to realise that her mum had splashed something volatile in earlier to kill the squirming blowfly larvae.

'Say your prayers, maggots!' the girl muttered, tossing in a lighted match. The whole thing went WHOOMP! The fright threw her back against the door, and she stared in alarm as the flames shot up and singed the wooden seat. Annie knew she had sinned "exceedingly" (the nuns always used that word to describe grievous mortal sins), and expected to be in serious trouble that day with her mother. But at least the family now knew that no red-back spiders were lurking under the seat – no live ones, anyway.

It occurred to her afterwards, as morosely she polished the mountain of cutlery which constituted the punishment for the crime, that setting fire to a lavatory pan was a strange and dangerous activity. 'Whoever heard of anyone doing such a peculiar thing?' she mumbled. 'And how will I explain it in confession?'

Annie consulted her Catechism, specifically the section dealing with the examination of one's conscience, which provided a lengthy list of sins to prompt memory before confession. She looked for a section relating to the destruction of property and more precisely, the singeing of lavatory seats, concluding from its omission that it was a misdemeanour of extreme rarity.

It astonished her sometime later when Herb admitted that he had once done the same thing. 'Amazing!' she marvelled incredulously. 'Both of us have set fire to a dunny tin! Probably the only two people in the whole world to do such a queer thing … and we're both from the same family.' It made her wonder seriously about their brains, and she solemnly resolved to eat more fish.

One of the most cherished dunny stories, which survived and grew fatter on the fodder of embellished accounts, went something like this:

One morning the Sanitary Man was in a great hurry and careered around the corner near Mr Gumm's shop – and the cart overturned! (There were still a few horse-drawn vehicles around after WWII.) Understandably it was a regrettable day for the Sanitary Man, and more so for the shopkeeper. Astounded shoppers gave the putrid mess ample room to spread and, hands to faces ceased breathing for as long as it took them to hurry past.

Naturally, the event spawned numerous jokes and stories. For a very long time, people laughed and talked, in an endearingly Aussie way, about the day the dunny cart went over. Some even regarded themselves unusually privileged to have such a unique I-was-there legacy to pass on to their grandchildren, visiting relatives, or any unfortunate individual who was socially penalised for not having the good luck to reside in the genteel, prestigious community of Oyster Bay.

And grinning Mr Mack, who owned the other grocery shop with Post Office some uncontaminated distance across the road from Gumm's, was heard to proclaim: 'Should happen every day; business has never been so good!'

The most memorable lavatory the Hughs family had ever encountered was at a friend's bush property on the outskirts of Heathcote. Externally, it appeared much the same as any ordinary outdoor edifice, although in noticeable terminal decline, but the floorboards and carpentry within concealed a pit, which obviated the need for a pan. The seat with standard-sized aperture and lid which crowned this foreboding crater was built of planks reaching across the full width of the little building.

But the pit! Annie's first curious investigation of its mysterious depths was her last. The grave-like excavation of indeterminate age, a repository for countless years of human excrement, and who-knew-what-else, gave her the horrors.

Several times after that, dreadful fantasies invaded her sleep – dreams that depicted her shrunken self falling into the pit, but mercifully never quite hitting the base, for its depth and overall dimensions were greatly exaggerated – typical in dreams. Naturally, if hell had been such a pit, Miss Annette Hughs would have led a most righteous life.

Nevertheless, casting aside all natural disdain, it had to be conceded that a pit was a practical alternative to a pan for there was no sanitary service at the friend's isolated property. An amusing, curious accessory – a thick rope – was secured around a gum tree just outside the lavatory, its frayed end lying conspicuously on the floor near the seat.

It was assumed that the springy, creaking floorboards were not to be entirely trusted and the rope offered an apparent means of self-rescue. Perhaps it was merely the manifestation of an unusual sense of humour; humour which entirely missed the idea of adding a safety harness … and snorkels in case the rope proved as decrepit as the lavatory!

29 Word Games

There were a few sounds that the innocent Hughs cherubs sometimes made, which their father found incredibly irritating. He could not endure, for example, the juicy consumption of apples, the crunching of nuts, slurping of soup, gulping of liquids. And yet, once he had lain himself down at night, his nasal strains always quickly escalated to heights imposing aural punishment upon any unfortunates still lying awake. Even the precise interval of silence – a count-down to the next reverberation – was itself a torture, as waiting for the next drip of a tap can be, and the kids grew rigid with tension anticipating the impending peace-shredding snore.

If one of the children had carelessly forgotten Jack's aversions and happened to be peering over his shoulder at *Sad Sack* or *Bluey and Curly* in the comic section of his paper, he would quietly lay it down on the table. (How sneakily calm he could be!) Then, turning in his chair with slow, dramatic deliberation, he would bore his glacial blue eyes into the opposing suddenly alarmed and staring ones.

'Do you have to crunch that apple right in my ear?' His displeasure would manifest itself in a low monotone of rapidly depleting forbearance. The offenders should have known better. Their father's abhorrence of eating-related noises was a fact with which each child was acquainted early in life, so there was no excuse for the imposition of such torture upon Jack's sensitive, war-weary ears.

But occasionally, this little idiosyncrasy of his would slip their lemming minds until suddenly becoming aware of the blunder. In such situations, they would stand there in the attitude of mental defectives, wide-eyed, mouths frozen in mid-chew, and hands still clutching their apples as though a *Kodak* snap-shot had fixed them thus. Not even an eye-blink would they risk because experience had taught that the low and steady tone Jack had used was indicative of the restless volcanic magma of his temperament. They knew that in the next second or two he would spontaneously combust!

'Get down the back and eat it, damn ya! Or over the other side,' he roared on one such occasion, flinging out his arm towards the wilderness on the remote side of the river. And then *thump!* A fist met the table, the sugar bowl jumped, and a sense of sudden eagerness to comply descended upon the munchers. And those who knew the drill ran!

'All a bloke wants on his day off is a bit of peace and quiet,' Jack complained to Margo, speaking in the third person as was his habit when lamenting his grievances, such as when his tribe got too much for him.

The scallywags faced banishment to the end of the expansive backyard or down to the river-bank to entertain themselves for a couple of hours. A touching motherly warning at the back door sent them along: 'Don't come back until I call you … or unless you've hurt yourselves.' Only then could Jack feel confidently protected from them all, and bask in his total eclipse.

There were other times, too, when Jack Hughs could not help but "do his block" with his kids, and after the dramatic telling-off, the extended punishment would begin: The Silent Treatment. The children much preferred to be whacked a few times than endure hours or days, according to their crime, of their father's ignoring them.

Most of the time though, Jack enjoyed having the family around, and he played games with the younger ones, wrestled the bigger kids and tossed the older infant and current toddler up into the air, much to Margo's consternation. 'Oh, f' heavens' sake Jack, be careful!' she'd gasp, hovering close, arms ready. Annie had expected her mother to show more confidence in his catching prowess, for had he not learnt the skill practising on the older ones before they grew too heavy. He never did drop any of them … that they knew of!

Jack's father, Otto, had long ago changed their German surname, Heinz, to Hughs in an endeavour to protect his four children against discrimination after the First World War. Jack knew some words of the German language, picked up from his grandparents. From this association, he became familiar with the varying inflexions of the speech and could often be found poring over his dog-eared German dictionary, attempting to further his knowledge. The children were an amused audience.

'Guten Morgen' was his greeting, or 'Guten Abend' if it was evening, and when he saw one of them slaking their thirst he would seize the opportunity, pointing: 'Aha! Das ist Glas Wasser!'

One year on his birthday, he announced his age, separating the German syllables and doing his best phonetically and grammatically. He was the same age that Jesus, Alexander the Great and Eva Peron had reached. Impressionable Annie saw this as ominous, realising that when her dad succeeded in walking out of the woods of his thirty-third year, her mum would be walking in.

Jack's childhood recall of the German language was something cherished. Equally, he was fascinated by the vast diversity of English expression and had a particular affinity for words. Annie was trying to bring her imagined coercive powers into play one evening, hoping to charm her father into completing her geography homework.

Jack was not receptive to the idea, however, and decided instead to write a story. He interspersed among the sentences the names of many countries and cities: "He wore a light Panama on his head; She peeled an onion, a Sweden a carrot; The knife slipped and Calcutta finger; Sydney asked her to pass the Turkey; and 'Are you Florence?' he asked. 'Yes Siam,' she answered". The story filled several pages, the narrative liberally ambiguous.

Jack's writing greatly impressed Annie and next day she took it to school to show Sister Bernadette, a good-natured Irish nun who still spoke in the delightful brogue of her own country. She had recently expressed a particular admiration of Mrs Hughs for 'raising so many little Cat'olic babies'.

It made Annie proud and happy to know that her mum had earned praise from Sister. (At her young age the girl could hardly appreciate the poignancy of the nun's apparent ignorance of labour pains, sleep deprivation and more of the same to follow for Catholic baby machines.) And so, with her mother nicely in favour, she hoped her father's essay also would gain credit … and obscure the unsettling fact that her geography homework had not been completed. She wondered briefly if that sly hope was a sin.

Earlier, Jack had voiced hostility when the Church sent notes out asking parents to "donate a brick" for the new presbytery. On the heels of this euphemistic request for money, curiosity prompted Annie to ask Sister why six nuns were crowded into an ordinary house and only three priests occupied the two-storey brick presbytery and yet still wanted to build a new one.

The permanently kind eyes of Sister Bernadette regarded the girl attentively for a moment, and after a short ironical laugh she replied: 'T'be sure, it *is* good to be inquisitive Annie, but I t'ink it best thut you confoine yer curiosity to ye're history and geography, m'dottie.'

Enlightenment was denied, but Annie judged by the endearment that Sister was not annoyed with her for creating a diversion during the lesson. *That* was a sin though, and she consigned it to her mental list of iniquitous crimes in preparation for her Thursday visit to the cubicle of contrite whispers.

Confession carried an additional benefit. In admitting wrongs, Catholic children felt a comforting, forgiving protection in the priest's absolution, in the assurance that the assigned penance would erase the stain of sin in preparation for Holy Communion. However, that meant remaining pure for the interminable time-stretch from the two o'clock confession on Thursday until one minute past Mass on Sunday. For some rascals, a hugely ambitious hope!

Father McKinley might have been bored comatose sometimes, by the minutiae of the inoffensive little sins (many of which were fabricated) of thirty or so whispering children. They whispered to deny knowledge to the waiting sinners of the sneaked biscuit, the utterance of the wicked red word and the lamb chop, eaten last Friday.

Jack's story presented a timely opportunity to bring to attention the fact that he was a word-wizard. Sister Bernadette quietly scanned the pages, no doubt to assess its contents for possible blunders. She lifted her beautiful green eyes (so wasted on a nun, Annie thought later) and smiled.

'Well Annie, I can see thut ye're father is a clever won wit' words, and he wroites in a foine, stoylish hand – almost calligraphy!' Her tone suggested surprise.

She glanced up and grinned mischievously – an endearing trait. 'Yer're a fortunate girl, an' no doubt about it,' she continued, 'and y' should be havin' no-o trouble a'toll wit' y' geography homework, m'dear … no-o trouble a'toll.' (Annie made a mental note here to ponder later on the inference of that statement. Sister Bernadette was a "shrewdy".) And then the kind nun read Jack's story to the class. Beaming Annie was immensely proud of her father that happy day. Puffed up with pride! 'Gawd –*Another* sin!' thought she.

Jack often played word games with his children. 'Stand on this spot!' he ordered Annie when it was her turn, and he pointed down at the kitchen lino in front of his chair. The giggling girl positioned herself where she thought the place was, and peremptorily he ordered, 'Closer!' She inched her toes nearer to him until she found the invisible location and he was satisfied.

He fixed upon her a steady, overpowering stare. She was compelled to eyeball him, neither blink nor smile, absolutely forbidden to move her gaze from his face. Perhaps this was some kind of training to support one of his teachings that you must always look into the eyes of whomever you were talking to ... but not *boggle-eyed*, it may be supposed!

When she was quite paralysed on his precise spot, he asked: 'Am I... salubrious? (He chose terms such as incorrigible, indispensable, mediocre, etc.) She stood there staring into his eyes, desperately trying to control her facial muscles which threatened betrayal by a grin or a smothered squeak of laughter. She had to decide whether the term was insulting to her father.

It was not easy. Jack possessed a vast stock of words that sounded similar to others but gave entirely different meanings and naturally caused confusion; the object of the game. Annie stood there aah-ing and um-ing and trying to sneak a glance at Margo who would nod or shake her head behind Jack's chair to give her the correct answer.

Jack, becoming aware of Margo's antics, laughed and said, 'Go on, buzz off y' little traitor!' He never allowed his stare to stray from Annie's face though, so it was almost impossible for her to solicit outside help.

Finally, a decision was demanded, and she blundered in regardless. If her guess was correct, hence acceptable, Jack's reply would be rather mild and somewhat disappointed, 'Hmmm, well that's all right then,' he'd mumble, his mind already advancing to the next enigmatic word – grotesque, erudite, illustrious, vexatious or deplorable, for example. His store of such terms seemed infinite.

This time Annie erred, blatantly insulting him. He roared in paradoxical delight: 'What! Y' cheeky little brat!' and grabbed her tightly. She shrieked and screeched with laughter, and he would not desist from his bear-hugging and tickling until she became so boisterous that Margo, as usual, had to yell at them to 'Pipe down!'

Once Annie had recovered, Jack resumed the word game, with Paul this time, and allowed extra time for more in-depth consideration. 'Am I ... flatulent?' (one who lives in a flat?), the boy wondered, or parsimonious (to do with parsnip owners?), or mendacious (able to mend things?), or senile (something to do with seeing the Nile River?), or stupendous – he thought carefully about *that* one. They went on and on, and it was impossible for Paul, and the gathered small audience to infer from Jack's expression which way to go, the master's face maintaining the cold stare of inquiry befitting a Commandant of the Gestapo.

At the end of the game, both children underwent a spelling test. The word "diarrhoea" was on the list and Annie stammered it out wrongly. However, everyone burst into laughter when witty Paul spelt out r-u-n-n-y p-o-o! (And after gorging themselves on passionfruit they readily related to the urgency this term suggested.)

30 Quids, Bobs and Pennies

Many post-war to mid-century children, including the Hughs kids, learnt the value of money early in life. To swell their fund of pocket money earned by odd jobbing for Margo, they joined a few other impoverished locals in establishing a tenacious little enterprise selling beer bottles. The "bottle-o" collected regularly and paid them "tuppence" (two pennies) for a dozen. If desperate for an "all-day" lollipop they faced a search for twelve bottles. Twenty-four had to be found for the new drink *Coca-Cola*, very novel in the small curvy bottle America introduced to thwart copy-cats.

Naturally, it became an advantage (and a mother-excluding secret) to know where resided the local beer drinkers – men, usually – who were either magnanimously happy to give up their "empties" or displayed indifference with a sleepy shrug. The manner in which a drinker relinquished the bottles depended on the state of sobriety at the time of collection. In any case, no adult particularly wanted to hoard the nuisance things.

Children thought differently; beer bottles were currency.

'How much for the lollipop, Billy?' (Moisture beneath disturbed cellophane betraying recent vendor-sampling.)

'Aw, tuppence … or thirteen bottles.'

'Thirteen? Aw, come off it y' robber!'

Kids were smart. The inflexible principles of business demanded profit, even from "shonky" transactions.

Thus, it was common to encounter children, driven by an addiction to all things sweet and tooth-rotting and assisted by burgeoning entrepreneurial skill, dragging billy-carts along, searching the grassy roadside and ditches and door-knocking for the prized resource. The best discovery was the large soft drink bottle. Returned to the shop it earned the three pence deposit someone had paid, and for that reason was not easily found.

There came a day in windy August, a day when men held down hats, women gripped skirts and children ran after inflated lolly bags and cavorting kites. Annie, on an errand to the new fruit shop farther along past the Community Hall, lost the pound note and shopping list her mother had pressed into her hand. She had taken the shortcut across the corner of Nancarrow's paddock, first establishing the location of the Friesian bull. There he was, a huge black-and-white beast with massive under-equipment hanging pendulously (an appendage Annie did not care to look at). There he was, plodding about under the gum trees, optimistically inspecting his harem.

And so, with her mind focused on staying un-trampled and un-gored, she sprinted across to the distant fence. It was this frantic haste that caused her to forget the precious money her fingers held,

265

and ten minutes later she faced a tearful retracing of steps to try to find the pound note. After searching the gravel road Annie returned to the wind-swept paddock, expecting the paper money to be up in a tree by this time or riding the choppy waves of the bay. The bull was safely occupied now.

To spot a green pound note on a paddock of rain-induced grass was difficult, especially as the oblique rays of the late sun cast long shadows east of everything, and impossible in the forest of bracken fern thriving near the nearby fence. There, newborns were unfurling, soft and lettuce-green, yawning and stretching to meet parents grown darker with maturity. Grandparent fronds stood nearby, faded to a mellow biscuit-brown in their twilight years, and over this cluster of relatives, the fawn-mauve long-dead still presided.

Nature always intrigued Annie. At another time, she might have turned over the leaf litter to spy on the bustling microcosm of life, but right now that pleasure would significantly hinder her quest. And so the search continued, but with the accompanying wish that the Royal Mint Master would be sensible in future and colour the notes bright telephone-box red!

The cost of a loaf of bread was, at that period, nine pence – less than one shilling. It may be appreciated therefore that a pound (*twenty* shillings) represented a significant loss from Margo Hughs' housekeeping money. Justifiably upset, she threw up her hands in exasperation and sent her careless daughter off to search again. Once more, Annie eased her way between the treacherous strands of barbed wire.

At school, all children had been given a bank-shaped tin moneybox and a booklet, which promoted the wisdom of saving for a "rainy day". Annie had used up a few rainy days since then. This time she was saving for the kaleidoscope displayed in Mr Gumm's window. Feeling the need to make amends, she offered to withdraw her savings to restore some of the lost money. Margo objected.

Ironically, her mother's generosity of spirit added to Annie's anxiety for it precluded the chance to atone. Annie's childish carelessness became a significant misery. Her conscience sneered, intimating that she was undeserving of further pocket money. This prompted the decision to forego her weekly allowance until restitution had been made, but before Annie could discuss this noble intention with her mother, something terrible happened.

A loud, shrill screaming exploded from the kitchen. Margo and Annie rushed in to find that Paul had been scalded. He had knocked over a saucepan on the stove, and the boiling water had cascaded onto his right leg. Overcoming her initial distress, Margo sat Pauly, still screaming, on a chair and Annie tried to comfort him while her mother gently eased down the long sock. They were horrified to see his skin peel off with the knitted wool.

Tony took a note across the road to Miss Gilbert, and she phoned Dr Sweeny. He arrived soon after and attended the burn, carefully showing Margo how to apply the dressing, and he gave her the flat tin of sterile *tulle gras* and a pair of forceps. The conscientious doctor made several further visits, and this reinforced the distraught mother's confidence in nursing Pauly back to healed comfort.

The painful daily sunshine treatment was always an ordeal for the young boy and Margo could do nothing but sit and read to him on the front veranda for the duration and then attend to the redressing of his leg. Pauly suffered a great deal, then and afterwards, and it took weeks for his shin to recover from the scalding. Ever mindful of the perennial kindness of Miss Gilbert, Margo baked a large cherry cake and took it over to her.

When eventually Pauly was over the worst, and his sister was able to take her mind off his poor injured leg, the former money problem re-emerged. Margo still refused to accept her daughter's savings or, alternatively, to deprive her of weekly pocket money. However, aware of Annie's need to salve her conscience, she suggested a compromise.

Thus, with a donation from Margo's purse to augment the withdrawal of her bank savings, Annie hurried off to Mr Gumm's store. Presently, Pauly became the happy recipient of an

entertaining kaleidoscope, which gave him hours of pleasure …
and which his sister expected to borrow regularly. Naturally.

31 Bathurst

Jack Hughs decided to buy a new bicycle. He relied on sturdy wheels to convey him to and from the railway station every workday, and his old red "mangle" was showing many signs of encroaching decrepitude, so he entrusted its palliative care to Herb and Annie. They were thrilled, and both wanted to ride it at once. Herb went first, tearing full-pelt along the gravel road to Daisy's corner, then back the other way to the Cheadles' place, and home again.

When it was Annie's turn, big brother held the bike while optimistic sister swung a leg over the bar. Her feet barely reached the down-position of the pedal, so he showed her how to ride "under-bar". It was an awkward, lopsided style of riding, the centre of gravity hovering precariously between listing-girland the bike, which corrected the imbalance by taking the opposite angle. Although that seemed better, Annie still crashed many times during the learning – and great was Herb's concern ... concern for the bike!

Margo's sister Enid was visiting from Bathurst at the time and noticing her niece's wobbly struggle, told Margo she would give Annie her ladies' bicycle – unused now that she drove the utility. As they were on holidays, Aunty Enid suggested that Annie travel back to Bathurst with her and son Dan for a short stay. She had intentions of returning to Marrickville to revisit Grandma and Grandad Carrington for, along with Margo, she was worried about her father's heart troubles. Enid offered to then bring the bicycle back with them, and Margo's agreement threw Annie into gasping rhapsodies.

How very much Annie admired Aunty Enid for her driving skill, as they set off from Oyster Bay! Apart from Miss Gilbert, she was the only woman the Hughs' children knew of who drove a car.

Some hours later as the travellers journeyed towards the Blue Mountains, Enid stopped at a junction to give way to the sporadic traffic. She was checking again that all was clear when the impatient driver behind leapt from his truck, threw up an arm and yelled, 'Yer s'posed to give *way*, lady – not give *up*! B-loody women drivers!' And, still snarling, he climbed back to his seat.

Enid eyed him in the rear vision mirror for a moment and muttered, 'Stupid nincompoop!' The highway was now clear, but she once more carefully and deliberately looked right, then left, then right again to punish him for his insult – and was entirely unruffled about it, Annie noticed admiringly.

As they continued on, Enid commented that she was fed up with the rude male taunts encountered on the road. She declared that a woman behind the wheel, who often had the safety of child passengers to consider, was naturally a more attentive driver than a lot of men appeared to be.

Sitting there with Dan and her aunt, watching the scenery flying past, Annie smiled as she thought of the spirit her driver had displayed. Enid and Margo were alike in that respect and had always been inseparable. During their childhood, Margo, older by a year and already a motherly little person, became a guardian angel for Enid because of her heart condition resulting from an early bout of rheumatic fever.

Somewhere along the way in the beautiful Great Dividing Range, they stopped to buy peaches. The Italian orchardist, pleased to be selling a whole boxful, also appreciated Enid's admiration of his blocks of well-shaped trees. His enthusiasm evolved into an impressive account of the hopes and dreams of migrants, made poignant by the heart-breaking wrench of leaving home and relatives to begin again in a new country. He told Enid he had arrived in Australia with almost nothing but his skills.

Again, the visitors looked beyond the house-yard at the acres of peach trees all growing in perfect symmetry. With a proud wave of his arm towards the green vista and passion in his voice that he was helpless to suppress, he said, 'First-a you have-a the dream, and then-a you make-a come true.' Those words and the example set by that life-embracing Italian orchardist were an inspiration to Aunty Enid, Dan, and especially Annie, who never forgot it.

The two weeks of busy activity at Bathurst passed quickly. Most of Annie's time was spent on her blue bicycle with its low-slung bar, and the bonus of the white basket clipped over the handlebars. She needed to keep reminding herself that the bike was *hers* now. Dan guided her on a tour of the district as far as Perthville one way and to Mt Panorama and Kelso in the other direction. Annie's sense of freedom was exquisite: she had her own bike; a bell to ring; there were new roads to travel and different places to see.

The happy girl frequently thought of her best friend and wished she was with them, for it was Ruthie, some weeks earlier, who had taught her to ride. After days of following Ruthie's patient instructions and almost giving up, it had happened. Quite suddenly the novice went hurtling downhill on the bike with enough speed to ward off the shoves of gravity. The difficult challenge of remaining vertical upon a moving object was at last met, and Annie felt euphoric – until realising there were no brakes! Her grazes recovered quickly, however, soothed by the great joy of having mastered balance.

Dan's father, Uncle Harry, treated the family to the Pictures on Saturday night and the next evening, carrying picnic fare, the family walked to Machattie Park. They selected a spot near some other groups and sat on the grass under a spreading old tree to listen to the thrilling WHOOMPA, WHOOMPA! of the band set up in the rotunda. To the ingenuous girl from Oyster Bay, it was novel and exciting to be right there under the deepening twilight sky with the powerful music pervading her senses. Indeed, the sound vibrations seemed to shake every cell of her body and even the ground she sat upon seemed to tremble.

While watching the animated movements of the uniformed musicians, Annie became aware of the fixed concentration evident on their faces as their eyes followed bars of minims, crotchets, and quavers, or drumbeat notation on their music sheets. Annie's feelings verged on reverence for the musicians. It was as though they occupied a different echelon, a little removed from other mortals. After that evening, she was able to appreciate the significant difference between music performed right there in the midst of an audience, and music relayed over the wireless.

On the second Sunday of Annie's visit, Uncle Harry took the family for a drive. They went first to the railway station and then took a street view of the house where Mr Chifley had lived. Aunty Enid passed on a few interesting points about his time as Prime Minister, also mentioning that she and Uncle Harry had stood in the main street of Bathurst to observe his funeral cortege.

They went along Bentick and Stewart Streets to view the houses where Margo and Enid and their siblings had spent some of their childhood. Lastly, the car cruised by the St Stanislaus College and then back to the main street past all the beautiful street-lamps and on to the showground near the Macquarie River.

Although Uncle Harry was often at home or taking the family to various places, he seldom spoke. During the first few days after her arrival, Annie thought he was annoyed by her presence or that perhaps she had offended him in some way and he was punishing her with the Silent Treatment, as her father occasionally did when angry with his kids, or in his *can't-stand-bloody-noise* mood.

The mystery of what might have displeased Uncle Harry grew daily more puzzling, and after three nights of fretful introspection Annie chose a private moment and asked Enid why he was annoyed. She told her of his reticence and asked if she knew the reason. The anxious girl had been helping her aunt to make the double bed. She smoothed her hands over the soft lemon chenille cover with its raised pink and green floral borders, trying in this action to mitigate her anxiety about what Aunty Enid was about to tell her.

Enid sighed and hugged her niece. She patted the bed, and they sat down. 'You mustn't mind Uncle Harry's silence, pet,' she said and went on to explain that he was a soldier and had suffered a great deal during the war. Enid revealed that he had been shell-shocked and seldom spoke to anyone except herself and Dan and that he had endured terrible pain and mental suffering during the war, seeing things that no one should ever have to see. Enid assured Annie that Uncle Harry was genuinely pleased that she was holidaying there. After that confidence had been imparted, his silence no longer disturbed Annie and after that uncle and niece often exchanged fond smiles. Uncle Harry was comforted by Annie's understanding about his silence – his cross.

There was so much to do in beautiful Bathurst. Sometimes the cousins spent time playing with Pal, the Border collie. Dan's previous dog also had been named Pal, which seemed strange to Annie. Likewise, when Dan visited the Hughs, he was puzzled by everything being painted green. (Perhaps there was some predestined genetic peculiarity in the entire family, which clung to the theory, "If it's good enough, why change it?")

Pally romped around chasing the ball and jumping on the children, excited to have *two* friends to play with him. One afternoon, as Annie fondled the warm black-and-white head, the memory of her own Peggy, Thumper and Rusty – all gone now – drew a curtain of sorrow over her bright day and she began to hope that another stray would turn up at Oyster Bay.

It was nearing the end of the holiday. The rosy-pink sky of early morning gave promise of a beautiful day and so, to make the most of it, the cousins took Pally for a well-earned walk. After lunch, while the dog slept and twitched his legs in joyful pursuit of rabbits on the sports oval, they cycled to the river for a final swim.

The water looked inviting as they wheeled their bikes down the incline through the river-sand, which had banked up near the bridge during the last flood. They selected a spot a short distance from a family picnicking there in the shade of the bridge.

The sun was past the zenith, but hotter. Dan and Annie, emerging from their first swim, noticed that the people near the bridge were peering into the water and looking up and down the river as though searching for something. The two stood there towelling their wet bodies, watching and wondering what it could be.

Presently to their dismay, two men came out of the water carrying a small boy. The family quickly crowded around where he had been placed on a towel. Hearing sudden loud cries, Dan and Annie became animated in their speculations, eager to learn what had happened. They watched, hoping to see the boy get up and run off to play.

But he did not get up. A short time later an ambulance arrived and bumped its way over the rough terrain down to where the family was huddled around the child. The ambulance men lifted him onto a stretcher. Annie and Dan could hardly believe what they were seeing and gasped when the grey blanket was drawn over the wet little head. And then the police arrived.

After the ambulance had driven away and when the police and the distraught family had left, the cousins approached a group of youths and asked if they knew how the boy had drowned. The oldest teenager explained that the boy's foot had become caught in a submerged branch, probably from the overhanging tree, he guessed and pointed his arm up at the suspected large gum.

They rode home slowly, subdued and thoughtful, and Dan told his mother the tragic news. She was shocked and also alarmed and, shaking her head, advised them never to swim in the river again – *any* river. Enid added that in future they should confine their swimming to Olympic pools or netted baths. Annie, still stunned by what she had witnessed, thought briefly of the wide Georges River with its intermittent edgings of mangroves, which flowed daily into Oyster Bay. As far as she was aware, no one had ever encountered snags in its depths.

It was a sad end to the holiday, but Annie's mood brightened when Enid told her to start packing in readiness for their trip back to Sydney tomorrow. Now that homecoming and beloved family faces were nigh, Annie found it difficult to fall asleep. Suddenly she longed to see them all again – Mum, Dad, Herb and all the kids, and even the chooks!

Despite a restless night, she was up early the next day. Uncle Harry lifted the sapphire-blue bicycle onto the back of the utility and tied it down securely. Annie could hardly wait to show it to everyone at home – especially Ruthie – and to ride it up and down their dusty section of Oyster Bay Road, but also to share it with Pauly who was learning to ride.

32   A boatload of Firewood

Another winter arrived, and it was a hard winter. The ground south of everything remained white with frost long after the sun had melted the rest of it. Later, a Perisher blast swept over Oyster Bay. People in overcoats struggled against the menacing, keening wind and girls with long hair sometimes found it flying out in front of them as they were buffeted along the road, fighting to keep their hats and berets on.

Even in the sheltered indoors, the children's toes felt frozen, and their fingers stung when they washed their hands in the dish of warm water Margo had placed on a chair near the fuel stove. But the chopped lengths of wood in the faithful old Bega stove kept burning away, and gradually the kitchen became cosy. The warmth inside fought against the chill outside and brought a steamy opacity to the windows, and when the children cleared circles through which to observe the winter world, they saw that chimneys everywhere puffed and plumed with white smoke.

The day came when Margo had burnt the last piece of firewood, and there was a great deal of washing and baking yet to do. She had used all of the best wood scrounged from the block between her place and Martins', and Jack had sawn up most of the old timber which for years had been stored under the house. There was no more firewood anywhere, so Jack grabbed the axe and, instructing Paul and Tony to follow, strode down to the wharf, boarded the Flattie and rowed to the other side of the river where there was fuel in abundance.

The Other Side, as it was commonly known, comprised a large hill sculptured high and rugged by massive sandstone boulders and a wide cluttering of smaller rocks that for aeons had amassed there. All else was covered with thick scrub and wildflowers, much of it shaded by smooth-barked gums with their sapling progeny, but utterly devoid of human habitation.

Jack had a fondness for visiting The Other Side, for there, in blessed isolation, visitors could not invade his precious hours of weekend freedom. In justifiable defence of her husband's reclusive attitude, Margo reminded that Jack worked very hard at the restaurant among many people. He deserved this recuperative respite, this rest from the mental fatigue caused by his bearing all the responsibility for maintaining happy, efficient and fast-working kitchen staff.

While Jack sawed and chopped up dead branches and old trunks, the boys scouted around for smaller wood to load into the boat. Energetic and willing toilers, they soon progressed to applying their muscles to Jack's pile of timber. It was a tremendous load, more considerable in bulk than he had intended the boat to carry, and much heavier than he had calculated upon.

When the boys climbed aboard, their father pulled up the anchor and stepped confidently into the middle where the oars were housed in the rowlocks. The Flattie immediately dropped low in the water. Paul worried that, like the *Pequod* of "Moby Dick" (his latest library book), it was about to go under. This gave way to his sudden panic, and he swiftly sought reassurance from Captain Ahab. Jack laughed with self-deluding complacency. 'It'd take more than a bit of old firewood to sink *this* ship,' he boasted affectionately and patted the side of the humble craft as though to say, 'Good old girl, I trust you!'

Josie and Annie were playing a game they called *The Wind in the Willows*, inspired by Kenneth Graham's delightful story. They were on the riverbank of the Hughs' side of the bay, busily building Water Rat's house. Josie lifted her arm and pointed to the river. 'What's that thing, Annie?' she asked. Her sister looked and instantly fell into laughter.

All they could see coming towards them across the smooth, wide river was a heap of firewood with two oars comically swinging. They could hear voices, but the heads that produced them were obscured. Fleetingly, the image came to Annie of the Master of Toad Hall in one of his comical adventures, and she wished her mum and the other children could have been present to enjoy the funny sight.

As the Flattie neared the channel, the halfway mark, a launch came *put-put-putting* down the river, past the island of mangroves and on towards The Point. Small waves from the launch began splashing against the Flattie, and some spilt onto the back seat. Paul and Tony jumped up at the same time, both with wet pants. 'The water's coming in, Dad!' Tony shouted above the receding noise of the other boat.

Jack blasphemed and yelled back. 'Siddown before you tip the boat.' They instantly obeyed. But, hastily reviewing that order, Jack said, 'No— move up here closer.' He was endeavouring to lighten the load on the back, but the boys' movements, hampered by the pile of firewood, caused the boat to list and more water poured in.

'Keep bailing!' Jack said, handing Paul the old saucepan kept for that purpose, and Pauly bailed furiously. Jack continued rowing hard, but it was a big load to pull with only two oars. The inflowing water quickly gained ... and the Flattie slowly went under.

It was a tame climax compared to any one of hapless Toad's calamities. The icy water was quite shallow, so the boys merely stepped out and hurriedly plodded to shore, but Margo's precious firewood floated all around like so much flotsam and jetsam and began drifting off with the outgoing tide. Strong Jack, however, was able to pull the boat back to the wharf. He retrieved as much of the wood as his legs could bear the cold and the three of them trudged on up to the house shivering and looking rather water-rattish.

With no dry wood for the Bega, Margo had to use the electric stove for all her baking and, conscious of the cost of electricity, considered this an ill-afforded indulgence. Reliable Herb got busy with his tomahawk and chopped up fruit boxes to feed the fire under the copper, at least long enough to boil up the sheets, towels and nappies, but Margo completed the remainder of the big wash by hand.

Annie saw how crinkled her mother's white fingers were and how dreadfully tired she was, yet she kept on working. Jack too, noticed Margo's weariness and the puffiness of her hands.

On odd occasions, often when Margo's day had been a hectic one, Herb and Annie cooked the evening meal. That water-logged wood day, they set about preparing scrambled eggs and baked beans on toast. Later, the extent of Margo's exhaustion became more apparent. She was barely able to sit upright long enough to finish her meal, and her eyelids kept closing. Jack left his chair, went quietly around to Margo and helped her to stand. 'I'm taking over now,' he said tenderly and with his arm supporting her, steered the tenacious little toiler towards the bedroom.

The older kids looked sadly at one another wondering if there was something more serious than tiredness wearing their mother down. After a few minutes, Jack came back, pulled out his chair, sat back in it and slapped both hands onto his thighs. 'Now,' he announced with renewed energy, 'we're going to have a pow-wow.'

The children had often encountered the Indian term in Cowboy films at the picture theatre, but it had never been applied to them. They understood its meaning though and listened deferentially to everything Big Chief Dad said in explanation of 'Mum's bone-weary' state. He enhanced their understanding of the consequences of over-work on a human body and inspired them to do more in the future to help their precious mother.

It was a long pow-wow, and so completely did Jack invigorate his children and win their support that they could hardly wait to "share the load, shoulder the yoke and pull together in the same furrow", and generally to get "stuck into" all the jobs they had been whinging about and neglecting. After Jack's edifying talk, there emerged eager unanimity that henceforth they would all "get cracking" and take on more responsibilities to help lighten Margo's workload and banish the terrible fatigue.

The next day at Mass, Annie prayed with renewed, solemn earnest for an improvement in her mum's health, realising how empty everyone's life would be without her. An hour later, she was back home and had just changed into her old clothes when visitors arrived. Aunty Mim, one of Margo's seven sisters, and cousins Robert and Doreen, came in with fragrant bread rolls and bananas for lunch.

Doreen instantly embraced Margo and kissed her, 'Oh, hello Aunty Marg!' she exclaimed, and stood with her arms hugging around her aunt's waist for several moments ... thoughtful moments for Annie.

This display of affection and familiarity sent Annie into a brief quiescence which revisited later and identified itself as guilt for a sin of omission – *Honour thy Father and thy Mother.* She had allowed the pleasant ritual of kissing her mum as she left for school to become extinct – always too hurried, always too impatient – and, reviewing cousin Doreen's actions, felt a sharp self-reproach for past neglect.

That night, the worry descended again before sleep could forestall it. Annie fretted, regretted and wished the little habit, perfunctory though it was, had never been allowed to lapse all that time ago, however long it had been.

The next morning, dressing for school, she decided to initiate the change; to kiss her mother quickly before racing off for the bus. She paused to reconsider: 'But– but maybe I'd ... perhaps she'd ... would Mum be embarrassed?' and remained quietly thoughtful as Margo smoothed out the crinkles of her ribbons over the hot oven door and then tied them around her waiting plaits. She patted her girl's shoulder, 'There you are dear. Off to school now, and be good.'

Annie turned to face her mum and in one rushed clumsy movement, kissed and hugged her, then grabbed her school case and dashed out the door. Margo smiled gently, pleasurably to herself that morning, knowing that Doreen's recent display of affection had been the catalyst for re-establishing the endearing practice.

Later that same week, two exciting new commodities, which Jack worked overtime to pay for, were carried into his house: a shiny, black kerosene heater, shaped in the mode of a lighthouse, and a round, white washing machine with a wringer. Margo was ecstatically happy – almost as though she had won the lottery!

33 The Home Dentist

About a year before World War II ended, Grandma Carrington had taken little Herbie and Annie to their first dental visit. She had minded the children to allow Margo, with her new baby Pauly, some essential rest and sought to do something more for her daughter.

The nearest dentist at that time was at Mortdale, several train-stops city-ward from Como. Once inside the surgery, the white-coated gentleman gave little Annie a ride in the strange-looking chair. He inspected her teeth, informed her grandmother that everything looked all right and down went the fun-chair. Grandma took Annie's hand, and they watched Herbie go through the same procedure.

Afterwards, Grandma bought ice creams, and they strolled to the invitingly green park, ablaze with beds of flowers, where there were swings, a seesaw and a slippery-dip. The excursion to the dentist had been an enjoyable experience, so neither Herbie nor his little sister had any reason to fear future visits.

The next dental appointment was several years later. Herb, Paul and Annie made the train trip to Mortdale and then walked to the same surgery. The nerve-shredding screech of the drill was hard to bear, and Pauly and Annie wondered what the dentist was doing to poor Herbie. Annie soon found out when he drilled one of her back teeth in preparation for a filling. Pauly was lucky; being so young his teeth had no cavities, but he might have been distressed by the high penetrating whine of the drilling.

Some years after that it was Annie's turn again. Part of a tooth had broken off, and the dentist moulded a small bit of gold into its place. The procedure had not hurt Annie at all and afterwards, during its novel period she smiled often. But practical Billy Meadows joked, 'Don't smile too much or y' might cop a punch in the gob by a gold robber!' Billy's many and varied gems of advice were always thus eloquently phrased.

Annie was anxious to show Ruthie her little nugget of gold, and when she arrived at her friend's house, affable Mrs Collins invited her to stay for lunch. At home later, talking to Margo's back and elbow – for her arm was busy in its vigorous stretch-and-retract motion as she cleaned the mantelpiece – Annie related points of interest. One being that Ruthie's Pop and Nan had been present ('Well, that was nice,') and they had all eaten pies with tomato sauce ('Oh, meat pies, mmm!'). Clearly, Margo's mind was not yet entirely receptive to chitchat.

After she had wiped the timber shelf dry, she asked Annie to pass up the canisters from the table and then to hand her the clock and the bill spike of impaled receipts. 'Good of Mrs Collins,' she murmured absently as she concentrated on aligning the green lettering of the cream Bakelite canisters, righted the green lids and then with more accuracy adjusted the adjustments. 'And what are the grandparents like?' she asked at last.

'Well, they're old ... but really nice,' answered Annie (not intending to express surprise that the two elements were actually compatible). But there was something more she was bursting to tell. 'Ruthie's Pop's sort of funny, y'know Mum, jokes a lot and all that, but you oughta hear the way he *eats!*'

Margo perceived that she undoubtedly ought *not!* Her job done, she sat at the table for a rest and to prepare herself for yet another unpleasant observation.

'Why?' The flat enquiry was voiced against better inclination. Margo, blest with the innate qualities of an effective educator, was well acquainted with her daughter's many faults. Correction, therefore, was looming.

'Well, instead of biting into his pie like you and me would do–'

'*I.* You and *I.*' (She was always quick to correct.)

'Yes, you and *I.* Well, he sucks the mince out of it! *Sucks* it! And it's so noisy.'

Margo frowned. 'But perhaps ... well, does he have teeth?'

'No – well, yes, but he puts them in a glass of water on the kitchen sink while he eats. And that's another thing that really—'

'Poor old fellow!' Margo interrupted, skilfully denying her whinging daughter the pleasure of her next complaint, and she levelled a look of enquiry at the girl. 'But don't you think that's sad Annie?' she asked, her head moving a little in the negative.

'Ooh, I s'pose,' came the reluctant, annoyed concession. 'But it's very disgusting. I don't know how Ruthie's family can stand it.'

Margo got up from the chair and pushed it in to the table. 'You mustn't let these things irritate you. They're not important. Try to imagine what it would be like eating *without* teeth. And look after yours ... and try to be more sympathetic and not so darn critical. You should hear yourself, Annette – you sound awful!' (The use of her full name meant 'watch your step!')

'But Mum, can I help it if things get on my nerves? I bet Dad wouldn't like it, either.'

'No,' said her mother in a moment of quiet, thoughtful agreement and, seeking to divert critical thoughts into pleasanter channels, she resorted to her old trick of distraction, exclaiming brightly, 'Oh, look! The sun's out again.' Grabbing her rags and sandsoap, she escaped to the tranquility of the laundry.

Annie stood there for a moment, struck by her new-born awareness of an affinity with her father and his abhorrence of eating noises. Presently, the new thought occurred to her, 'Well ... looks like I take after Dad, then!'

After a while, yet another dentist opened a surgery at Jannali which proved very handy to anyone in Oyster Bay suffering a sudden toothache. Eventually, that misfortune befell Annie. It was heralded by a needle-sharp pain piercing her jaw while biting into an ice block and recurred that night as she drank hot cocoa. Margo shook her head regretfully and said, 'Looks like a trip to the dentist for you, my girl.'

The following day, Annie cringed in the waiting room futilely trying to use mind-power to deflect the terrible sound of drilling going on in the torture chamber. She felt as Marie Antoinette might have done when approaching the guillotine, and tried to focus her attention on the pictures in the *Pix* magazine. When her turn came, the dentist imparted his absurd order: "relax".

'*Relax!* He might as well have said laugh!' nervous Annie silently scoffed.

Injections of local anaesthetic were not usually given for fillings in those *good old days*, and dental appointments loomed as nightmares.Annie's attempt to ease her stranglehold on the chair arms failed when the drill touched a nerve, expected at every moment. Her hands grabbed and hung on white-knuckled as though she were being electrocuted. Throat noises became primitive and guttural. Annie wanted to yell, but there were particular impedimenta to that indulgence, and her mouth seemed to be stretching to tearing point, the corners burning.

Later, the dentist left the room for a few minutes, and Annie relayed her concerns to the nurse who assured the girl that her medium-sized mouth would not tear. She added that it was difficult for people with small mouths, especially in relation to dentists who had big fingers, and also for people with thick tongues, a new concept to Annie. The nurse told her that the combination of small mouth, large tongue and big fingers would make dentistry difficult, perhaps impossible. Those unfortunate people, she said, would have to search for a dentist with small hands to end their suffering. (Perhaps Marie Antoinette could not find one!)

Annie took particular notice of the dentist's medium-sized hands when he brought them back into the surgery and again he told Annie to relax and open wide her mouth. But when he started drilling, her right foot began to rise independently of her will and hovered rigidly above the footrest.

She let it drop, realising the comedy, but when he drilled again, up went the self-initiating foot. An attempt to control the rebellious extremity while enduring agony proved unsuccessful and, regardless of Annie's fight to anchor it, the drilling always triumphed. Her foot continued to rise and fall throughout the ordeal, and this presented a challenge for the attendant nurse as she fought to keep her features composed, and thereby her job secure.

A few years later, the Hughs received notice of yet another dental surgery soon to open right there in Oyster Bay. *What was the cause of this sudden influx of tooth people?* It was, predominantly, the sugar. While the Hughs children were growing up, the general consumption of sugar, relative to present day use, was excessive, and it was inevitable that tooth enamel would succumb to erosion. The Hughs' family's diet, although rich in all foods healthful, still included sugar. Cocky's Joy (golden syrup) was always on the table alongside the bowls of sugar and jam. Treats, such as cordial, soft drink, ice cream and lollies, were regular indulgences rather than occasional.

It was a disconcerting fact; in Annie's estimation dentists were encroaching too fast and too close. But none could be closer than their own "Home Dentist" from whom there was no escape. When Herb, Paul and Annie were younger and losing their baby teeth, Margo always gently pulled them out, for usually they were just hanging there, and she never forgot to inform the tooth fairy who faithfully visited them that night and left a silver coin.

Sometimes though, their father would perform the extraction. He was by nature always methodical and completely organised in everything he undertook, especially when associated with something as crucial as a tooth extraction. And when the skill of acting also was required, Jack Hughs excelled.

One of Tony's baby teeth was "hanging by a thread" – as Margo termed it. This drew an enthusiastic response from Jack (if not Tony!). As soon as the breakfast dishes had been cleared away, he began carefully preparing the table with a white sheet upon which he placed his "instruments" in proper order, as would a theatre nurse for a surgeon.

Adopting the professional, impersonal detachment of an elite Macquarie Street specialist, Jack issued the correctly enunciated, formal instruction: 'Next patient, please. Step into the surgery, if you will. I am now ready to extract the tooth.' His acting was remarkably good and the pantomime entertaining – if you were not the victim.

The prerequisite always, of course, was the patient. This usually required several dental assistants to fly around the house or down the backyard to find the little escapee. Perhaps it would be necessary to drag him down out of a tree or from under a bed, or even to force the lavvy door open to grab hold of him. But on this occasion, Tony was obligingly right there under the house. (It takes time to develop cunning strategies of escape.)

The understandable reason for the absconding was the painful sight of Jack's "instruments": claw hammer, chisel, saw, pliers, a string tied to the weighty shoe last, and a ten-pound sledgehammer for the anaesthetic. Every one of the older kids had once been a protagonist in a similar kitchen-surgery drama and knew that when the wide-eyed patient was rigidly supine upon the table, the procedure would be dragged out for as long as possible.

Dentist Jack took up each tool in turn and speculated upon how it might be used in his approach to the problem. 'Well, what about this one, then, will *this* do the trick?' he asked. Tony wildly shook his head and stared round-eyed at the hand drill his father was seriously inspecting.

Jack applied this pretended in-depth consideration to each implement, while Margo sought to counter the effect by making dismissing little laughing noises (equally feigned) and sincere and comforting assurances to Tony that 'Dad is just pretending.' Presently though, deciding that her precious child had been subjected to quite enough terror, she brought down her brows and delivered a stern look of warning to accompany a low-voiced threat to her husband to get on with it, or she would "dong" him and take over.

Finally, Dentist Hughs came to the only tool necessary – a small pair of pliers. With one hand holding Tony's head in an inescapable position he slipped a section of a clean handkerchief over the tooth and deftly nipped it out "before you could say *Jack Robinson*" … which takes less than three seconds if you merge the middle syllables!

Tony blinked, amazed at the sight of his tooth in the pliers' jaws and the speck of blood on the handkerchief. His father asked if it had hurt. 'Nope!' was the surprised reply. No, the actual extraction never did hurt – the painful part of the procedure was all the fear, panic and drama that preceded it!

34 Biddy's Calf

Some of the Hughs children had made the train journey to their grandparents' south coast farm for a short holiday. It was late autumn. Almost all the leaves had fallen from the fruit trees, the grass was browning, and everything was spent. Mother Earth gathered the dead herbage around her and prepared for a winter's sleep. One long sigh she emitted, sending the last of the russet leaves fluttering to the ground – and then she rested.

Silently, Annie crept from her bed early one particular morning to accompany Grandpa and the two dogs on a walk to the western boundary fence. Biddy was due to calve and Grandpa, unsure of where the cow had camped, naturally was concerned. When they left the house, they could see no farther than the tea trees at the south. The fog was a "real pea-souper", reducing visibility to about the same distance all around them.

But how beautiful it was! The whole bushland had become enshrouded in an enchanting nebulosity. The trees stood tall, still and wet, their towering heads lost in the fog. Below them, veiling every hakea and prickle bush and uniting the diverse array of wild plants which formed the undergrowth, were magnificent structures of dewy-beaded gossamer, principal engineers nowhere to be seen.

Banjo and Trixie quietened, aware of the difference. Sounds were trapped beneath the fog as if enclosed in a low-ceilinged cave, but from above the trees, the lonely, mournful caw of a crow could still be heard. Elsewhere, under the misty canopy, bright little birds were already twittering to one another.

Suddenly, the dogs ran off along the fence. Grandpa assumed they were chasing a "roo" – their usual delight – but as he whistled them a fox shot out from the bush in a frantic effort to escape. Under the fence, it zipped and was fast away, the dogs in hopeless pursuit. Annie and her grandfather walked on. By the time they had almost completed the circuit of several fences, Trixie had caught up, and soon Banjo's throaty noises announced his worn-out *I'm-too-old-for-this* presence.

Annie's hair became damp from the fog. Grandpa had very few hairs to worry about, but his head shone with the moisture. By the time they were treading the last stretch and had turned towards home, the fog had almost lifted. Soon, they could see everything again ... and there at the edge of the bush was Biddy.

'Ah! She's having it now,' Grandpa said in a relieved but apprehensive voice, and they slackened their pace and moved gradually closer to the labouring animal. 'We'll stay just here,' Grandpa said in a lowered tone. 'Be very quiet now and let her concentrate on what she has to do.' They stood half obscured by a clump of bushes and waited.

The young girl became both fearful and excited, never before having witnessed such an important event. The cow slowly

298

waddled a short distance away from them to the farthermost corner of the paddock, her back legs widely straddling the large udder. Annie watched in wonder as Grandpa explained what was happening. Biddy made several directionless turns and then lay down. A few moments later she stood, and a small bag or sack appeared beneath her tail.

She walked a short distance further. The bag fell to the ground, and she spun around to examine it. After stomping about on the grass, the cow lifted her tail, and the two anxious observers saw that a little white hoof had appeared. The sturdy brown body strained again, and another one emerged.

Clearly distressed now, Biddy lay down but immediately heaved up the burden of her bulk, repeating the action several times. 'This is so awful Grandpa! It's too hard for her ... what if she can't get it out!' Annie cried fretfully, appealing to him for reassurance that Biddy would not rip open or die in her struggle to deliver the calf. But Grandpa shook his head and assured the anxious girl that it would soon be born.

The exhausted cow stood and kicked up dirt and grass with her front leg then strained again ... and suddenly the calf emerged, then to hang right out into the world, head almost touching the ground. Its whole length finally flopped heavily onto the grass where it lay stretched out and steaming. Biddy spun around and began licking, sending short, soft *moos* to the blinking calf, and

Annie imagined she was saying: "Lie still my baby while mother cleans you up."

At last, it was over. Beaming Grandpa moved closer to inspect the little fellow. It was almost a replica of its Hereford father, complacently chewing his cud over there in the paddock of the adjoining farm, and entirely oblivious of Biddy's ordeal and the calf he had sired. Practical Grandpa had ready two names for the occasion and right away, without even thinking about it, he said, 'Well, young Sammy ... you finally got here, eh?'

35 Uncle Owen

Of Jack's two brothers, Owen was closest to him in age. Although of similar appearance, their personalities differed significantly. Jack's nature was down-to-earth with a warm sense of humour which quickly recognised the comical aspects of various situations. Contrastingly, Owen was usually serious-faced and always refined, yet his sometimes-droll manner often invited much amusement.

Not everyone nurtures a passion for rivers, boats, fishing and swimming. Uncle Owen had become disenchanted with these activities while he was still a young man. He had fallen prey to his brothers' penchant for practical jokes and had allowed Jack and Charlie to persuade him to go swimming farther up the river, a distance from the farm, where the whole family was picnicking on the grassy bank.

It was a hot day, and the water's mirror-smooth surface sent a message of coolness and tranquillity. The three youths had not brought along their swimming "togs", and so they trekked a short way through the bush, stripped off and plunged into the creek. Before Owen knew what was happening, larrikin Charlie sneaked out under cover of overhanging branches and hid his brother's clothes. Owen, by nature excessively modest, underwent a lengthy and angry search before retrieving them from a high limb of a river oak. Forgiveness was a long time coming.

A tall, commanding figure like his mother, Owen was devoted to his religion and emanated a cultivated, almost aloof air. He had acquired from books and various other influences outside the family, vast knowledge and an extensive vocabulary. His speech, therefore, was often eloquent, even pompous and sometimes comically so. While Jack might say: 'C'mon kids, get inside for a wash, Uncle Owen's going to take your photo,' Owen would express it differently.

Smiling almost gleefully, he would rub his hands together, and with the self-possessed air of one who has confident verbal skills, he would carefully articulate: 'Come along children and attend to your morning ablutions. I'll be photographing you presently, and I require clean, smiling countenances!' He would pause between certain words to pronounce the final consonants correctly, speaking in the manner of an elocution teacher or an imperious headmaster.

The fun-loving Hughs children might have responded to Uncle Owen with solemnity and deference, but they suspected that the "carry-on" was performed for their amusement. Owen never swore or used slang or nicknames, but he had a humorous way of addressing the children. '*What*! Still rotting in bed?' he would exclaim if they happened to be sleeping in. 'Idle monsters and wenches lazing the day away, squandering the precious early hours!' Laughter was never far from their lips and always in their eyes, and they skylarked with him all the time.

Jack's sister, Eva, was every bit as religious as Owen and their mother. In that respect, there was a clear division in the family. The unsophisticated Hughs were Grandpa, Jack and Uncle Charlie, the last being the most coarse and jocular. Charlie was the indulged scallywag of the family and the one about whose deplorable antics and risqué jokes Owen would tut-tut, roll his eyes heavenward and mutter to God: 'Appalling want of refinement!'

Nana faithfully attended Mass every Sunday, but Grandpa rebelled against her futile efforts to assimilate him into the flock and so they established a satisfactory compromise. Grandpa drove Nana to Mass at Nowra's St Michael's, and she happily disappeared inside for an hour to hear Mass and receive Holy Communion. Grandpa patiently waited out the time in the Oldsmobile, content enough with his Sunday newspaper.

Uncle Owen had once been engaged to his sister's best friend, but the romance faded and died, and she married someone else. Owen remained a bachelor and therefore had no children, but needing someone to care about he developed an affectionate interest in the welfare of his monstersand wenches. He built his own house at Jannali and, after Sunday Mass, often walked to

Oyster Bay to visit his brother's family. Margo, conscious of his loneliness, always prepared a special meal.

Lunch over, Jack and Owen usually sat back with their beer or cups of tea to enjoy an analysis of the current deplorable state of politics or communism. They spoke too of the homeless drunks sleeping in the park near Central Railway Station, but sometimes they just talked about family news – all the usual things fathers and uncles tended to discuss. The children did not bother to eavesdrop (because of indifference, not virtue), but passing through the kitchen, they could not fail to hear fragments of conversation often associated with *Menzies' White Australia Policy* and the oft-repeated slogan *Populate or Perish.*

Jack one day, was hotly criticising Arthur Calwell for allowing more migrants into the country. Owen's general outlook was broader and less prejudicial than his brother's, and he sat back, crossed his ankles and reminded Jack of their German heritage.

'You may as well accept it Jack', he said, 'because we *will* become a multicultural Australia in the future. Australia Day is already a day for naturalisation ceremonies.'

Jack's indignant response was: 'Well and good. But we aren't like those Greeks and Italians! White Australia? Not much longer!' It was a burst of discrimination Jack soon regretted, for after meeting some of the skilled, hard-working foreigners, and recognising their value to Australia's development, his negative attitude changed significantly.

Owen was always kind to the children and, being a photographer, often afforded them the opportunity to be his subjects. He used backdrops and improvised props to lend the photographs a professional presentation. Tony was sitting one day on the blanket-covered, curtain-backed sewing machine table, smiling away happily. Uncle Owen looked up from the camera and said: 'Close your mouth, little monster, the absence of front teeth is not your most outstanding attribute!'

Of course, the child grasped only the first part of the sentence and did not care much about his gappy grin. Margo drew a curious amusement from the droll tone in which her brother-in-law had expressed the command.

Religion became increasingly important to Uncle Owen. He built a small altar in his lounge room so that he could kneel before the crucifix and the statue of Our Lady and pray fervently more often. It was as though the presence of the altar provided a personal, direct and speedier route to God. Jack remarked that his brother would have made a good priest. It was a fair appraisal and quite natural to picture Uncle Owen in a black soutane and white lacy surplice or beautifully fashioned outer vestments of shining green and gold.

It was easy, too, for Annie to visualise him swinging the smoky thurible of incense at Benediction; easy to imagine him watching from the rear of the church as the children progressed self-consciously from pew to pew and, under his blue gaze, genuflecting at the pictures depicting the Stations of the Cross. She visualised herself kneeling before him to receive Holy Communion and saw his covered arms raising the chalice before he drank the wine. *That* was not difficult to imagine because he loved wine. His florid complexion with its web of damaged capillaries always betrayed recent enjoyment, especially after he had shared a bottle of *Penfold's Port* with her father.

The Ecclesiastic life would have suited Uncle Owen. It would have made his mother and sister extremely proud had he entered the priesthood and oversaw his relatives' spiritual nourishment. However, that would create a certain problem for Jack's kids – confession. The idea of revealing to a close relation all their mortal sins, or even venial ones, was most disturbing to them because apart from embarrassment, there was the likelihood that penance imposed by Uncle Owen would be severe. For instance, he might order the recitation of the entire Rosary rather than the usual few prayers. And what was worse – forever after he would be in cerebral possession of all the terrible sins his impious relatives had committed.

But Uncle Owen did not become a priest and the children's relationship with him continued to be happy and entertaining.

However, on the day Herb and Annie were making their Confirmation, with sponsors Uncle Owen and Aunty Eva, something happened which made Owen extremely angry.

It was a lovely sunny day and not such a trial to be standing out there in a long queue on the asphalt. Herb seemed subdued and bored, and Annie was impatient to get on with the business of being confirmed; to impart the promise to love God and serve Him for the rest of her life. But she was keener to return home where she knew there awaited a mysterious Confirmation Day present for her consecrated self.

At last, the queue began shuffling forward. With appropriate reverence children and sponsors dipped fingers into the holy water font and made the sign of the cross and then sat in the packed but hushed church where masses of pink belladonna lilies scented the air. Everyone was waiting for the bishop to emerge from the sacristy and begin the ceremony. Just as he appeared in his splendid garments and impressive mitred hat and crossed in front of the candle-lit altar, there arose an unceasing, ear-splitting shrilling coming from a smuggled-in cicada in Herb's coat pocket.

Aunty Eva and Annie were seated in the pew directly behind their shameful relation, and Annie saw her Uncle's neck go a bright wine-red as he turned to glare at Herb. 'Shut it up!' he hissed – somewhat louder than he intended and quite forgetting to be eloquent. Obediently Herb's hand slapped hard against his pocket.

The jubilant singing of God's little creature came to a spluttering halt in that hallowed and cavernous place of worship, and a hundred eyes, which had turned Herb's way in appalled wonder, now focused again on the momentarily stunned bishop at the altar.

Annie's heart went out to her brother. How awful it was for Herbie and his favourite '*Yellow Monday*' to part company in that sacrificial way! Later, the impish thought sashayed across her mind lamenting the great pity that Herb had not simply thrown the cicada up to winged liberty above all the devout, white-veiled heads. She imagined the eruption of feminine squeals and felt deprived because of the missed opportunity and the conception of a more entertaining tale to relate to Ruthie, who was curious about the mysteries of the Catholic religion.

(Once, when Ruthie had asked what Mass was like, Annie had shrugged and replied, 'It's just … you know … a lot of Latin and very, very sacred. And so *boring!*' she added as the rebellious afterthought struck her. But later, she became troubled by a conviction that she was indeed a very sinful person for having uttered such irreverent thoughts.)

The ceremony began. Eventually, it was time for the four Hughs to stand and take their places in the queue shuffling towards the altar. Herb had to forgo recovery time. By sheer strength of will, he banished the unfortunate incident from his mind and stepped forward to present himself to the bishop and to have his forehead anointed with the holy oil.

Later, Herb well-knew, he would face the wrath of hostile Uncle Owen (still smouldering away there) and after that, endure the merciless teasing from his dad and visiting Uncle Charlie, both rendered irresponsible by an hour of beer and jocularity at the Como pub.

36 Johnno

One balmy wattle-scented day a high-class car pulled up in front of the Hughs' house. Margo and the children were surprised to see that the driver was John O'Dwyer, an older mate of Herb's and an employee of a boat hire place. Johnno grinned broadly, basking in the awed reverence that Herb's young siblings were vocally conferring upon the gleaming beauty, and he asked if they would like to go for a "burn."

'Oh boy! Would we? Yeees!' rose the chorused response.

The excited youngsters crowded around the sleek Hudson Hornet to lay reverent hands upon it. Mrs Hughs, with babe in arms and toddler trailing, sauntered outside for a closer investigation. She eyed the vehicle with a glint of scorn, somewhat sceptical about Johnno's proprietary claim. However, she discerned credibility in his glib comment connecting the car with a visitor – for he had always evinced pride in his wealthy relative.

Johnno, no respecter of truth and not one to dwell upon incriminating inconsistencies, quickly evaded the danger of awkward probing questions by switching the focus most appropriately to the seating arrangements. His successful diversion, Margo later reflected, revealed much skill in the art of distraction and subterfuge.

Before ten minutes had passed, Margo Hughs, excited despite her reservations, had taken off her apron, put on a hat and closed the front door. The energised younger kids competed to be first to slide onto the plush rear seat. That settled, Margo passed in the infants and then climbed in. Annie and two of her young brothers were promised the next trip, and so they waited impatiently at the gate.

'Let's go!' said grinning Herb as he took his place next to the driver, and the beautiful car cruised off down the gravel road towards the bitumen at the shops. The excited Deserted, watching through the sinking dust, could hardly wait to have their turn.

In those old mid-century days, the children's prospect of a drive was exhilarating, for along with many people, the Hughs did not own a car. Only on essential occasions did they travel in such a conveyance – usually a taxi. But those short trips were often of an urgent nature, too pressing for an appreciation of scenery flashing past and definitely not comparable to a leisurely tour of the entire district in a "posh"Hudson Hornet.

This was especially so on such a pleasant spring noon when fragrant blossoms were opening, and the sun was noticeably brighter. It was a day deserving of the word "glorious", and all were out and enjoying it.

At length, Annie and the boys could hear the exciting low purr of the car mounting the hill, advancing sedately over the corrugations, skirting pot-holes and making slow, careful progress towards them, which at least reflected merit on Johnno's driving.

The young passengers beamed as they tumbled out, but when Margo alighted, her expression promised thunder.

She ushered the little ones indoors and followed without sending a single glance to her generous chauffeur. That was not like Margo – one of her maxims was: 'Having good manners shows that you care about others.'

Annie's whispered enquiries to Herb wrested the fact that cavalier Johnno had laughingly boasted: 'The car's hot!' The young girl wondered why he would be so happy that his car was hot and therefore uncomfortable ... and if the discomfort had caused her mother to be upset. She hurried indoors to elicit further information.

Meanwhile Johnno, whose conscience was unaccustomed to exercise and who had forgotten the Holy Commandment concerning pilfering, quickly devised some pretext which facilitated his immediate removal from further censure and smoothed his course swiftly onward. Disappointed Paul and Tony were left with the distinct impression that their excursion in the "swanky" dream car was probably *off*.

When faced with her daughter's questioning about the temperature in Johnno's car, Margo replied in low, angry tones: '*Hot* is a slang word meaning stolen'. She raised her arms to remove the hatpin. 'And to think we went all over the place in it ... and there were people everywhere today.' She heaved a sigh of defeat. 'And that infernal busy-bo— Mrs Next Door, saw us too. Wouldn't it?' she said, adding her oft-repeated aborted phrase. 'And even worse ... so did Father McKinley!' She plonked her plump body onto a chair at the table and tried to exorcise the anguish of what she perceived to be irreparable damage to her reputation.

Margo Hughs, in fact, was entirely unaware that the priest, having suspiciously surveyed the vehicle, had extracted a promise from repentant Johnno to visit the confessional on Saturday. Father wanted to point out to the youth the downward slide of his errant conduct, to guide his wayward feet back onto the correct path. His intended private sermon, he felt sure, would produce the crucial turnabout in Johnno's life of petty crime. Father McKinley was humbly proud of his winning way with words.

After a moment, Annie asked, 'But how come Father saw the car?'

Margo sighed. 'Well, John drove to the church where the fete was on, and I took the little ones in for some fairy floss.' She cradled her head in her hands. 'While I was doing that, Father went over to look at the car,' she said to the table. 'Oh, Lord! To think he was actually admiring a stolen car. If this ever gets out we'll *never* live it down,' she grieved. 'And I suppose Mrs Next Door will make very sure of *that*.'

The concerned young girl yearned to soothe her mother. 'But Mum, you didn't know.'

Surfacing from the depths of indignation and remorse, Margo turned in the chair and patted Annie's caressing hand. 'No … no pet, I didn't, but I shouldn't have trusted Johnno and paraded around as if I lived in Vaucluse.'

She drew a little comfort, however, from the thought that Johnno's story had seemed valid and she had seen no reason flatly to disbelieve him. 'But one of his relatives *is* well-off,' she continued, 'so I just assumed–' She nodded to Annie. 'Well, it serves me right for being a darn fool, doesn't it?' Thus, Margo Hughs attempted to establish some equilibrium between self-justification and self-condemnation.

Herb, who had been mending a punctured tyre of his pushbike while he waited for the tempest to abate, sauntered inside and looked across at his mother from beneath his apprehensive brows. Margo sighed, tied on her apron and, in keeping with her usual stern precepts, warned him to avoid Johnno in the future. This latest escapade confirmed her belief that the youth's notoriety was well-founded. She made wise use of the example, issuing a timely reminder to her children of the risk of being judged by the company kept.

But the renouncing of Johnno's services imposed feelings of painful disappointment to Annie and the boys; the opportunity of 'a burn in his hot car' – as Pauly so imitatively expressed it – having vanished with Johnno's retreat.

Jack and Margo lived modestly and had never aspired to the ownership of an expensive car or of any such high rungs of the social ladder. Nevertheless, Margo had enjoyed the drive even more than she had expected and therefore it took some time for her to get over the sullying of the experience. 'I know I'll laugh about it one day,' she muttered wryly to Jack that night – 'in about twenty years.'

Herb tried to comply with his mother's wishes, but Johnno had long been his friend, and it was difficult, therefore, to avoid contact. Johnno, unfazed by adult disapproval, had acquired the companionable habit of dropping by occasionally with some exciting activity in mind. Naturally, the Hughs kids always looked forward to seeing him.

Johnno was a rascal, everyone knew that, but he was a harmless, *Sherwood Forest* rascal who always felt the generous need to share the spoils of his sometimes-hazardous escapades. Never, to anyone's knowledge, did he consider mercenary gains.

But in Johnno's estimation, veracity was a flexible and expendable quality, and he felt at perfect liberty to relate entertaining and elaborate stories. He was crafty, and always conflated his tales with a dash of truth to lend plausibility to his slick explanations of how he happened to find certain goods in his resourceful possession.

Contemplating this, Annie began to regard lorry drivers as a very negligent lot who often failed to secure the goods correctly on the back of their trucks, and she remained in this charming state of naiveté for quite some time afterwards.

Predictably, Johnno did not stay away from the Hughs crowd for long. Despite Father McKinley's astute counsel, the lost sheep, easily led into temptation, embarked nonchalantly on his next folly. This involved the removal of a large number of packeted chocolates from a riverside kiosk, quality and quantity uniting with doubtful anonymity in a coarse-weave hessian bag. On the premise that he may as well be hanged for a "quid as a bob", he borrowed a canoe from his absent employer's boatshed, dumped the chocolates in and paddled up the river to the Hughs' wharf.

On first sighting of the bag of treasure, Margo stared in alarmed wonder. She shook her finger at the grinning youth, who appeared to be blind to the sinfulness of his deed. He lapsed into an impervious silence – no doubt already planning his next venture – so that Margo's kindly meant lecture seemed to flit around the periphery of his mind with the efficacy of a whisper from Father McKinley's distant pulpit.

Just as Johnno was on the point of making a speedy escape, Margo slung a belated two-word lasso: 'The police!' That caught him. For five full seconds, he was wide-eyed attentiveness. 'The police might come here!' cried Margo, appalled. 'Oh John, what a thing to do!' she scorned. 'No, *don't* shrug and look away. Listen to me! Think of the seriousness of this and how it'll affect you – and your mother – if you're found out. And what about us? Stop smirking, John, it's not funny. Think of the consequences!'

She scowled darkly at him and sent him on his wicked way to absorb that wisdom, and this kept him in feigned frowning contemplation until he had descended the four back steps.

To the Hughs family, Johnno was an enigma. The gains he scored in the children's affection were often negated by the common sense of their mother's words and by an instilled appreciation of the difference between right and wrong. Despite this, Annie and her brothers nurtured an indulgent soft spot for their Robyn Hood's character flaws; he had a natural charisma, which vested him with certain virtues that always seemed to beg levity and leniency.

Margo perceived it, too, and there was never contempt in her tone when she berated Johnno. Like Father McKinley, she recognised that although the youth did not know it, he hungered for guidance and firm boundaries. She also surmised that as Private Patrick O'Dwyer had not survived the war, Johnno had probably felt only feather smacks from the maternal hand for his "high-spiritedness" – Mrs O'Dwyer's smiling, exonerating term for his misbehaviour.

Any scolding from his mother's gentle kissing lips was always wrapped up in cajoling appeals to "do better next time dear", for the vision of her beloved Paddy was ever-present in the younger face. Indeed, it was there for all to see: same grin, same laughing blue eyes and same forward-falling dark hair which thwarted the comb's attempt to clear the forehead.

Most local people were sympathetic to the plight of Paddy O'Dwyer's widow. She was the Presbytery cook, hardworking and respected by everyone. Margo, in her kindness, endeavoured to "walk in another's shoes" when dealing with Johnno, but she occasionally became irritated by the pretended obtuseness of the jovial incarnate. She would exhale a heavy sigh, shrug her shoulders, turn up her hands and move on to the more rewarding pursuit of potty-training her toddler. After all, the reformation of Johnno was his mother'sresponsibility, not hers.

Despite their knowledge of right and wrong, Margo's children had not yet developed the same reverence for principles as she possessed and they quickly dismissed nudging concerns of how or why the chocolates had arrived at their house. Exuberantly, they followed Johnno's Pied Piper departure, hopeful of becoming the beneficiaries of the delicious largesse.

The reward for loyalty was swiftly awarded, and they yelped and scampered about to catch the cascade of packets he tossed to them on his grinning way down to the wharf. Gluttony reigning supreme, the kids disappeared behind the chook-house to gratify their greed before their mother became aware and until they were remorsefully sick and had forfeited the right to maternal sympathy.

As well, they had acquired a brand-new sin for the ears of kind-hearted old Father McKinley, and they whispered it the following Saturday in the diminutive sanctum of the confessional. Father conferred absolution, made gentler by the music of his soft brogue, and assigned proportionate penance … and in the interim, he thought about dinner and Mrs O'Dwyer's Irish stew and dumplings.

The pious old fellow from County Clare regarded his priestly duties seriously. After assimilating Johnno's confession, pondering a moment and issuing a few "hmmms", he delivered an edifying oration. It was meant to be severe but was rendered somewhat mellowed, by fond patriarchal influence: 'Aah t'be sure, tis a *troble*some lad, y' are, John, no-o sense a'toll. Yet, 'tis a fact thut in many ways ye've the makings of a foine young man.'

He swayed his head sadly and turned to look sternly at the face behind the screen. 'Y'll be puttin' a stop to oll this stealin' now m'lad, and confoine y' energies to y' *work*, John,' he said, bringing down his bushy brows. 'But, then again,' his natural, gentle voice conceded, 'now thut I t'ink on it, I recoll Patrick was the very same ... hmmm, the very same.'

It was past Father's naptime. He opened his jaws in a loud yawn, too tired to care that it gaped, and rubbed his cheeks to encourage a restorative blood-rush to the thinking powerhouse. 'Aye, t'be sure, a handsome man was Paddy ... and himself a foine war hero an' oll.'

Later, in the peaceful seclusion of the Presbytery, Father McKinley returned to the solace of his reading and deferred until morning all concerns about Johnno and his criminal activities. 'Aah well,' he reflected as he drifted into a doze, 'Himself up there will take care of the lad.'

Providence, it seemed, much favoured the contented old priest and the scallywag clone of Paddy O'Dwyer.

37 Mr Toobey

Spring arrived when the buzzing racemes of wisteria and tight pink buds of the Hughs' nectarine tree told them to expect it, and Annie went for another short holiday to her grandparents' farm.Margo had sent her children in all directions to stay with relatives so that she would be free to help and comfort Grandma Carrington while Grandad was recovering from a stroke. She saw Annie safely onto the train with a final reminder of instructions, and from that point, the apprehensive but excited young girl travelled the two-hour trip alone (reasonably safe to do so in those days).

At Bomaderry station the bus was waiting. Relieved, Annie joined the queue, and soon the bus was heading south. Her competence in managing all this imbued her with an elevated feeling of confidence, maturity and independence. However, pride soon fell, complacency soon withered, for upon the bus's arrival at the village shop where Nana awaited, it became apparent that something of great importance had been overlooked.

An abrupt enquiry addressed Annie's departing back, 'Have you got y' fare, girlie?' Startled, she turned and stumbled back up into the bus.

There followed some awful moments of discomfit for Annie while she searched first her pockets and then the tightly packed school case, trying at the same time to keep her embarrassing bloomers and singlets from escaping. And then she remembered that the ticket was safely pinned inside her jacket. Further delay and frustration ensued as fingers fumbled with the obstinate safety pin. All the while, Annie was becoming more conscious that these activities, so impeded by her nervousness, were the focus of every eye. Her cheeks burned.

At last the pin yielded, and she handed over the much-mauled ticket. The driver's fatherly face was smiling – *every* facewas! In fact, no one appeared to have minded the delay for good-natured amusement had been drawn from the girl's predicament.

Thus, Annie Hughs blundered her clumsy way off the bus and into her grandmother's outstretched arms. Laughing and kissing, Nana said, 'Hello *Calamity Jane!*' Annie felt so joyously comforted to be with her at last as they strolled into the post office-store where Nana sent a reassuring telegram to Margo.

Although the fortnights' stay at the farm had a holiday zest to it with a different ambience and the novelty of farmyard creatures, school attendance was nevertheless required. The nearest school was at Wandandian, a typical country-style building consisting of a single area for the combined classes.

In 1970 this quaint schoolroom was moved to St Georges Basin and continued its life as before. Little did young Annie

Hughs imagine all those years ago as she sat in that classroom wearing her gingham frock, hair ribbons and sandshoes, that three of her own children would one day sit there, one of them perhaps at the very same desk she had occupied. The building was later moved to the Lady Denman site near the Currambine Creek at Huskisson where it now serves very nicely as a museum.

The Headmaster, Mr Toobey stopped at the farm gate for Annie each morning in his green Austin car. A small boy and Annie's holiday friend, Katie Miller, were already seated. At the end of the school day Mr Toobey usually stayed back to tidy up and prepare for the next day's lessons, and so Uncle Charlie, working as a timber-cutter in the Jerrawangala forest near the school, drove her home in his utility. On the way, he would sing: 'I got the blu-u-ues ... those old Jerra-wan-gala blu-ues.' Annie loved his voice and the swinging jazzy rhythm and often threw herself into the song with him.

On that first day, all the boys and girls in the little school room enjoyed a hearty laugh when Mr Toobey's resonant bass suddenly commanded: 'Stand up fifth class!' and no one did ... except astonished Annie! How come there's no fifth class? she wondered. *That* grade at St Mary's numbered about twenty.

Mr Toobey beamed. The endearingly "buck-toothed" smile stretching widely under his moustache was in complete harmony with the merriment of his brown eyes. 'Who wouldn't like him?'

323

mused Annie. He extended a formally worded but warm welcome to her and remarked on the "fifth class" novelty, expressing regret that it would be of short duration. His large hands initiated applause and the grinning, clapping children all looked at Annie – a pleasant, but a self-conscious moment for her.

It soon became apparent that Mr Toobey was indeed a character and an exceptional teacher, the kind you remember all your life, and the children appeared to respond spiritedly to his theatrical demeanour. After lunch, he asked the new girl how far she had progressed in the subject of Australian history.

That established, he wrote several reference points relating to the current lesson on the blackboard, regularly consulting the book in his left hand. Almost squatting, he dotted a loud full-stop at the end, unfolded his tall frame and inspected his handiwork, then swung around and slapped the book onto the desk. This, in the one flowing movement.

'Ludwig Leichardt led an expedition from the Darling Downs to Port Essington,' he boomed. 'In– what– year?'

He rocked on his heels while his eyes searched about for an enlightened countenance. Every child in the fourth and sixth classes glanced around unconcerned as though the question had been directed at someone else, and all of them hoped that the "someone else" would speak up soon. No one did, and with commendable patience, the headmaster repeated the question and attempted to put away his teeth. It was not easy for Mr Toobey to wear a stern face.

Silence prevailed. The tall fellow sighed wearily, passed a hand over his forest of peppery hair and paced the leather-smoothed floor that had creaked beneath the tread of his shoes for more than two decades.

'I don't know why I expect you all to remember something you read in the dim, remote past of fifteen minutes. Unreasonable of me, yes?' He shrugged a shoulder and raised his caterpillar eyebrows in a gesture of helplessness.

Katie's smiling twitch infected Annie. Glancing around, she saw that everyone was similarly amused and thought delightedly, 'This school is good fun!' Indeed, the convent seemed staid by comparison, because Mr Toobey possessed the natural talent of a comedian. Moreover, his pantomime method of teaching greatly assisted the children's learning.

Pacing again, hands behind his back, the headmaster went on, 'One realises intellectual energy is a precious resource to be used sparingly at all times. One notices, also, that every child in this room has the propensity to expect the rewards of maximum result for minimum effort.' He stopped his pacing abruptly for dramatic effect and to stare at the history class in feigned bewilderment. 'So, why not I? *Tragic*, is it not?' Annie saw a renegade smile tugging at his mouth and lending sparkle to his

eyes, and she began to realise what everyone else already knew –
that he thoroughly enjoyed his own performances.

He clapped his hands authoritatively several times. 'Come
on now, wake up everyone! We are not pre-verbal beings – Homo
sapiens has advanced somewhat! Rattle those heads now, liberate
the moths, brush away the cobwebs and all that corrosive holiday
rust. What year? – **Ernie**.' he said with loud, startling suddenness
and pointing to the most promising (or least inert) countenance.

Ernie stood up slowly. 'I think it was 1842, Sir,' he said in
a hesitant, hopeful voice.

Mr Toobey's arms shot up to heaven. 'Hall-e-lujah! All is
not lost,' he told the ceiling. 'No, don't sit down boy ... not while
cerebral life is at last stirring. How *long* did it take – the journey,
mmm?' He extended his neck comically forward, smiled
encouragingly to assist the chrysalis from its cocoon and rubbed
his hands to keep his growing impatience at bay.

Through flickering eyelids, Ernie considered the vast
geography of The World Map. 'Umm ...' and shifted his attention
to the window's geometry, his busy eyes seeming to be counting
its many panes. He saw clearly now why the angles of a square
will always be equal. And then he stared with profundity at the
portrait of King George VI, wherein, behind the glass, might lurk
the answer – 'Umm'– and tilted sideways to observe His Majesty

from a better angle. Only Ernie knew what scholarly advantage this listing stance conferred.

But metamorphosis proved too slow. Mr Toobey, who had been gravely contemplating his shoes as he rocked to and fro, then rose and sank in them, looked up now, frowned his disappointment and signalled Ernie to be seated. He searched the vacant expressions again with dying hope lengthening his own features.

But Hope is a resilient quality. Before it quite passed away, the headmaster noticed a promising twinkle in this otherwise unyielding cluster of faces – one shining star. Katie Miller raised her hand somewhat diffidently, not comfortable with her stellar status. 'Was – was it fifteen months, Sir?'

'Yes! Yes! Splennndid! Well done Katie!' Mr Toobey exclaimed, beaming at his gifted pupil. He tapped at the blackboard with the pointer. 'Now who can fill in these names, mmm?' he asked with an inquiring lift of brows, and he looked about with wide-eyed, revived optimism and again rocked on his heels.

One morning Mr Toobey brought along a large block of cake Mrs Miller had donated to the school tuckshop. 'Today we are going to learn about fractions!' he announced and, placing the cake on his desk, began slicing. 'Now, recite as I cut the sections:

Two halves, four quarters, eighths then sixteenths...' Thus, he divided until the hand of every child held a generous slice.

The world of insects fascinated him. He "detained" a spider in a jar one day and encouraged every child to examine and then sketch the long-legged creature including as much detail as possible while it obligingly struck new poses.

For the sheer fun of it, Mr Toobey drew his own impression on the blackboard: a large circle doing double duty as head and body, and legs as long as the depth of the board would allow. The spider's smiling face with overhanging teeth was adorned with a brush moustache, thick-rimmed glasses and comical high hair on top. Grinning, he moved aside and there it was for all to laugh at – a caricature of himself.

Later he took the spider outdoors and using his most eloquent diction, thanked it for posing for the nature students and, wishing it good fortune and prosperous future, he gently set it free. In this way, he sought to teach respect for, and value of, all life however small ... and no doubt hoped for an improvement in everyone's vocabulary.

The excellent teacher loved words; the melody and rhythm of words and had a fondness for alliteration. During one lunch hour, Annie found him kneeling on the playground mending someone's bicycle before an admiring little gathering. A small boy bent forward, hands on knees, and asked: 'What's wrong wif the bike, Sir?'

Mr Toobey moistened his lips and looked up from the bicycle: 'Well Tommy, there seems to be a slight irregularity with the springing of the sprocket and the straining and the spacing of the spokes!' Tommy immediately straightened and applied a sleeve to his rapidly blinking face. The teacher smiled teasingly, made a soft fist to the little chin and explained that the chain had only slipped off.

That same afternoon, a storm of unusual violence pounded the schoolhouse. The thrashing on the iron roof nullified the children's startled exclamations, and they stared in wonder at the windows, dark and foreboding. The smaller children became round-eyed and fearful, and Mr Toobey motioned the older pupils to comfort them. He went over to the blackboard and chalked in large lettering: "Ten Green Bottles" – the invitation to sing the favourite.

The conductor elevated his ruler-baton, established a *moderato* tempo and, with uplifting gestures, increased the volume to *sforzando* and the children exercised their vocal cords accordingly. It was all such riotous fun – their shouting and screeching in the schoolhouse actually sanctioned! And as they progressed through the stanzas the little ones lost their anxious look and sang as robustly and jubilantly as the rest.

They were almost sorry that afternoon when the pounding on the roof fell to a pattering and then ceased. But the sun brought a return of joy to the day as it speared golden shafts through a rent in the last, *wait-for-me* cloud, and the storm eventually grumbled off westward to frighten the little children in the primary schools of Braidwood and Bungendore.

Thus, every lesson in the country schoolhouse was conducted and enjoyed. Annie quickly grew to love Mr Toobey, and as the days passed, she began to wish her "holiday" would never end.

38 MollyMartin

The Hughs' "sunrise" neighbour, Mrs Molly Martin, visited one morning carrying a plate of cupcakes brightly decorated with "hundreds-and-thousands", mint leaf jubes and, endearingly, her "desecrated" coconut. Margo had invited Molly to see her very first carpet square, lovely in its autumn leaf colours, but more especially to try out the *Dustette*, a small vacuum cleaner bought to service it, for Mrs Martin was interested in buying one.

Another reason for the visit was for a further inspection of the old woman's forearm where recently a skin cancer had been removed. Margo was happy to provide this small service and glad also to give Molly a respite from the boisterous, all-male household from which the woman so badly needed to escape occasionally.

Annie, dreaming of one day becoming a nurse, looked on with keen interest as Margo examined the stitched wound. Mrs Martin, sitting there, still in her apron and with stockings rolled down around her ankles, mentioned Dr Sweeny's comment that Australia had more incidents of skin cancer than anywhere else in the world. Margo had heard the disturbing report on the wireless and replied that, because her children were all fair complexioned, she always ensured they wore hats during summer.

Having inspected the stitched wound, she assured the old lady that it was healing well, and gently began rewinding the bandage around the freckled arm. Mrs Martin smiled at Margo's serenely confident expression while she was doing this and remarked admiringly, 'You shoulda been a nurse, y'know. You'd make a bonzer one.'

Margo's *'Ho!'* disclaimed the praise. 'Well, I suppose you have to be a bit of everything when you have a family as large as mine,' she said.

'Yeah, I reckon y' would – I don't know how y' cope. My two have always been more than enough for me.'

Margo, an intuitive, sensitive person, was gifted with the ability to hear well beyond what was said and could read even the subtlest changes of facial expression. She perceived on this occasion that, because of the disruptive sons, Molly had reached some sort of emotional precipice and needed to talk about it. Indeed, the Martin "boys" had always been a trial to their parents.

Molly's sons were shearers. Wally was a hot-head, Ned somewhat tamer, being married. He and his wife, Gwen, both worked on sheep properties. Gwen was a magnificent cook. Whenever they came home, the brothers always argued and after a few more beers, fought with closed fists.

Brawls usually started out the back, heralded by shouts of blasphemy and swear words (of which "bastard" was the softest)

332

followed by swinging punches. The beery men always managed to stumble over the startled, squealing pig. Thus, sufficiently announced, they progressed through the house with such noise and violence that the Hughs kids, gawking in trepidation and glee over their side fence, could hear the walls being thumped and the furniture crashing. Interspersed with all were the shrill and frantic entreaties of Mrs Martin and Gwen: 'Ned! Wally! Gawd love-a-duck, stop it, will ya? *Stop* it! Stop 'em will ya Pop?'

Oh, that the spectators might have occupied the dress circle of the Martins' side fence!

On one memorable occasion, the sons battled their way out onto the front veranda where Pop Martin was enduring stoically behind the *Sydney Morning Herald*. By some well-practised command over his first inclinations he had rendered himself to a phlegmatic state, almost comatose, or so it seemed to the spies. Thus, he remained throughout all the thumping and crashing until one of the "boys" fell against his cane chair, all but dethroning him.

Then he exploded. Waving his arms about, he stood his great height, and a lion's roar commanded: 'Get to f'n buggery, and f'n kill each other but stop knocking the f'n furniture around y' ratbag pair of nitwits,' and back to his dishevelled paper, he went. He righted it and resumed his seat with such aplomb as to suggest the interruption had never occurred.

In relating the details next day, Molly Martin had spared Margo the indelicacy of the full expletive Pop had shouted to the world. Molly had also mentioned that, while still annoyed with Pop because of his failure to stop the fight before the teapot was smashed, she had taken her nightie from the wash basket and pegged it up on the near end of the line. The spirited lady hung his pyjamas distantly at the other – coat by the throat and pants by the ankles with legs spread painfully apart. This display of protest had seemed to afford her some kind of private satisfaction or revenge and, belatedly perceiving the humour of it, she bent forward chuckling merrily.

With their energies expended, Wally and Ned had been glad to calm down. One battle-weary body stretched its length on the lawn under the shady stringy-bark, chest heaving for a while. The other, breathing gustily, hung over the front fence and watched the blood drip from the soon-to-swell nose. Shortly afterwards, with paradoxical camaraderie, they threw themselves into Ned's utility and in a burst of exhaust fumes and road dust, took off for "a couple of snorts" at the Como pub, locally known as The Bloodhouse.

They knew that in that much-frequented environment, their injuries and the battle-blood proudly displayed on the navy singlets would be sure to promote delighted speculation, banter and laughter from the work-toughened labourers. In fact, the worker's natural toughness predisposed them to believe that a show of concern or sympathy compromised their masculinity and earned them the epithets "softies" and "old women" – and other demeaning titles, undeserving of print.

With this neighbour history in mind, Margo prepared herself for an extended visit from Molly. She asked Annie to make a pot of tea while she and Molly took chairs out to the shady rear of the house. On the steps, Josie was busily rolling plasticine snakes of merging colours, occasionally watching the squatting boys thumb-firing marbles and clay-dibs into a dirt ring.

'No fudging!' Paul warned Tony, about to fire his prized "cat's eye".

By the time Annie had carried out the tray of tea, cupcakes and mint cordial, Mrs Martin was well into an earnest discussion, justifying her support for the shearer's strike, recently.

'No one should expect them to accept a five percent cut in the award wage, not the way *they* hafta work. My boys – well, not *boys* no more, are they? Middle-aged more like – there've both got crook backs from it. The trouble is though, now they're on strike they've got nothin' to do, so they fight! Hubby just reads his paper and ignores them … but I s'pose I shouldn't whinge about that – the poor blighter's miserable – he's got piles,' she said in a sombre and subdued tone.

Annie waited. Piles of *what?* She looked at her mother, wondering why she did not ask. Indeed, Margo seemed oddly lacking in curiosity and merely shook her head slowly. Annie thought it equally strange that Molly had not expected an enquiry, but just continued … 'and the boys don't listen to *me.* Even Gwenny got fed up and cleared out last night after a big blue with Ned, She's stayin' with her mum at Cronulla. Half her luck! I'll miss her though.' Her face softened with the genuine fondness she felt for her daughter-in-law.

Being very interested in woman-talk, Annie settled down on the back steps to listen. The colours of Josie's plasticine had succumbed to the influence of warm hands and vigorous rolling, and she abandoned the now drab-grey lump for the rag doll Margo had made. Inspired recently, by the film *The Wizard of Oz*, Josie had named the button-eyed doll with its brown woollen hair, after Dorothy, portrayed so wonderfully by Judy Garland.

Meanwhile, their neighbour, sipping tea, sank back into her chair and resumed the unburdening of complaints against her men. Margo, keeping an eye on the emotional barometer, offered supportive and diplomatic comments and assurances.

With renewed energy, Mrs Martin said, 'And their blasted smoking! I've told 'em percifically to smoke *outside.* But do they? Not on your life! They forget I s'pose, and the house *reeks* of tobacco. Anyhow, I for one am *bloomin'* glad that the floods have wiped out the Queensland crop. Less tobacca is a very good thing, *I* say!' Listening to the conversation, Annie gained a clearer insight into the injustice suffered by some unfortunate women who had become trampled, oppressed and even displaced, by their own men in their own homes.

To add to Molly's anxieties, poker machines were being legalised in clubs, and she became hotly animated in her denunciation of them. 'To me, the pokies are as bad as the horses – Wally and Ned will gamble on anything, and now there's even more possibility. I sometimes wonder what the world's comin' to, I do. It's a man's world, Margo, no doubt about that!'

She shook her head and sipped some more tea, and even Annie could tell that tears were not far away, and she thought, 'Poor, good Mrs Martin!'

'It doesn't make no sense, Margo,' she continued. 'The two silly blighters work so hard at shearin' with their backs bent all day, and then they throw most of their earnin's away! I can't understand 'em. It's drink, fight, and smoke, two-up, bett'n on horses. That's all they ever bloomin' do! And here's me makin' aprons outa chaff bags and darnin' the worn-out darns in their socks.' Her cup slipped a bit on its saucer. 'And when I remember how long I had to fight an' strain to bring the buggers inta the world – both of 'em ten-pounders too – I think I shoulda spared meself the bloomin' agony, I really... do.' She recollected herself, quickly looked over at Annie and fell silent.

Margo did not belong to the society of maternity martyrs who regularly polish the memory of excruciating labour pains. She shot a concerned glance at her daughter – who did not fully understand why at the time. The older woman's tears suddenly burst forth, and comforting arms encircled her in an instant. 'This'll do you a world of good, Molly. We all need to have a good cry when things get too much.' She sent Annie a significant look, over the grey hair, and indicated with the swing of her eyes and a slight head motion, the more distant area of the backyard.

The message was conveyed without a word uttered. Annie felt proud and important that her mother had trusted her to understand the reason for the subtle transaction. Believing she had gained privileged admittance to the mature realm of womenfolk, she shepherded the children away from the immediate scene, saying brightly, 'Righto then kids, let's go and raid the fruit trees!'– a sure way to gain their immediate compliance.

By the time they returned, fingers and mouths mulberry-red, the visitor had already left and Margo, quiet and thoughtful, was busily preparing a meatloaf. As Annie gathered the vegetable scraps for the chooks, she pondered on the miserable plight of Mrs Martin, and it became clear to her that the woman was entirely subordinate to her husband and sons. A strong impression began to form in Annie's mind then that *some* men, relatively few she supposed, were more trouble than justified the task of cooking for them, and the contrast helped her to appreciate the full worth of her own good father.

The February heat was growing fiercer. The concreted path scorched the feet that could not quickly locate shoes, and they sprinted all the faster to reach the lavatory. In the chook yard, the gasping hens received a hose-down. Jack's garden suffered dismally. His beautiful tomatoes cooked on the vines, spinach and lettuce lay flat and lifeless and the climbing beans withered amongst their crisping leaves.

As the sun slid past the meridian, the reflected heat from the fibro house and the shed walls, along with the radiated heat from the ground, seemed to increase the temperature. The children noticed shimmering wriggles of heatwaves above every smooth surface, reminding them of the mirages depicted in the cactus-studded deserts of American cowboy films.

One late afternoon when the worst of the heat was over, Mrs Martin called out across the vacant block. Margo put down the washing basket and went over to see what she wanted. The old lady was inviting her in for a cold shandy with her family – a shandy which, by Margo's polite insistence, would be nine-tenths lemonade. Drinking with the Martins was the last thing Margo wanted to do, but her kind heart would not allow the risk of offending Molly by refusing. She called back to her children, all watching from the yard, that she would not be away for long and told them to get on with the afternoon jobs.

As Annie pulled off the dolly pegs, paired up socks and folded nappies, a queer sensation enveloped her of her now being "mother". She became increasingly concerned for her mum's welfare, being in the company of those rough fighting sons of the Martins – and Pixie the pig, which always charged about squealing excitedly and placing its barrel-body in everyone's way.

But Annie had worried needlessly. She slipped back into her carefree, young girl persona when, a short time later, her mother came walking through the trees at the roadside, her hand clutching the string handles of a weighted brown paper bag – the everyday sixpence carry-all of the times. Margo's bag contained three bottles: wine for Jack, *Blue Bow* lemonade for the kids, and Sherry for herself, a generous and ill-afforded Christmas gift which Margo believed was an expression of appreciation from Molly for recent attention and friendship.

Sometime before Pixie the "pigling" arrived at the Martins, they had owned a pet ram – "Mr Bojangles", so named for his tap-dance-like movements when trying to dodge anyone who approached. Mrs Martin greatly valued the bag of merino fleece she had kept and often sat on the front veranda with her old spinning wheel, transforming the raw, burry wool into yarn.

One morning, when Margo, Josie and Annie were returning from their walk up the road, taking turns to wheel the pram with its occupant, new baby Maree, they paused to greet Molly and to observe the fascinating activity. The old hands spun an excellent, durable thread from the staples of fleece, still crinkled and dirty. The wisps of wool slipped speedily through her fingers onto the spool of the whirring wheel, and soon the yarn bore a resemblance to greasy string. The next day, and three soapy washes later, the soft, creamy-white skeins hung drying in the sun. To Margo and Annie, when they saw the skeins, the transformation seemed almost magical.

'Molly, you're a whizz!' Margo exclaimed. The old lady shrugged off the praise in that humble way of hers but drew much pleasure from the appreciation. A week later she walked over to Margo's place with two skeins of finely spun, rose-scented wool. The beautiful gift from Molly and Mr Bojangles begged to be knitted, and shortly afterwards under Margo's talented fingers, it grew into a pretty shell-patterned jacket for cute little baby Maree.

39 Little Siblings

Sometime after Margo had brought new baby Maree home – her ninth, and last – Peter became unusually subdued, often behaving entirely out of character. Busy Margo drew him onto her lap and asked, 'What's up, Pete … don't you feel very well?' The little fellow remained silent and stared at the floor, incapable of finding the words or voice to explain what was breaking his heart, but Margo realised and asked, 'Do you like your new little sister, darling?'

Peter nodded – and then broke into sobs. 'But now you don't love *me* anymore!'

Margo rocked him and crooned, 'There, there! *Of course,* I love you. We *all* do, pet.'

Peter felt comforted then, and his body-shaking sobs began to subside. 'But you're always cuddling to Mawee,' he whimpered in a small, hurt voice. It was difficult, after being the youngest for so many years, suddenly to move over for someone else. Everyone had unconsciously contributed to his misery by doting on baby Maree. After that, Margo and Jack ensured that everyone gave more attention to Peter and he soon became his cheerful, playful self again.

Around that time Clivey also was in favour, having almost drowned. Herb, his rescuer, became his hero. Clivey seemed to be accident-prone. Shortly after that fright, there was a fast taxi ride to the hospital after he was discovered gleefully gobbling up Margo's forbidden chocolates – laxatives! Later, when Jack had absorbed all the details of *that* drama and Clivey was tucked into bed, they all sat around talking about it and Tony, wanting to make sure that Jack had been fully informed, told him 'He hadta have his *pumik stumped!'* and wondered at the laughter.

That set Jack's fertile mind to witticisms. He thought for a moment, looked at Margo, and quipped: 'Sounds like you had a dizzy bay!' The children's initial puzzlement evolved into amusement, and after a grinning pause, Jack again concentrated on rearranging consonants. Presently, he looked up again and added: 'Just as well he didn't trap the caxi!' Once the kids had grasped the reversal idea, they spent the next twenty minutes or so creating new spoonerisms.

Clivey and Pete one day declared a sudden wish to escape the chaotic household of nappies, dummies and crying baby in favour of camping. They asked Jack if they could pitch their small tent in the nearby bush and sleep there all night. Margo had no intention of allowing such an escapade, but Jack insisted that it would be a good experience for them.

'Yes, of course, you can!' He imparted this with great magnanimity and enthusiasm, and the story-teller wheels in his head began turning. 'But first I'd better warn you about a few things campers have to be very wary of – especially around *here*.'

Margo walked into the room just then with the baby in her arms. 'Yeees ...' she commented sardonically, 'I thought you probably would!' and she wore that little smirk which so clearly said: 'Here we go again – more B.S.!' Those initials were the nearest Margo had ever descended towards real swearing. It was enough, Annie thought, to grant tacit leniency to *bummy*.

Ignoring wifely sarcasm, Jack embarked upon a frightening sequence of yarns – ostensibly so the boys would be better informed before advancing into the perilous night, but actually because he was powerless to suppress his imaginative creativity. He proceeded to enumerate the mythical misfortunes that befell people who braved the eerie, hostile bush.

Listening to him, Annie muttered to Josie, 'Gawd, it's a long, dark way to the lavvy!'

Practical Josie replied, 'We'd better go *now*, Annie – and take the torch.'

The boys' eyes grew larger as Jack's stories underwent impromptu evolution and he became the recipient of regular whacks from Margo as she went about her evening work. 'They'll grow up frightened of their own shadows if you keep this up,' she warned scornfully.

Jack was well practised in feigning innocence. 'What'd I say?' he asked. 'I'm just doing my fatherly duty letting them know it's not all twinkle, twinkle little star out there in the big black night.' And he affected an injured look, implying offence taken that she should doubt and sully the innocence of his motive.

Margo resumed clearing the table, but her ear remained receptive to Jack's mischief. At intervals, in response to his narration, she commented: 'Oh, what a lot of rubbish,' or 'For heaven's sake!' or 'I'm warning you, Jack!' Unperturbed Jack took no notice but pursued the fancy of his imagination with an air of absolute impunity.

Presently, he reached over to draw back the curtain. 'Gee, it's as black as the inside of a tomb tonight,' he said, his tone evincing a terrible omen. 'Just the sort of night vampire bats like.' His shoulder received another whack for that, but he continued on regardless. It was obvious that Jack revelled in Margo's heavy caresses! 'Yes, a real blood-sucker's night,' he muttered forebodingly. 'And d'you know? I've seen the ground crawling with snakes on nights like this,' he said, a side-to-side motion of his head expressing sham incredulity.

Margo replied, 'Yes, I guessed you might have!' Annie saw by the constrained merriment in her face that she drew a sneaking amusement from the repartee.

Jack lowered his voice to a more secretive tone. 'They come out after the bats,' he said, pleased that this idea fitted in so well with the last, and wondering why his name was not up there with Poe or the Brothers Grimm. 'But they get so hungry sometimes waiting for the bats to land that they gobble up anything they can find – mice, possums, cats' …

But before he could deliver his deliberately suspended punch line, Peter spoke up and stole it from him: 'And does they eat human beans, Dad?'

Margo's voice could be heard in the kitchen, 'Don't believe a *word* he says, Peter.'

Jack was not one to endure contradiction. By sheer strength of will, he rendered himself impervious to her interruptions, tenaciously adhering to his own thoughts. His eyes swung dramatically back to the window. 'And then there's the *other thing*… as big as this!' He spread his arms to indicate size but then dropped them in feigned reluctance, conveying regret that he had injudiciously mentioned the subject – which tactic promptly served its purpose.

'What uvver fing, Dad?' asked wide-eyed Pete. Jack pretended a disinclination to reveal anything further – he required more time for fabrication. 'What was *the thing*, Dad?' Clivey persisted impatiently.

After he had submitted to sufficient persuasion, Jack explained with a pained expression: 'Well, the problem is that if I tell you about ...*the Thing,* you'll only get scared and won't want to go camping.'

That was the tenor of talk Margo was waiting for. 'Yes, and a very good thing that will be, too,' she said, dismissing their camping aspirations as a mere half-hour fantasy. 'Now, come on boys, off to bed.'

'Ooh, Mum!' they wailed. 'But we wanta go camping!'

Margo drew in a breath and released an elongated sigh. 'What, after all that nonsense?' she asked, and the little clones nodded eagerly. ("All that nonsense" was *déjà vu* to laughing Paul and Tony. They had been through it some years before with the "monster" in the bay.)

Margo glared at Jack who was having some trouble keeping his expression neutral, but she could see in his clear eyes the same merry devilment observed many times before. Later, when she was settling Maree into her cot, Jack slipped away into the darkened yard.

The chattering in the tiny tent stopped at the first throaty growl.

'Wha'wazzat?' Pete gasped in a catch of breath.

'D-dunno!' answered Clivey, his voice a high tone of alarm.

There came the sudden loud crashing of branches, and then another growl, animal-like and blood-chilling (to ears suitably preconditioned). Frantic voices emanated from the tent.

'Might be the Fing! ... S'comin' closer – geez!' There followed a savage swipe at the tent with a branch of she-oak. The little boys' voices escalated inside the tent, and before Jack could reveal the joke and identity of the jester, Pete and Clivey charged out – Clivey swinging a meat-cleaver!

Jack received the bigger fright and, stumbling back out of reach, tripped and fell into the undergrowth. 'Hey! Cut it out!' he yelled before he had time to review his careless choice of words, preoccupied as he was with the nearing thrash of the cleaver. 'Stop it, damn ya – it's me ... Dad!'

'Geez, Dad,' Clivey exclaimed when, after much panting and swearing, Jack had dragged himself shakily upright. 'We were gunna chop you up!'

When enough breath had been restored to Jack's lungs he exclaimed, 'Yairs! ... and y' bloody-well nearly succeeded, too!' He sat down on a rock to wait for his heart to stop hammering, vowing never to pull that trick again, and to 'hide that blasted meat-cleaver.'

'Little buggers nearly killed me.' He told Margo later, as he hid the cleaver behind the canisters on the mantelpiece. 'Just missed out being castrated, y'know!' he joked.

Mother-of-nine glanced contemplatively at Jack's comically indignant face; at the pile of nappies she had been folding; towards the chair loaded with socks to be darned; and down at her hand which held the dummy she had searched the whole house for while baby Maree screamed in her cot. Pensively, she shook her head, and a mysterious little smile lit those gentle blue eyes as she replied: 'And what a terrible *tragedy* that would have been!'

As they grew older, Peter and Maree fell into many fights, one of which was over a spaghetti sandwich. Margo heard them fighting with tiger ferocity and went to investigate. When she had quietened them, she asked, 'Now, what's all this about?'

Maree glared at Pete, her very blue eyes swimming, and with energy and fury exploding in every syllable, she said, 'He pinched my b-sketti samich!'

Jack was always quick to correct mispronounced words and having heard Maree's complaint, immediately began teasing her about *her* unique version of "spaghetti".

Margo frowned and said, 'Well don't tease her Jack, teach her to say it properly.'

And so, Jack agreed to that challenge. 'Righto,' he said, positioning Maree's small form in front of his chair. 'Now, watch my mouth: spa – get – i … spa-get-i – spaghetti!'

Maree giggled at that and said: 'Bah – sket – i … ba-sket-i … b-sketti!' and smiled happily at her elocution teacher. But Jack shook his head and said, 'No, no, Dolly' – using his special nickname for the pretty little thing – 'Look, just copy me,' and he went through it all again, concentrating mainly on the sibilant sound. 'Sss – pah – getti.'

Maree was studying her daddy's lips intently, her own little mouth silently going over the syllables with his as a guide. The other kids began taking notice of this most interesting exercise, and Jack told her to try it again.

She slowly grasped the idea of keeping her tongue behind her teeth in readiness to try the "sp" and started with 'Sssss (everyone's breathing was suspended – as though waiting for that second sneeze) … sssss … b-sketti!' They let out their breaths with laughter, and Maree looked around puzzled.

It was not long though before this youngest of Hughs could speak as well as any of them and she used that mighty power to counter the boy's regular infringements upon her rights. But when words proved too tardy for impatient Maree, she and Pete flew into vigorous fights.

Margo would then instruct Josie to keep her little sister occupied in the peace-promoting front garden, where there was a bench surrounded by masses of perfumed stocks and jonquils. Josie always took along a few dolls and storybooks to calm Maree and keep her amused. Margo usually sent Peter in the opposite direction to play with Clivey in the nearby bush where they played Cowboys and Indians.

There came a day one September, when Margo was spring-cleaning. She had removed all the food from the refrigerator and was waiting for it to defrost. Meanwhile, she took another load of washing out to the clothesline, but upon her return, there was no sign of young Pete. The worried mother went from room to room calling, but there was neither sight nor sound of him. Out in the yard – still no response. External dangers became an urgent concern. She looked towards the cliff and the river. Trying to keep panic subdued, she *yelled*: 'Peter, Peter, where *are* you?'

There came a faint cry, which seemed to be a long way off. Utterly bewildered, she looked this way and that – and then spotted

351

the three refrigerator trays half hidden under the table. In a flash, Margo spun round, yanked open the fridge – and out fell Peter, cyanosed and almost on his goodbye gasp!

Naturally, little brother was swamped with affection after that close advance of death, and he cheerfully accepted all the attention, his new happy demeanour promoting even greater indulgence. Jack, feeling the full force of the near tragedy, decided to devote more of his time to Pete and began by taking him on a bus ride to Como.

They walked around the swimming baths area and then climbed the small hill to The Pleasure Ground Lookout, from where they could see an exciting variety of boats and sailing yachts rocking with the breeze upon the choppy water.

After a while, they came back to the bus stop reserve near the station and watched the trains rattling across the bridge. The sun climbed higher, and Pete announced that he was hungry. Jack, treating him with more than usual importance, fished in his pocket for coins and sat outside the shop to enjoy a cigarette and to think again about Clarrie, while Pete went in to buy fish and chips.

Presently the little fellow returned with arms around the hot newspaper-wrapped parcel and a smile beaming proudly across his face – never before had such a weighty responsibility involving choice and purchase been entrusted to the plucky young boy. He sat down companionably close to his dependent parent and with the air of having made an important, self-initiated decision remarked, 'I got some skobbits wif 'em, Dad.'

The paternal brow became corrugated. 'Skobbits? What're skobbits?'

Pete looked up sideways at his not-too-bright father, and said 'Well, y'know when they cut the spuds into stircles and dip 'em in stuff and then fry 'em? ... Scobbits!' he explained with patient condescension.

All was clear. 'Ah! Scallops,' Jack exclaimed.

Pete nodded his head tolerantly at his slow old dad. 'Yeah – *that's* what I *said*, scobbits!'

Peter may be forgiven for his disdainful attitude. It was probably retaliation for the time when Jack, looking puzzlingly at the end of the garden hose, asked him to peer into it to see why the water was not coming out ... and Herb, waiting, turned on the tap. It was an old trick but not so to the new victim. The stunt had followed Jack's request for Pete and Clivey to go into the shed to find the long weight and the left-handed screwdriver – and after that, he asked the two little boys to dig half a hole! No wonder Margo shook her head!

40 The Chook-house School

A marked division had begun to establish itself between Herb and his siblings sometime after he turned sixteen. Naturally, he was often out or away with his friends Allan and Johnno, whereas Annie was still the minder of the brood. The children always became bored towards the end of the summer school holidays, seeking new forms of amusement, and Annie decided to try Margo's mother-benefitting suggestion to play "schools". It had the promise of an excellent idea in terms both of activity for the kids and peace for their mum.

Margo suggested that a classroom could be set up under the willow tree, and there in the shade, Annie's doubtful teaching skills could be imposed upon all the younger ones along with several of the neighbourhood children who seemed always to be drawn to the Hughs' place. In fact, so many were there at times that the yard resembled a child-minding establishment ... and a brief mercenary thought or two did cross Annie's mind.

However, not over-keen on an outdoor arrangement, she sought an improvement. Jack was clever with a hammer and saw, therefore, the most logical person to build her a small classroom (also, his being the only one available did tend to steer her request in his direction). But the young girl had no real grasp of what the granting of that request would entail. Her father drew on his

354

cigarette, thought for a moment and, gesturing in the direction of the red building, he said, 'How about using the chook shed?'

'Oh gee, Dad,' Annie laughed, 'the *chook shed!*' She supposed he was joking.

'Well,' he said seriously, 'it's big enough, and there's only a couple of hens left now. I could fix it up for you.' He was *not* joking.

After further consideration, Annie began to see the merit of the idea. About the size of a small garage, the Hughs' chook-house was the best any of the kids had ever seen – a mark of status in their provincial environment. Credit for this belonged to Jack and Grandad Carrington who had built it soon after Jack had returned from the war.

The roof, high enough for the men to walk around underneath without bumping their heads had over the years protected scores of hens, happy on their floor of smooth concrete. Three walls, one housing the door, were constructed of red tin and the fourth side was enclosed in wire netting with a door-sized opening into the chooks' yard. This was where Jack grew his magnificent fruit trees. He knew his horticulture – the symbiosis of chooks and trees assured the family of a superabundance of luscious fruit every summer.

The dearth of live poultry was a seasonal fact. The family had been feasting on fowl regularly (relative to that period) after the egg production had ceased and Jack planned to buy new layers later in the season. Only three hens remained.

Although troubled by regret and sorrow on behalf of the fowls, greater was Annie's impatience for the school to become a reality and she almost begrudged the time to wait for the hens' arrival at the table with their roast vegetable companions. However, the alternative was toleration of a space-stealing perch in the corner and three death-row hens making a lavatory of her schoolroom floor while she ambitiously "gave lessons".

Jack roused her from her reverie. 'Well? The chook shed will do, won't it?'

Already Annie's imagination was responding to the reminder of splattering messes and the sensation brought on an automatic nose crinkling. 'S'pose so …but gee whiz Dad, fancy having chooks running around my feet while I'm trying to teach! And what about the *smell*?'

Mr Quickwit grinned, gave his head that familiar sideways jerk and said, 'Aw, they're not fussy love … they'll soon get used to y' pongy old feet.'

'Oh, very funny, Dad!' she laughed.

The child-minder agreed to wait and became busy in the meantime making butcher-paper charts of numbers, letters and tables, and a drunken hand-drawn map of Australia. Dependable

Jack honoured his promise and after the last of the hens had been sacrificed to the noble pursuit of learning, he removed the perches and nesting boxes and subjected the shed to a thorough scrub and hose-down. The next day it was dry and ready.

To their credit, Paul, Tony and Josie abandoned their games to help carry in all the fruit box "desks" and then distributed paper and pencils. After tacking up the charts, the novice teacher placed her important person before the Masonite blackboard Jack had affixed to the end wall. Upon this, for the grand opening, a name was written in sloping, curly script: *Miss Hughs*... although none of the merry-eyed pupils was comfortable with such and after the carefully spoken 'Good morning children' was delivered they spluttered explosively into their grubby little hands. Not an auspicious beginning, but time, Annie hoped, would damp down the comedy.

From her temporary perspective, pretending to be a schoolteacher was the pinnacle of pleasure and an activity of which Margo, of course, heartily approved. She felt contented, glancing from the kitchen door at her children's activities and pausing in her path-sweeping to watch the marching. And later, while pegging nappies onto the clothesline, she was amused to hear the recitation of the tables and poems, such as:

"Hist! ...... Hark! The night is very dark,

And we've to go a mile or so across the Possum Park ..."

C.J.Dennis

Sometimes Margo paused to chuckle over a comical rhyme of the children's choosing and modification:

"Sam, Sam the funny old man, washed his face in a frying pan.

Combed his hair with the leg of a chair and went to town in his underwear."

As the days went by, a few more neighbour-scallywags drifted curiously into the classroom. With so many scholars it grew crowded, noisy and quite a strain on the seating provision and stationery allowance. Presently it became necessary for Miss Hughs to strike hard the plum tree "cane" (merely a pointer for the charts) on the table with the order: 'Silence!' in the sharp, authoritative tone a grown-up teacher would surely use under such circumstances of anarchy. But the command might as well have been 'Laughter!'

Besides lessons, the pupils practised physical culture, or PT, for which the class was marshalled outdoors. 'Come along children, into the chookyar— the playground,' the teacher instructed happily. Soon they were all throwing up their knees and swinging rigidly straight arms around the perimeter of the yard to the tune of *Twinkle, Twinkle Little Star,* which Herb had taught his sister to play on his *Tonette,* a kind of recorder.

On alternate days, they performed the PT routine to the more vigorous shake of the powdered-milk tin of nails borrowed from Jack's shed, and the unsynchronised beat of a wooden spoon on Josie's biscuit-tin drum. The children responded with exuberance to the *outdoor* aspect of the primitive little school, but when again seated behind their fruit box desks, enthusiasm became flaccid and rebellion brewed. There was something very confronting about a chook shed full of mutinous kids! Annie soon realised.

She thought with longing of her brief attendance at Mr Toobey's School a few years earlier; of that funny headmaster with his horn-rimmed glasses, moustache and humorous teeth, and especially the novel, entertaining method of his teaching. Annie knew that she did not have the knack and wondered grimly what she had better do.

'G'day Annie!' Just at the timeliest moment, the Inspector of Schools, Billy Meadows, who had been appointed to fulfil that duty, arrived and saved her. Awkward and chuckling, hands buried in pockets, he threaded his way past all the fruit boxes, protruding legs and grubby feet to the front of the class. 'G'day kids,' he said wearing his endearingly lop-sided grin.

'*No, no!*' she protested, 'that's not very – you should say: "Good morning children."'

He snorted an abashed laugh and made a wry face. 'Gawd! Do I hafta?'

'Well, you *promised*,' Annie reminded, unwillingly grinning at his comical, entreating expression. And so, faced with this appeal to his good nature and questionable integrity, Billy complied.

Eagerly, the children responded: 'Good morn-ing Mis-ter Snoooo-dles.' (They all listened to the evening wireless episodes of "Yes What". Mr Snoodles, with his tremulous voice, was a favourite.)

'*Now* what?' asked the shrugging Inspector of Schools.

The Mistress also shrugged. 'Well, I s'pose you should ask some questions about general knowledge and things. Or how about geography?'

A moment of Billy's floor-gazing contemplation inspired the brain-straining question on geography: 'Righto you lot – what's the name of our country?'

A gleeful chorus went up. 'Aust-raaal-yah!'

This tremendous success was followed by his brief meditation upon a subject close to his heart: 'And who won the big fight last Fridy night at the Stadium, eh?'

'Oh f' heaven's sake!' Annie mumbled disapprovingly and surveyed the sea of blank faces. 'Look, Billy— Mr Snoodles...' It was hard to maintain a serious school teacher look on her face; somehow the humble and diffident "Mr Snoodles" persona did not quite fit Billy's larrikin features. 'How about something to do with arithmetic?' she managed, fighting to prevent her querying inflexion from rippling into laughter.

Good-natured Billy readily agreed. Warming now to his role, he adopted a more confident stance with arms akimbo. 'Now for some mental arithmetic.' He leant forward, quite unconsciously employing the posture known to capture greater attention. 'How far can John Landy run while you boil an egg?' He straightened up and folded his arms to await the reply – which never came. 'From here to Como!' he said jubilantly, arms out, palms up.

'A mile,' the tolerant teacher clarified, but then she turned to Billy and suggested: 'What about names of rivers or something ... or, you know ... nature?'

Instant illumination! Billy shot her a mischievous smirk and turned to the class. 'Righteo, nature it is. What goes ninety-nine clop, ninety-nine clops, ninety-nine clop?'

Pauly had learnt that one from Grandpa Hughs. Up went his hand. 'A centipede with a wooden leg ... *Sir*,' he answered, laughing at the title.

'Hmm. Well, what about this one … why did the chicken go over the road?'

'To get to the other si-i-ide!' The children's confidence clearly betrayed the antiquity of the original joke.

'Aha! Tricked ya!' gloried the Inspector. 'Because it couldn't go *under* it.' (They were having nature study, apparently … or a lesson on prepositions.)

The children loved Mr Snoodles and his jokes, but soon the inspection was over, and he made ready to leave. Annie had expected that he would maintain the pantomime ambience by declaring something concluding, such as: 'Good day Miss Hughs. Your school has passed inspection.' But he said, 'Could I use y' dunny? – I'm bustin' and I still have to go to the shop for Mum.'

With his urgent request for departure sanctioned, off ran the Inspector to the lavatory and the class zipped out to the table under the willow tree to feast on the chocolate crackles and lemon drinks Margo had just brought out for them all.

After a week or so of this activity, Annie's temporary aspirations towards the noble profession of teaching began to wane, for the mounting discontent of pupils could not be ignored. A number of the neighbourhood children had already decamped from the hallowed House of Learning to the sanctity of their own homes and well-rested mothers, but loyal Josie remained to clean the blackboard. Female solidarity!

A big question mark now hung over a career as a teacher and Annie swung back to her original choice, nursing ... or mother-of-many-babes. Perhaps both? The young girl pulled rein, however, when remembering that to achieve the latter a husband would have to be thrown in somewhere – not in her plan of things at that particular moment!

In the meantime, her tutorial endeavours in the chook-house came to an abrupt end when Paul, chief delegate of the insurrection, complained to Margo, the union, that: 'Annie's too bossy.'

Tony's plaintive accents corroborated: 'We fort it was gunna be fun.'

And together they chorused: 'We don't wanta play schools anymore, Mum.'

So *that*, most indisputably, was *that!*

41 The Three Kings

When 'big news' occurs, often we are left with an indelible memory of our surroundings at the moment of receiving that news. Thus, it was for Annie when her father arrived home from work and said: 'The King's dead!' His family stood there in the lounge room gaping at him, hardly able to believe that their likeable King George VI was gone from their world.

He was a shy man; he stuttered and therefore experienced difficulty delivering the many speeches required of him throughout his reign. Bertie, as he was called, had reluctantly taken the throne when his brother Edward abdicated to marry the American divorcee Mrs Simpson. Soon, at schools and theatres and certain public gatherings children would stand to sing "God save our gracious Queen" for Elizabeth II.

There came to the Hughs, during the next few years, two more sobering milestones – the passing of both grandfathers. The king's death had engendered deep sadness, but the second and third blows brought profound, abiding sorrow. Of the patriarchs, Grandpa Hughs was first to leave. Annie's psyche had always been closely aligned with this beloved man whom her father so much resembled, and therefore she was incredulous of the concept of never seeing him again. Surely, it was not true! Surely, in some distant reach of time …?

Grandpa Hughs was not old when he died, but Annie had thought him so. On the farmhouse veranda one sunset hour, he complained to Nana of a backache. Annie observed him with a sympathetic eye as he eased himself into his old cane chair and sighed, comfortable at last. Grandpa sank into deep slumber, his head held up by a hand, elbow resting on the chair-arm. Watching him, the girl became fascinated as each gentle breath drew in his cheeks and the expiration fluttered them out again in a slow rhythm and with a slight nasal whistle to accompany the departure of each breath.

Presently he awoke, and concernedly she asked, 'Is it very awful being old, Grandpa?'

He might have expressed some poignancy in the alternative. But he glanced at his granddaughter with amusement and replied, 'Well, when old age finally catches up with me, Annie, I'll tell you all about it', and his chuckles mingled with Nana's as he turned back to admire the pinking heavens.

It is easy to fall into the habit of placing on a pedestal a person who has died. It was that way for Annie with Grandpa Hughs. She knew him as the personification of kindness; a sage with knowledge of all things relating to nature, farming and self-sufficiency. He stirred the girl's sense of wonder: told her how the cuckoo bird cheated by laying its egg in another bird's nest, relinquishing all responsibility for its raising. He said that rabbits are almost mute; that dingoes do not bark, but howl; that water goes down a sink clockwise in the southern hemisphere, anti-clockwise in the northern … and together they counted the concentric rings of a felled tree to estimate its age.

Grandpa advised Annie to do no less than her best in whatever she later chose to do in life and to have *stick-to-it-ivity*. He possessed a wry wit, which he exercised often. Annie liked that, and many more notable things about him, and as she grew older and discovered further attributes, so Grandpa in her mind became even more worthy of the metaphorical kingly cloak she had fashioned, embroidered and maintained for him.

The Hughs all loved Grandpa and felt cheated that he had been taken from them so soon. It was at first almost too painful to recall their last sight of him as he waved goodbye, no one realising that it was forever. No one could know that the dear image of him standing with Nana at Bomaderry station as the train moved away from them, would remain fixed in the family's life bank of painful impressions. And later, after the news of his heart attack, it was difficult to accept that they would never see him again. The very word *never* moved into Annie's consciousness, took up prominent residence and hit her with the full force of its powerful, definitive meaning.

Sometime after this, the Hughs experienced another family tragedy when Grandad Carrington passed away, another blow to hurl them back into the abyss of sorrow and despondency. Annie thought they would never be happy again and she understood why people often resort to euphemism to avoid the pain of uttering the word *died*.

Grief was not a new visitor to Margo and Jack. When Annie was very young, she had asked Margo about the baby girl she had lost, for at that time Annie was particularly lonely for a sister-companion. Margo described the tiny white coffin and abruptly broke into sobs. Annie learnt that day that it was not right to satisfy her own curiosity at the expense of another's grief. Herb and Annie had no memory of their baby sister Lorraine, who had lived for only two weeks, for Herbie was then a small child and Annie, a mere toddler. The grief of losing Grandpa and Granddad was a new and painful experience for them.

Both grandfathers were heaven-bound. Margo and Jack, faced with the reality of losing their fathers, supported each other and sought to carry on with the everyday routine and gradually to find a return to happiness in life. And the little ones, restless but silent, looked perplexedly at the sad parental faces and worried about their mother's sudden weeping, her long periods of staring into the middle distance and their father's continued melancholy.

42 Herb's Wheels

It seemed entirely in tune with the Hughs family's sunken spirit and indeed, quite fitting that it was colder than usual that June when Grandad Carrington passed away. The days were sunny but windswept, and trees shivered, some species yielding up the secrets of their leaves' lighter undersides. Strands of honeysuckle lifted to the east; the oleander slapped and thudded against the fibro wall, and the pines at Gilberts' place thrashed their branches at everyone in a wild duet with the wind. "Lie low; take shelter", they seemed to howl. But at last the wind lost its energy, and the pines stood straight again. The worst was over.

Josie and Annie were pressing wildflowers between the pages of an encyclopaedia one morning, content in the warmth of the sun captured in the glassed-in front veranda. They were not listening, just hearing the murmur of conversation between Margo and her visiting sister, Dulce. The adults were seated at the window with their tea and *Saos*-with-cheese, dabbing eyes with handkerchiefs and lamenting Grandad's funeral.

'Mum's crying, Annie,' Josie whispered, and the girls lifted sad eyes to the women.

Margo blew her nose again. 'And he was *only* sixty-three,' she said in her distress. Annie wondered how "only" could be applied to such seeming longevity, but more importantly, how her mum would cope with the loss of the father she had always been so close to. (In a quixotic way, Grandad Carrington lived again in Tony.)

For Annie, the thought of losing her own father was too painful – recent anxiety had been prompted by the discovery that linked cigarettes with cancer and by Margo's regular plea to Jack to give up the habit before his lungs succumbed to the disease.

Margo's closeness with Grandad stemmed to some degree from his devotion after she had fallen, when a child, from a moving horse-drawn cart. The wheel had run over her right foot. For some time afterwards, she was particularly clumsy and often stumbled while trying to keep up with her siblings.

Refined, sensitive and compassionate Grandad bestowed particular attention upon his little girl and took her with him whenever he was checking his yabby and rabbit traps or collecting firewood, blackberries or mushrooms. Later, "Margie" became her father's off-sider working on their poultry farm. Her foot eventually recovered … but now her heart was broken.

But just when the sisters were at their most dismal and when merciful distraction was most required, there it was in the pleasing visage of Herb on his pushbike.

Dulce emerged from her sad reverie. 'My *word*, Marg, that boy's grown!'

'*Hasn't* he, though!' Margo marvelled, composing herself. 'He went from being one of the smallest boys in the class to one of the tallest – and so quickly, too!'

'Ha! Just *look* at him … what do you feed him on? – And who's that with him?'

'That's his friend, Alan – nice boy.'

Aunty Dulce, unable to quell astonishment at her nephew's phenomenal growth and glad to focus upon something cheerful, kept watching the activities with the bikes on the dirt road yonder, exclaiming yet again that he had 'stretched like magic'.

Herb was growing up. His pants no longer needed braces to hold them up. His hair appeared darker for the hair oil, and he was becoming a magnet for feminine eyes – childhood definitely over. The affectionate name *Herbie* had some time earlier met the end of its service, gradually receding into the past in deference to the more mature *Herb*. But that's where the metamorphosis ceased, *Herbert* being reserved for the formal use and the filling in of forms.

One exciting day Herb bought a horse, Bonnie. She was a great novelty at first, but this proved transient. Her upkeep became a liability owing to the cost of feeding and to the fact that she needed to be tethered for varying periods on the vacant block between Hughs' place and Martin's. When the prolonged spell of dry weather welcomed a full day of heavy rain, concern was roused from its complacency to acknowledge the worrying fact that there was no suitable animal-shelter. In the interim, Bonnie spent the wet hours standing beneath the canopy of a kind old scribbly-gum.

After the clouds had scudded off allowing supremacy to the sun, Annie ventured out with a towel to confer more fuss and honeyed adoration over Bonnie. She had been feeding the horse with oats, bestowing soft nothings upon the flicking ear: 'How magnificent are thine eyes,' and such nonsense, and voicing rash, unsupported promises to learn horse riding. Besotted by her, she was in the act of kissing the velvety muzzle when the creature she had so lovingly fed and lavished much poetic adulation upon, put down her head and bit Annie's cotton-covered belly! The fright, anger and shock drew from her a loud squawk and left a bruise, purple and painful.

Later Herb sold the mare to some farmer, and for a brief vengeful time it was Annie's merciless wish that Mr Clag had bought her, but as the pain receded and the bruise changed hue and then faded, she overcame that infantile nastiness. With the sale of the horse to supplement his savings, Herb now had sufficient funds to purchase an old Chevrolet, an open-sided vehicle with running boards and a horn which blurted out comically.

During the period when Herb worked part-time at the local grocery shop and also at Nancarrow's dairy, he was able to buy such things as unruly horses and vehicles (of such decrepitude that they had to be cranked to wake them up). But what he *really* wanted was a motorbike as good as the Norton that Uncle Charlie roared around on.

While waiting to begin an apprenticeship with an electrician, Herb was offered another temporary job timber-cutting with Uncle Charlie at Captains Flat near Braidwood. Off he went and toiled resolutely for six months. He sold the "Chevy" and at last bought his longed-for motorbike – not a Norton, but a Triumph. Just as good, Annie thought, not knowing one from another. After that, the peace of the neighbourhood was occasionally disturbed, and the air currents around the Hughs' front gate often carried the drifts of petrol fumes.

Since the first amazing day her infant eyes could clearly see, Annie had known Herb was there. Unsurprising then, that while he was away, she felt the lonely void in her life. His absence fulfilled its function in the way absence often does, and this evinced a new conviction in the young girl's heart, that she loved her big brother more than previously realised and, far from becoming accustomed to his being away, she yearned for his company.

At last, Herb returned home from Captains Flat and his presence wholly restored the equilibrium to Annie's existence. She was amazed at the change in him. He was taller with shoulders squarely defined, and his voice had deepened. Furthermore, he had developed a mature kindness of spirit providing his penniless sister with an opportunity to earn some pocket money. He-of-the-pay-packet handed over a generous two shillings and sixpence every time she ironed his trousers with the essential finish of sharp vertical creases in preparation for his taking Annie's school friend Laura, now the love of his life, to the local dance.

Herb had met Laura at Christmastime when she was spending the day with Annie, swimming and rowing the boat. Annie was glad the two had finally met. In recent times, Herb had sometimes cruised his motorbike up to the school fence at lunchtime. Standing there, proudly talking to him, Annie always became aware of an instant gathering of admiring girls, all eyes on the handsome youth astride the black bike. But *his* eyes had lingered upon the one in the background, the tall, attractive one with the excellent figure, the girl he was destined to marry, the girl who was to bear him a daughter and seven sons.

Herb's second love was always his motorbike. He appreciated Annie's admiration of his shining Triumph and took her for terrifyingly fast rides, her arms and grip unyieldingly prehensile for the duration. At every corner of the road he yelled over his shoulder to the leech on his back: 'LEAN WITH THE BIKE!' as the road surface loomed threateningly close to their heads and Annie responded to a natural human desire to distance her precious skin from the peril of the bitumen flesh-grater.

At home, Herb lavished much attention on his motorcycle, submitting it to regular washing and polishing, even to the extreme of placing some of its greasy parts into the bathtub for cleaning. When Jack saw this, he bellowed at Herb to throw the bike parts to "buggery" and scrub the bath, or he'd 'heave the whole bloody bike over the cliff.'

It became part of life for the Hughs family to hear the Triumph roaring up Oyster Bay Road and sputtering to a stop at the front gate. This was always followed by Margo's remark: 'Aah! Herb's home,' and accompanied with a grateful sigh. That sigh is surely universal among mothers of daring, adventurous sons and daughters addicted to the exquisite exhilaration of speed experienced above only two wheels. Margo's sigh, so replete with satisfaction, revealed how very much she had been quietly worrying.

But one evening Herb did not return home. Nor did he arrive during that long anxious night. Miss Gilbert hurried over at breakfast with a telephoned message from the police. Margo dropped onto a chair as the hard slap hit her: Herb had been taken to hospital after a road accident down the coast somewhere near Berry.

Uncle Charlie, boarding with them that year, wasted no time in starting up his utility. Jack and Margo hastily shrugged on coats. Margo, her strong, quiet equanimity returning, issued instructions to Annie, who was now to be in charge at home. Soon, Charlie, Jack and Margo were on their way to the hospital at Wollongong.

Later, they learnt that Herb's motorbike had hit a rut in the road. A jolt, as he approached a bend, caused the light to fail and the bike went straight ahead and crashed into a ditch, the impact dislocating Herb's hips. It had been a moonless night. Many vehicles went by but no one saw him lying there, and he endured hours of cold, lonely pain. At daybreak, the accident was discovered. Someone at the hospital later informed Margo, Jack and Charlie that it had taken four men to manoeuvre Herb's joints back into place while he lay on the floor of the Casualty department.

When Mrs Birtles, a few doors down from the Hughs' house, heard the news of Herb's accident and of Margo's intention to take all her children by train the next day to visit him, she immediately wanted to help. Grabbing her purse, she hastened to the public telephone and rang her sister, who lived close to Wollongong hospital. That kind action meant a great deal to Margo – she and the children were assured now of somewhere to rest and lunch after the train journey while they waited for the hospital's visiting hour.

The children sat at Mrs Orth's table and ate the sandwiches Margo had packed. The kind-hearted woman gave them lemonade drinks and lamingtons and then made tea for Margo and herself. Mrs Orth closely resembled her sister, Mrs Birtles, and in response to the children's curious stares, she told them they were twins. Annie had never before seen adult twins; had never even thought about it. Now, she felt that it was odd, almost as though the privileged novelty of being twins belonged only to children.

The visiting hour drew near. Margo expressed her gratitude to Mrs Orth for the generous hospitality, gave her the box of chocolates she had bought near the railway station, and accepted the invitation to visit again when next she came to see Herb. Much refreshed, but now with returned anxiety, the Hughs tribe trailed up the hill to the hospital.

Herb was in a ward on an upper floor. Margo, Annie and the younger children were relieved to see that he looked comfortable propped up there with sterile-looking white pillows. The bed seemed unusually high, and there was a cage under the white cover to keep its weight off the painful hips. The patient's broad smile assured them that, apart from his injury, he was reasonably well and very relieved to see them all. Annie, with her revised nursing aspirations, took in every detail of the ward, of the nurses in their blue and white uniforms and their brisk efficiency as they came and went. She so dearly wanted to be one of them.

Later, out in the corridor, a regretful and sympathetic doctor astounded Margo with the grim prognosis that Herb would never walk again. It was a thunderclap shock to the family. Their previously happy world had turned upside-down. Anxious Annie wished instead to have something ordinary, and by contrast petty, to worry about, such as unfinished homework or confession day looming or her fingernail-biting habit – all Lilliputian now in the shadow of this menacing colossus; this thief of their happiness.

It was incredible! … active, energetic Herb, never to walk again? The prophecy was difficult, almost impossible, for them to accept and Jack and Margo clung to the fact that doctors are sometimes mistaken. This time the doctors were indeed wrong. After Herb came home, it appeared that nothing could impede his progress. Gradually he learnt to walk again. He danced with Laura, and they rode their pushbikes, swam at Cronulla beach and bushwalked to the Royal National Park.

Cold weather always prompted painful reminders of Herb's injury, but Laura and his family knew he was suffering only if it was suspected and enquired about, because he never complained. The courageous youth had inherited his father's steely resilience – which, ironically, may sometimes work against such seemingly invincible humans.

Herb sold the Triumph and progressed to the higher ambition of *car* ownership. Ever since Prime Minister Chifley unveiled Australia's first car in 1948, Herb, like many youths and young men then, had set his heart on a Holden. Until that dream could be realised, he looked about for a vehicle that at least had fewer wrinkles than the old Chevrolet – which nevertheless had given him, and his siblings, much pleasure.

But higher goals required further saving which took longer to accrue. In the meantime, Herb studied books on automobiles and became increasingly knowledgeable about the intricate mechanical mysteries of car motors.

There was a great deal of interest at that time in "Gelignite" Jack Murray, and the Redex Trial and that infused more energy into discussions of all things concerned with motor cars. New words began to infiltrate the Hughs' household: differentials, carburettors, brake shoes, pistons, spark plugs, gearboxes, gaskets ... It was all double-Dutch to Annie, and quite a long way from the big rubber-band concept which Jack, joking with his laughing young sons, declared, 'made cars go!'

43 Best Friend Ruthie

They had been friends since about age five, Ruthie older by six months. Their homes were a five-minute walk apart, and they knew each other's house and backyard with equal intimacy. With worried frowns befitting little motherhood, Annie and Ruthie discussed the ever-changing health problems of their dolls, spotted them with red-crayon measles one day and bandaged fractured limbs the next.

Tenderly they rocked their babies to soothe away the effects of concussion inflicted by the violence of teasing neighbourhood boys – lowly creatures who impaled live flies with pins and plundered the nests of birds. And yet, these barbaric rascals sought at every opportunity to shout their ludicrously misguided mantra: *boys are better than girls.*

Together Ruthie and Annie began kindergarten at the local two-roomed village school snug in its playground of gumtrees, where Herb was already a pupil, but at the third class, they separated. Annie continued her education at St Marys Convent a few miles train ride distant, and at the same time, Herb was sent to The Marist Brothers boys' school. Although the little girls' closeness was breached during school hours, they compensated on weekends by sharing much petty gossip, and as time skipped on they grew in stature and wisdom and for many years remained the very best of friends.

Summer was ripening. Ruthie and Annie, teenagers now, were spending a few hours at Como Public Swimming Baths. They had been in the salty water for some time and were glad to climb out, spread their towels on the boardwalk and bask in the warm caress of the sun.

"Big-head Butch" and several of his larrikin mates were talking and laughing nearby. They kept glancing at the girls, their eyes resting briefly on Annie's freckled face and sun-bleached plaits and lingering interestedly on the pleasing, suntanned visage of pretty Ruthie.

Noticing the attention, the girls proceeded carefully to ignore them, deeming it beneath their dignity to respond to ruffians (whom Jack would label "boofheads"). The bored youths were crude pranksters, coarse exhibitionism being the criterion they set to qualify for admittance to their gang, and in this select fraternity, Butch the bully was king.

Ruthie leaned over to whisper something in Annie's ear, and suddenly the biggest youth came thumping along the boardwalk. He plunged into the water and performed a somersault directly in front of them – which would have been a non-event had he not pulled down his trunks! Annie was better acquainted than Ruthie with boys' anatomy, having little brothers who often ran naked down the yard to the lavatory. But the sight of an older boy's rear end displayed so brazenly was a severe shock to her and, face afire, she glanced quickly away, while Ruthie fell against her squawking with laughter.

Much encouraged by the hilarity, the big boys guffawed, nudged one another and continued to gawk at convulsive Ruthie. And then one youth called out: 'Hey, youse two sheilas! Hey, Blinky Bill! (to Annie, for her latest bad habit) do y' know what a *lesbian* is?'

Ruthie recovered sufficiently to wipe her eyes and exchange Annie's look of enquiry, and she cast down her mouth corners and shrugged. The word was alien to them. The innocent young girls were utterly ignorant of specific terms and, unlike the free-to-roam sexually-focused rough youths, did not spend Saturday nights prowling around King's Cross where such new words and their meanings were discovered.

Annie had intended to remain haughtily silent but, puzzled by the odd question, made an effort to retrieve something from a recent history lesson relating to Vasco da Gama. She half-turned and with crushing condescension (and oblivious of her blunder) threw over her shoulder: 'A person from *Les*bon, *of course*,' muttering smugly, 'That put the ignorant mug in his place'.

An explosion of laughter shot up from the group, and the girls raised naive eyebrows at each other and wondered at the absurd hilarity. Some of the boys, affecting to be weak with mirth, leant against the dressing-shed wall and another flopped down groaning in parallel charade on the boardwalk. Butch, for some warped reason, imitated the awkward movements of a polio victim – just what the girls expected from someone whose party trick it always was to eat a fat, wriggling worm.

Upon returning home, Annie relayed everything to her mother and sought an explanation. Margo looked at her somewhat startled for a moment and then turned away to attend to something on the stove (a frequent retreat when more profound thought was required). Time and Margo's explanation moved slowly. Annie managed three extra blinks while her mum, gaining thinking time, bent to retrieve the half-chewed rusk she had just spied under the table.

'Well?' asked the impatient girl, hot on the trail of a suspected secret. 'What does it mean, Mum?'

Feeling uncomfortable, Margo grew silent while arranging her reply. Facing her daughter, at last, she said falteringly, 'Well I– I believe it means – well, there are some girls and – and women who prefer to – who prefer the company of other females to males.' She drew out a chair and sat heavily at the table. Annie presumed she'd had a busy day.

'Y'mean – like Ruthie and me?' she pursued ingenuously, 'and the nuns at school?' This puzzlement prompted a few more blinks – good hard ones to stave off the urge for longer. 'Are we all lesbians then?'

'No!' sparkle-eyed Margo cried out appalled, yet maintaining strong command of her features. 'No, that's *different!*' She drew in a tranquilising breath. 'You see ... nuns consider themselves married to ... to Christ, but, unless you become a nun– –'

'Fat chance!' interrupted Annie and rolled her eyes as Sister Agatha's formidable image obtruded upon her consciousness.

'Well then – you'll get married one day, and so will Ruthie. Not the same thing at all, dear,' she assured and shaking her head, managed the difficult contortion of frowning and smiling simultaneously. Margo imagined Jack's probable response later. (He was the sage from whom she acquired such intriguing knowledge, often producing bouts of bedroom laughter.)

Yet the mist lingered. 'But I still don't see— So why was that so funny?' Annie persisted. 'And anyhow, what do you call people from Lesbon, then?' Blink blink.

This was safer ground. Margo sighed and relaxed. 'They're Portuguese ... and it's *Lisbon* – LIS-bon,' she articulated to drum it safely in. 'Make sure you remember that!' Suddenly, expediently, she rose from her chair, for she had heard the postman's whistle and was glad to escape Annie's interrogative presence in favour of the less disturbing pursuit of over-due bills in the letterbox.

American preacher and poet, Ralph Waldo Emerson might have had a friend like Ruthie – "… a friend you can afford to be stupid with …"

It was one of the blessings of Annie's life that she once regarded Ruthie as her best friend. The fun-loving girl was almost a sister to her, and together they made many precious memories over the years, as sisters and best friends do.

One morning Margo asked her daughter to go to the Jannali chemist for her – there was no chemist at Oyster Bay at that time. As well, Pauly's corrective shoes needed new heels. Usually, Jack mended his children's shoes using a "last", so named, the curious kids all thought because it made shoes *last*. Pauly's shoes were unique though, and during the period he required their corrective design, the bootmaker repaired them.

Annie invited her best friend along. Ruthie was entertaining, being endowed with a premature elegance instilled in her by her older sister who was instructing her in the art of sophistication. Annie's understanding of that mature word, often slipping so effortlessly from Ruthie's tongue, was still somewhat vague but seemed to be synonymous with Gloria, lipstick, earrings and high heels. And Gloriahad a boyfriend – Ruthie learnt much from her sophisticated sibling.

But sometimes the sisters fought, just as Herb and Annie used to. Ruthie had collected an arsenal of combative words – which Gloria considered offensive – to fire at big sister during their skirmishes, the most emotive being "vomit". She used this weapon in various imaginative forms: 'Here comes your *vomity* old boyfriend'. Or, after snarling across the breakfast table: 'Looks like it's going to be a *vomitus* day, eh, vomit-face!'

The magic word and its derivatives always enraged Gloria, much to Ruthie's glee, and a cat-fight usually erupted with their mother wedged between and slapping them both to quell the riot. Small wonder Mrs Collins sought peace at the beer garden of the Como Pub!

The best friends set off towards the shops to await the bus. Seated outside the grocery, Ruthie stretched out her legs, twisted around and with a dark pencil, drew a line up the back of each one, happy now in the knowledge that people with poor eyesight would admire her "stockings." Standing, she playfully asked, 'Are my seams straight?' and turned this way and that for Annie's grinning, blinking inspection.

Seated again, Ruthie revealed the treasures of her mother's cast-off handbag. An impish smile played about her lips as she ferreted out powder, rouge, lipstick, the black pencil again, and applied the lot to their faces on the erroneous theory: heavier paint – more beauty.

Despite their bursts of giggles, the transformation convinced them that glamour had easily been achieved by the application of colour and black pencil upon pristine canvasses. They stepped towards the approaching bus feeling at least eighteen – that magical age so coveted by new-teens – believing they looked absolutely gorgeous.

As they boarded the bus, Clarrie, the driver who had known the girls for more than a decade, stared at their sudden beautification and his face broke out in a broad smile showing even his back teeth, not often seen. A jerk of the head and a wink – 'By the jingoes, there's some good sorts around here!' he exclaimed and driving on, they heard him joking: 'Watch out Lana Turner!'

The beauties accepted this homage as their due and smiled serenely in emulation of the newly crowned Queen Elizabeth – Did Her Majesty ever have the terrible blinking habit? Annie briefly wondered – and they made their regal way past grinning faces to the rear of the bus where they sat with pretended posture-improving books on their heads. *Oh, bliss!*

At Jannali, the girls encountered two rough urchins, often noticed during excursions to the "flicks", also known as The Como Fleahouse in the elite location they frequented. It became apparent when the boys began laughing and slinging derogatory nouns at

Ruthie and Annie, that they were not blest with a capacity to recognise panache.

'Those boys are just silly, ignorant children,' explained wise old Ruthie. Forgetting to be sophisticated she hissed, 'Go on, *shoo,* snotty brats!' and as if slipping on a stole, she resumed her lofty manner. Annie took care in imitating her mentor's superior demeanour. She tossed the tongue-exhibiting underlings a dismissive glare punctuated by no fewer than four intimidating blinks and followed Ruthie's confident lead into the milk bar.

As they awaited their milkshakes, Annie noticed two women in one of the booths attempting to stifle their laughter over something and their eyes kept returning to the two young girls. Even the man at the counter appeared jovial (more teeth) as he attended them. Slowly the suspicion began to permeate Annie's brain that, quite apart from her regular comical blinks, there wassomething peculiar about their appearance. She sought the wall mirror. The awful truth dawned.

With rosy embarrassment, Annie shrank down in the booth and stared into her malted milk. After the last noisy slurp had ascended their straws (sophistication a frequent sacrifice), she urged Ruthie to accompany her to the railway station "Ladies", there to remove their clown facade. A clean, blinking, freckled face was suddenly the most desirable thing in the world to Annie Hughs.

But Ruthie was reluctant to discard all that newly acquired beauty and remarked in an annoyed tone, 'Oh gawd, this place is *so* unsophisticated.'

Anniesaw by the proud tilt of Ruthie's chin and the quick assessing glance she threw her way that her friend derived immense pleasure from slipping out those syllables again. Ruthie further remonstrated that had they been visiting the city their enchanting presence would have drawn enormous appreciation.

To Ruthie Collins, a train ride to town, an empty-pursed visit to David Jones and a peanut butter sandwich in Hyde Park provided sufficient temporary gratification in her quest for freedom and sophistication. In fact, it comprised all either of them could economically aspire to, usually possessing only lunch in a brown paper bag and the stub of a train ticket. The pretty girl was a romantic dreamer, yet most learned in the essential subjects of beauty and boys. Eagerly, she snatched up every nugget of wisdom Gloria discarded from her mine of experience and felt an educator's duty to convey her gleanings to whoever was in most need of it – usually Annie Hughs.

Consequently, she exposed the world-shaking revelation that if *one* (Ruthie had lately adopted the habit of using the pompous pronoun – incongruously with idioms) ... if one had the great fortune to be a stunning humdinger of a good sort, the admiring boys would say: 'Hubber, hub-ber!' as one walked aloofly by … *aloofly*, mind. Annie did not experiment with "one" – she knew that everyone in her house would fall over laughing.

Ruthie informed her ingenuous friend that other youths would whistle, not in a commanding manner such as Annie's brothers used when summoning the dog, but a long whistle followed immediately by a short, which carried the ultimate compliment: Whacko! With befitting solemnity, Ruthie's light blue eyes stared into Annie's ignorant soul, and she warned never to look their way when boys whistled.

In effect, she explained the puzzling fact that even the slightest acknowledgement of uncouth flattery would shatter the veneer of one's carefully nurtured sophistication. Here, a kind pause in the tutoring allowed Annie time to appreciate the profundity of her best friend's wisdom.

The inference Annie drew from this mentoring, was that a young girl had no choice but to pretend annoyance at any male attention, and just keep walking. Thatshowed *class*, Ruthie most emphatically assured her. When combined with the June Dally-Watkins lessons on deportment and poise, it was supposed to represent the apogee of every young lady's aspirations. To many girls, of course, it was merely a forerunner to marriage and maternity.

At age thirteen, however, Annie still competed with boys in the occasional tree-climbing venture and always enjoyed participating in a bare-footed game of rounders out on the dirt road. As well, she revelled in adding to the thunder of protesting feet with the mutinous horde at the Como Pictures whenever the old projector malfunctioned, and in summer it gave her the greatest of pleasures to wait in ambush with a bucket of water and administer the sudden, triumphant baptising of her pesky brothers.

Clearly, Annie Hughs was not ready for *class*. Moreover, not yet willing to relinquish ownership of her precious dolls to Josie, expanding the little girl's brood, she felt an insecurity of identity – neither child nor adult – and swung from one to the other entity. And so, uneasy in the pursuit of class and deeming such artificial behaviour counter-productive, Annie told her sandy-haired instructress, 'Well I think that's a pretty stupid way of getting a boyfriend.'

'Ha! So what?' injured Ruthie retorted, spreading her hands. 'You got any better ideas?'

'Heck!' Annie said. 'If a boy ever whistled at me I'd say, "Thanks a lot, mate and the same to you."'

Ruthie's hands dropped with a slap against her thighs, and her sedate little frame slumped. She surveyed Annie, sighed and looked skyward, and in an attitude of long-sufferance conceded, 'It must be *awful* having lots of brothers!'

Clearly, there was a problem, but to resilient Ruthie the prospect of the new challenge was restorative. Taper touched tinder; the flame of enthusiasm grew, and soon she was promising to do all in her power, not only to help her friend overcome her fingernail-biting and blinking habits but to teach her to become as sophisticated as she was – a task of inestimable dimensions.

Soon afterwards with the aid of a tonic, Annie overcame her terrible blinking habit, but while it held her prisoner, she gained an insight into what it meant to be addicted to some action or thing and understood how hard it was for her dad to give up smoking. A sense of purpose washed over her then, and she fancied that God had imposed the blinking habit upon her specifically so that she would be able to help her father – a suitable mission in life for an aspirant nurse.

But there were times when it seemed Jack did not deserve Annie's help – such as when he teased or criticised. One day, for example, her peculiar habit drew from him an irate, 'Will you stop that stupid blinking?' Sensitive Margo asked him not to draw attention to the habit so that Annie would get over it sooner. But Jack, raising his brows at Margo, had the final sardonic word: 'Huh! What happened little Mother Hen? Did we hatch an idiot, then?'

Besides her other accomplishments, Ruthie's ear detected the differences in cultured speech and the contrasting broad vernacular. She had a flair for dramatic phrases derived from the films at the picture house and also was endowed with a sparkling wit, which earned much laughter from friends and acquaintances.

One hot day while queued outside the picture theatre, a small boy asked the large-breasted girl in front of him: 'Why do y' wear that harness fing?' the back of which was visible through her thin blouse.

She turned, her pretty face dimpling into a wicked smirk, and said, 'Well if I didn't, kiddo, me bosoms would hang down to me belly, and I'd have to tuck 'em into me bloomers.'

Ruthie emitted a squeal of mirth, and with superb spontaneity, her bird-like soprano chirped: 'Or into her socks!' The good-natured big girl gave her a playful shove and laughed all the louder. Such comical response was typical of Ruthie's quick wit whenever she condescended to sacrifice sophistication to earthy humour.

Equally, she could imitate the many glamorous actresses she had been studying. While walking home after another Saturday matinee, she adopted a languid, unsociable demeanour and directed a statement in low and sultry accents to the other kids trailing along. Out came Greta Garbo's famous line: 'I *vont* to be alone!' And flapping a hand, she prosaically reinforced it by telling them to "buzz off". Annie greatly admired her timing and accuracy in repeating the little phrases and decided to find one to try out on her dear old dad.

A week later the group of children were again ambling home from the matinee and Annie was ruminating over something uttered by *goddess eyes* Bette Davis (or someone of her ilk). With aloof superiority, the actress had delivered a soul-maiming little phrase to some "moron" who was mouthing crass comments to gain her attention.

Finally, her unusually large eyes glared at him as though he were a birthing blowfly and in a bored, cultured tone, she drawled: 'I am *not* amused!' She turned her head, adorned in elegant coiffure away from his offensive presence, dispatching him to obscurity. The scarlet slash of lips drew on the cigarette in its long black holder and with a disdainful chin-lift she blew a plume of smoke to the chandelier, all in one elegant motion.

Such style! Annie was much impressed by the actress's suavity and could hardly wait to imitate her at home. However, delivering the sacred phrase would not be easy. The difficulty confronting the freckled-faced young girl was the lack of opportunity and appreciation in the Hughs' household to voice such a polished gem. And she did not have a cigarette, much less a holder. Moreover, dangling plaits were an additional impediment, and even Annie's overworked imagination could not hope to transform a forty-watt light globe under the ubiquitous white enamel shade into a chandelier, glittering with opulence.

Eventually, Jack came out with something humorous while teasing Annie about her jam tarts – which he called fibro tarts. Typically, the girl would laughingly defend her baking endeavours, but she could not resist the opportunity finally to articulate with calm confidence (gained from much practice), *'I am not amused.'* It sounded so mature to her ears, thrilling the histrionic young heart. She expected her dad to be stunned by this new sophistication – but he let out a laughing yelp!

'Huh!'he said, flinging up his hand. 'Who's trying to amuse you, y' crummy little sheila?'which ruined the whole effect. 'Come here so I can bash you up,'he commanded, grabbing her, and soon she was laughing and shrieking as befitted the silly thirteen-year-old she happened to be.

Jack's sobering words, however, quickly recalled Annie to her correct stratum of society and chased away forever all foolish yearnings for sophistication and *class*. Moreover, she welcomed the exemption from the Ruthie-imposed duty of having to strut after those dubious pleasures. Indeed, Annie Hughs was glad to be cured!

44 The Humpy

The Hughs children regarded the Blairs, who lived farther up the road, as rich and "posh". Their house was unusual. Brown weatherboard covered the lower half of the walls, and the upper was clad in fibro, painted mushroom-pink. The house was fronted by a circular rose garden in a lawn of exquisite neatness and bordered by hedges whose new leaves had hardly reached for the sun when they were shorn. To the Hughs youngsters, a most significant outward sign of wealth was the classic bird-bath. It resembled the marble holy water font at St Mary's church, except that a chubby little cherub presided over it and rudely supplied its chuckling water.

The external presentation of the house, although attractive in that particular style, was free of architectural pretentions. But the interior, to the Hughs children at least, evoked an aura of modernity: carpet, wall-paper, ceiling cornices of moulded plaster depicting fruiting grape vines, a shelf radio, *gorgeous* lamps … and a velvet lounge suite, its smooth elegance almost forbidding buttock contact.

As well, adjoining the laundry was a *Hygeia Dissolvenator* lavatory, its pan resembling the white ceramic variety – almost as civilised. This style of toilet, "the chocolate wheel" to all the plebeians, was so named because of the disc underneath that whirled the effluent away, and this then became sterile compost for the garden.

The Blairs displayed beautiful manners and spoke ever so nicely in cultured English. Therefore, from such gracious hosts, one does not expect an invitation merely to "sit down" upon floral-patterned velvet but to please, be seated. The scrumptious-looking "horses' doover" was offered but the visiting Hughs children did not eat it – they partook of it in the proper observance of the respect always owed to the decorative *hors-d'oeuvre*.

Mr Blair was a jolly "what-ho" sort of a fellow who transcended the kids' common-place terms beaut and bonzer, which they attributed to his bright little fish "O-ing" at them through the glass, by elevating them to first-rate, sterling and capital.

Naturally, this difference of manner added to the children's enjoyment of the Blairs' hospitality in the picture-book house – which was, to impressionable Annie Hughs, the epitome of outer-suburban standard wealth. However, most intriguing to the children and the chief object of the visits was the newly-acquired film projector with its stock of favourite films: Charlie Chaplin, The Three Stooges and the Marx Brothers. Quaint, and rather less interesting, were the old black-and-white cartoons, the characters' movements synchronised in an unnatural rhythmic sequence.

In the selection of cartoons offered at the Como Pictures local kids were moderately indulged: Donald Duck, Mickey Mouse, Popeye and many others, the newer technique pioneered by Walt Disney, a vast improvement. Animators excelled in the creation of Technicoloured characters of independent motion – rendering the early black and white cartoons dull by comparison. But that aside, the Hughs children always regarded a visit to kind Mr and Mrs Blair as a special treat.

At the conclusion of each visit, their hooroo or ta-tah was never echoed, but a cheerio or tootle-pipaccompanied them out the gate. The Blairs were nice, top-drawer people and didn't mind the provincialism of their Oyster Bay address with a pot-holed gravel road out the front, and they were well-regarded by the neighbours. Margo, too, formed a favourable impression of them, but Jack thought they were a bit on the "loony" side, although he appreciated their comically entertaining ways.

The Blairs' perceived wealth was mostly a misconception, but by sad contrast, the poverty of the Cheadle family was genuine. They lived a few doors down, the other side of the Hughs. Their grey weatherboard house, a build-on to the first built-on edifice with few hints of symmetry, had never known the stroke of a paintbrush. The board floors had no coverings, and there was no bathroom; Mrs Cheadle always bathed her children in a large tin tub on the kitchen table.

This deprivation made Annie feel thankful that her family at least had a proper bathtub, even though it was in the laundry. Later, she felt humbled to recall that before Jack and Grandad Carrington built the extensions, there were only the laundry taps to service the house, and just one power point, which was in the kitchen. In the time of the house's construction, this would have been considered adequate for a one-bed-roomed dwelling. Being near the water, it was initially classified as a holiday cottage, as were many others in the developing days of the holiday settlement of Oyster Bay.

It has often been said that all things and experiences in life are comparative; a truism that may be applied to a group of unfortunate people who dwelt in humpies in the bush some miles distant from Oyster Bay. The contrast of their living conditions significantly elevated the status of the Cheadles, whose house at least had wooden flooring, electricity, a tap in the kitchen and a roof which kept out most of the rain – relative wealth to the humpy dwellers.

The residents of the edge-of-town humpies endured great privation. They had neither plumbing nor an electricity service. The typical hut or shack built during the depression generally consisted of a single room roofed by spreads of other people's cast-off corrugated iron. The roof was sometimes the sole catchment area for rainwater, funnelled with a collection of gum leaves and dust into barrels or drums.

Before a single tap was eventually provided near the dwellings, every ounce of drinking water had to be carried in containers such as billy-cans or the larger kerosene tins, from a tap in the nearest park – a more cumbersome task in the pre-plastic days. A sad aspect here; some humpy-dwellers' pride demanded that their *Gunga Din* excursion was undertaken only after sunset, one of the many indignities of poverty.

When Queen Elizabeth first visited Australia, the route she was to travel happened to be near the humpies. Sometime before the royal visit, the dwellings were dismantled and removed. No one seemed to know what became of the occupants, struggling year after year on the margins of society, but it was generally believed the authorities had provided some form of emergency accommodation.

Not many girls at the school associated with Nancy Flynn. The justification for leaving her in solitary humiliation at the back of the class ("she smells like she wets the bed") was perhaps forgivable. Annie too, usually maintained a distance, for the ammonia odour was sometimes hard to ignore. Indeed, on occasion compassionate Mother Superior invited the girl to tea and cake at the convent home and ran a bath for her. Moreover, as Nancy lived in one of the humpies, she was exempt from paying school fees. St Marys Convent school had much to recommend it.

This stark poverty did not strike Annie as a situation of shame, but of sorrow. Owing to Margo's compassionate influence the young teenager saw only hardship arising from misfortune. However, some pupils, who were not blest with a mother as kind as Margo Hughs and who lived within handy reach of taps and light switches; within brick walls beneath tiled roofs and with carpet underfoot, openly shunned her. She was avoided, too, in church, even as Mother Mary's stature and the picture of Jesus and the Sacred Heart looked down sadly upon them.

'Don't go near the humpies', someone's mother warned one day, 'they probably have fleas and lice,' – an unkind assumption which so easily might have been applied to many other families at some time, and did not pose a severe threat to society.

Occasionally, after Saturday Confession it became the duty of a few of the convent girls to help Sister Joseph arrange the flowers in the church ready for Mass the next morning. Annie was surprised one day to encounter Nancy there washing a vase and filling it with a tap near the bubblers. The girl pushed back an unruly swathe of dark hair and tucked it around an ear for a better peripheral view of Annie. 'Sister told me that if I help her, I can have the milk,' she said self-consciously.

Her gaze flicked to the wooden suitcase nearby, and Annie saw about six small bottles of school milk issue (introduced by Prime Minister Menzies in 1951) left over from the previous day, lined up in the case ready for transport back to her home. The surplus milk was given to any girl willing to carry it. There also was half a pound of butter in Nancy's case.

'Gave me that as well,' she said, almost apologetically, the brief shoulder-shrug expressing a pretended indifference – born of embarrassment. She was a proud girl, Annie realised, knowing full-well that the butter was prized. 'Swept the convent paths and verandas.' Annie was sorry that Nancy felt the need to explain about the milk and butter; sorry never to have befriended her before, and this regret prompted her to invite the girl home for an hour or so. Nancy quickly looked at Annie and then returned her attention to the vases.

'I can't, Mum needs my help. But – but thanks,' she said.

Annie was disappointed. 'Well how about I help you carry the case?' She didn't want that either, but Annie's wish to be friendly and a growing curiosity about her home set her feet in pace with the other girl's. And so, they walked out through the school gates and along the footpath shaded by jacarandas, past the brick houses and ordered lawns and gardens. At some point, Nancy glanced sideways at Annie's wrist watch.

'That's nice,' she remarked, and as they paced along Annie told her about her dog and that her dad had given her the watch after Rusty's death. Nancy was thoughtfully silent for a few more yards and then, still walking, she turned her sad eyes to Annie and said, 'We had a dog once, but a tick got him.' After a moment she added, 'You're lucky to have a watch.' Annie immediately sought to disarm her of envy by telling her how easy it was to forget the watch was on your wrist, and then ruin it when you were washing up.

It was a long walk to the other side of town. The pavement yielded its concrete solidity to undulating foot-worn grass verges, and soon the last house was behind them. Past the cattle sale yards, they went, and along a lonely stretch of road towards the railway line and the bushland fringe of town.

Avoiding the busy highway, they followed a narrow, unfrequented track. Annie glanced at the first makeshift dwelling and felt the onset of a queer nervousness evoking the sensation of their being Hansel and Gretel emerging from the dark, silent woods. It was a relief to be startled by the sudden, cheery, familiar preaching of magpies from their leafy rostrums.

"Shanty Town" as some people labelled this settlement, formerly of about 130 people, was spread out through the bush with several primitive lavatories to service all. Nancy's place was last in a crooked row, the smallest and most humble little home Annie's saddened eyes had ever seen.

The shacks were occupied by people who, along with others in various parts of Australia, had met their lowest ebb and were forced to endure the privations of the Depression. Some were unable to find jobs; others were incapable of working and had no money for rent even if a house could be located, and therefore had nowhere else to go. At the initial, extreme cost to pride, a few of them sank too far, some irredeemably so, into the bog of hopelessness. They had given up trying and found solace in alcohol – and one would need to walk a mile in *their* shoes (if shoes they had) before casting disdainful glances or issuing criticism.

Others, it appeared, were doing their best to get through the day-to-day living with scant comforts and fraying hopes of the availability of government housing. Passive victims or otherwise, they were all at the farthest reach of justice and social equity. Even a thirteen-year-old could see that, and it seemed outrageously unfair – the war was over, years had passed, but *still,* they were waiting!

'H'lo girlie! Watcha got there?' A drunk, Degradation personified, swayed towards the two girls and stumbled over his empty beer bottles.

'Hello Athol,' Nancy replied and, scarcely looking at him, set a faster pace.

Two grubby little boys ran out in front of them, the trouser-less imp chasing the apple-stealer. 'Gimme that, you–' (A few descriptive crudities followed.)

'Aah, get lorst!' shouted the escapee, and both ran off.

And then, from another shack, a lacerating voice: 'Git in 'ere youse or I'll beltcha!'

Nancy remained silent as the girls hurried on. She was guarding against the hurt of expected, dismayed comment on the poverty of the people and the primitivism of their huts. But Annie kept a quiet tongue, and yet wished to lessen without delay the perceived difference between them.

She wanted to speak of her war-imposed calico flour-bag clothes; of the occasions when she'd had to wear Herb's school socks, long, grey and hated; of the two pennies which stabilised the leg of the Hughs' kitchen dresser and were removed only for emergency telephone calls. She wanted Nancy to know about their going to bed with hot bricks wrapped in jumpers to warm their feet; of the cups without handles; of the Christmases when Margo re-painted the worn lino ... But whichever hardship Annie resurrected, Nancy's remained more profound and, unlike the Hughs' lean post-war struggle when stringent economy ruled their lives, now well past, hers was present and continuing.

'This is our place,' Nancy said, eyeing her companion with that sidelong mannerism she had, and her defensive expression appealed: *Please don't pity us*. She turned into a makeshift yard and after a brief hesitation, entered the humpy. Annie presumed she would return in a moment and so used that time to observe.

The dwelling was about the size of the Hughs' kitchen, which Annie knew was twelve by twelve feet. The doorposts were bush poles, and the roof and walls were covered with nail-holed corrugated iron oddments, taken from the nearby tip. There were long red sheets, short green ones; some were rusted, others were cut diagonally, and all united to form walls and roof in the rough design of an asymmetrical patchwork quilt.

A shallow trench had been dug along one of the walls where, at some time, rainwater had seeped in. There was a length of guttering secured by wire beneath the lower edge of the skillion roof, and at the end of the building, a forty-four-gallon drum collected rainwater. A pipe jutted obliquely from the south wall and smoke puffing vigorously from it ascended to the tree canopy announcing a fire recently lit within.

The sudden aroma of mint warned Annie that her feet were trespassing upon a crude garden plot. She moved away and looked up at the steely sky darkening ominously with storm clouds.

Presently a small girl appeared and leaned shyly against the door. The visitor smiled at the pixie face and offered a warm 'Hello.' Not a syllable came forth – Annie's much-mended black leather school shoes captured the little one's mind and gaze.

'I'm gettin' shoes for my birfday,' she said as distinctly as finger-in-mouth allowed.

Annie moved closer. 'Oh! And how old will you be?'

'Fi-ive,' she said, without the impeding finger, and raised her little eyebrows wonderingly. 'An' I'm goin' to school too … when I get me new fings.' This confidence, intimately imparted, cemented the fledgeling friendship. To reinforce that trust she quaintly enumerated on her fingers the treasures coming to her: 'Sho-oes, rib-bons, pen-cils-s-s…' she said, elongating the words to assist memory, as one sometimes does when compiling a list.

Nancy appeared behind her. 'Mum said to come in. There's a storm. Better wait here.' They looked up at the rumbling expanse turning midday into dusk. Annie was glad to go in.

Mrs Flynn was a slim woman whose facial bone under taut brown skin suggested former beauty. Her eyes had learnt to view the world from deeper recesses – the dim glow of lamplight and candles exacting a harsh toll.

Her thin upper lip stretched to a mere line upon smiling but this smile, self-consciously attempted, might have flashed with vivacity when it had not been necessary quickly to conceal gaps. Dentists were well-sunken in the quick-sand of priorities when you had to improvise in every possible way to create some semblance of a home.

'You can sit over there,' she said, gesturing to a bed. The bed was simply a mattress laid out upon fruit boxes, an over-spread of a floral curtain lending it some brightness and dignity. Annie sat on the hard, horse-hair mattress and smiled back at Mrs Flynn when asked: 'You in Nancy's class then?'

As Annie responded, the woman's eyes flicked about the room checking that all was in order and the girl then realised it had not been lack of manners which had her waiting outside, but the courtesy of a quick tidy for a visitor. 'You like Sister Agatha?' Annie suspected that Mrs Flynn was not really listening to her cautious reply but merely trying to generate conversation. 'And whereabouts do you live, Ann— *Annie* is it?' she asked.

Attentive now, Mrs Flynn leaned back wearily against a pole while Annie told her about Oyster Bay. The woman sighed. 'Waiting for a house,' she said in weary explanation of … *everything.* 'Housing commission – there's a long waiting list. Bit worried about the council. Threatened to move us on.' She spoke in a desultory manner with a habit of omitting pronouns.

'They're very nice, the houses they build,' Annie remarked. Nancy, seated on a smaller bed with the little girl, had offered nothing to support or vary the conversation. During a moment of quietness – seeming more so for the sound of the clock clacking away the seconds– something occurred to Annie. 'They must share that bed, and it's the little girl who wets'.

'I'll make some tea,' Mrs Flynn said, suddenly upon her feet. She shifted the flat-iron to the back of the stove, moved the kettle and bent to stoke the fire. Annie surmised that the black cast iron stove was their most valued possession. 'Do y' like scones then?' the kind woman asked, still bending but turning her head to glance back. 'Making them for hubby, but there'll be plenty.' She moved the pad of blanket and sheeting from the table, and the visitor realised her arrival had interrupted the woman's ironing.

And so, they sat around the table on fruit boxes and drank tea and buttered the scones, hot and fragrant, while Mrs Flynn poured the milk from the small bottles into a large tin can and stood it in a bucket of water.

'What's your name?' Annie asked the little girl, who had been eyeing her unblinking all the while over her cracked cup of milky tea.

'Emma,' she replied and swung her bright brown eyes to Nancy and then to Mrs Flynn. 'Same as Mummy's,' she said, livening up a little, the last residue of shyness gone. 'Cause she nearly *died* having me! Me bruvver died. We was twins, and—'

'Emmy,' her mother softly interrupted, 'go and see if Daddy's coming yet.' Mrs Flynn glanced across at Annie, and the girl discerned gentleness and proud dignity in her bearing. 'Takes whatever jobs he can get. Shifting bricks today … pulling down an old chimney at Oatley,' she said. 'Be home soon.'

Emma, at the doorway, shook her dark curls. 'No, not yet Mummy.' A clap of thunder propelled her to her mother's side. They all jumped. It shook the whole dwelling. For about half an hour heavy rain pummelled the roof and they had to shout at one another, so close to their heads was the corrugated iron protection.

Mrs Flynn began dismembering a rabbit for a stew while Nancy found tin cans to catch the drips coming in from the roof holes. The floor was earthen with several hessian bags serving as mats. Annie glanced around while not under scrutiny and saw neatness, cleanliness and resourcefulness everywhere.

The cream jars lined up on a shelf were used as drinking glasses, she knew, for the Hughs, just after the war, had used such receptacles for that same purpose. Annie noticed a sealed jar of lentils containing an adult dead moth … If that's all there is to life, why the wings? the sad sight suggested.

The only window gained curtained privacy by the hanging of a skirt attached to a wire by a dozen metal washers sewn onto the waistband. Fruit boxes stacked two- and three-high made tidy cupboards, and suitcases, their edges just visible underneath the smaller bed, substituted for wardrobes. Mrs Flynn's modest dress was no longer best nor even second best, but it had been mended and washed by hands bearing grim testimony to the regular scrubbing of clothes in the tub now hanging on the wall.

Over the head of the larger bed were a crucifix and framed photograph of two boys – Nancy's younger brothers. They were staying with an aunt at Herne Bay, waiting to re-join their family when a house became available. How awful to be separated! Annie meditated later, and she tried to imagine her home without the sometimes rowdy, teasing but comforting presence of her own tribe of brothers.

Tall, lean Mr Flynn, thoroughly drenched, arrived home as Annie was about to leave. He spoke first to his wife, lowered tones informing her that the job was finished and that he would hunt around for another in the morning. Shyly, Annie looked at him. There was something in his face which was reflected in Nancy's. It was the eyes – they evoked that same feeling of melancholy that touched Annie's sensitivities and brought sadness to her own. Nevertheless, the sad eyes did light up for one moment as he smiled and remarked that he was pleased Nancy had a friend and he invited Annie to come again sometime. A nod and a quick gesture resembling a wave were bestowed, and indoors he went. The others also said goodbye and, with a head full of new impressions, Annie Hughs made her pensive way towards the railway station and home.

During the next few months, the two girls became friends and therefore shared such feelings of ambivalence when Nancy brought the news to school that her family had been allocated a government house at far away Greenacre. They wrote to each other for a while but other things intervened in their lives and, apart from the magic day of Queen Elizabeth's visit, the correspondence dwindled and then ceased.

However, for years afterwards, it gave Annie pleasure to recall that a happier, more confident Nancy returned for a brief stay with a relative. She stood alongside her friend that day in 1954 to cheer and wave when the gleaming royal conveyance flashed Her Majesty past the very site where once had existed the humble little humpies.

45 Sister Agatha

At school, Annie Hughs eagerly embraced the subject of English, especially essay-writing. Sister Agatha, a nun the girl was inclined to admire for her tall, almost regal stature, often observed her, she thought, with particular disdain, sapping her self-esteem. However, the big woman stepped out of character one memorable day to praise Annie's composition, and then read it out to the class.

After the reading, she regarded the girl through narrowed eyes and asked if someone had helped her to write it; the wrong, insulting implication taking Annie halfway back to her original estimation. Nevertheless, the first acclamation seemed worth cherishing, and so she dismissed the sceptical query as an unintended extension of praise.

Confidence filled Annie's young heart that golden afternoon. Sister handed back the pages and conferred upon her a rare smile, conveying: *well done!* That praise sent Annie's spirits soaring with a transient sort of love – hard to discriminate from grovelling gratitude.

"Old Aggy" was not *old* of course, but from a pubescent schoolgirl's myopic perspective anyone who had struggled past the age of thirty had surmounted the pinnacle of midlife and was about to descend into infirmity. "Teetering on the abyss of senility," was the extreme hyperbole which had issued from the mouth of an individual haughty girl of a more senior class. And so, it seemed that Sister Agatha, having survived hill-top thirty about a decade before, was aspiring to great longevity.

Large and loud, she was the archetypal ruler and her dominance rendered Annie despairing. Conversely, her milder moments elevated the girl's mood to an awed, child-like reverence. On that inspiring afternoon, however, her manner evoked happiness in Annie, and for a while, she applied proper diligence to studies for the prize of further approval. Wishing more than ever to rise in Sister's evaluation, she wrote and read with greater assiduity, sacrificing much leisure time to her English homework; always hoping for another "Well done!" smile.

The often-insensitive nun had her occasional kind moments, though. She taught Annie to draft dress patterns and praised the H-line dress and three-tiered gingham skirt the girl had recently completed. As well, she kept a corrective eye on the roses Annie's needle-pricked fingers were cross-stitching onto a doily for Margo.

In moments of contemplation, Annie, influenced by her mother's good and sympathetic counsel, acknowledged that not all nuns at the convent were blighted by a Jekyll and Hyde disposition. Indeed, several teachers were akin to angels. Sister Clare, an older nun who taught the fifth and sixth classes, came instantly to the girl's mind. She thought with longing sometimes of her years in Sister Clare's classroom – such enjoyable years under the kind tutorial eye. Understandably, the gentle angelic nun had been the recipient of Annie's school-girlish admiration and affection.

No one liked Tuesday afternoons. After the recital of the Rosary, the young ladies of St Marys were subjected to elocution lessons. This interlude of linguistic culture was deemed essential by the rarely seen Mother Superior, whose status of antiquity kept her among the convent pots and pans and also, when she remembered to water them, her geraniums wilting on the sunny veranda. It is probable that the dear old nun had forgotten that not one of the girls had aspirations or the qualifications for a place in the English aristocracy.

The energetic elocution teacher, Miss Boyle was of a restless mien, displaying the daintiness and quick mobility of a ballerina. It was her habit to flit, bird-like, from one side of the room to the other as she spoke, her narrow throat emitting a voice of a high-pitch, which grated on everyone's nerves. (Sister's most of all, Annie suspected after catching a look which conveyed: *Oh, for pity's sake, give – me – str-ength!)* Indeed, the disparity between the two women could not have been more significant.

The pupils of St Mary's were unfairly infused with the misconception that their everyday Australian speech was inferior.

They saw it differently and debated: 'Why should we copy England in everything? Do we really want to sound like the newsreaders on the wireless?' Furthermore, it seemed pointless to expect them to pronounce a word such as "park" in a phonetic fusion of *park* and *pork,* for they knew of no common vowel to represent that particular sound.

Nevertheless, as the girls were virtually trapped, they had no choice but to grimace and contort their way through the half-hour eternity and with their "instruments" attempt sounds so far removed from natural speech as to verge on the ridiculous.

"How now brown cow?" had never won favour with the "true-blue" Aussie pupils – they could not desist from laughing. Nor could they stretch their mouths wide enough to satisfy Miss Boyle with the "Rain in Spain" weather announcement.

Later, on their merry homeward exodus through the school gates, several clowns expressed aversion in *goofy* parody: 'The rine in Spine falls minely on the pline.' And ultra-*posh,* with lips rounded as if to blow out a candle: 'Ho no brone co!' It was not unexpected then that the foray into pretty speech laughed its way into rapid decline.

Annie Hughs' primary talent for irritating Sister Agatha surfaced again one afternoon in a discussion during which one brave pupil questioned the sense of a certain proverb concerning "camel" and "needle". Annie wanted to support the girl by adding something gleaned from a past casual friend. Her hand shot up, and then down with the self-warning: 'Don't be stupid!' However, against her own intuitive wisdom, she raised it again and was granted brief audience ... or toleration.

Tentatively, Annie repeated her casual friend's theory while Sister, at her desk, took up papers and began shuffling them. Presently she ceased the noisy tidying and glared over her spectacles at the nervous girl. After a silent moment of meditative lip-pursing, Sister drew in a long disdainful sniff and asked if the friend was a Catholic. No sooner had the profanity "Jehovah's Witness" glanced off her ear than she curtly dismissed Annie's contribution.

The rebuff sank Annie into a mire of black thoughts. Neat phrases sprang to mind, things she wished she had said, ideas which might have prompted debate on the point. Furthermore, she regretted that she had not offered at least a simple challenge to Sister's negativity, for Annie was past the age when belief in the omnipotence of adults was unshakeable. But in truth, brave retrospective musings aside, she would never dare respond with sword drawn.

Anyhow, it was now too late. Sister had briskly moved on to the more familiar enigma of The Immaculate Conception. Incidental to the subject, she found a cleverly ambiguous way to include a comment, denouncing people who are too forward in their remarks, and continued to indoctrinate the virtue of Mary theme for another half-hour until the offender was mercifully anaesthetised and rendered impervious to further boredom.

One Saturday morning, Annie was again imposing her persistent view upon Margo, that a short hair-style similar to that of Miss Boyle would be much easier to look after. Craving a little peace and having reminded her daughter that 'a girl's hair is her crowning glory,' Margo submitted to pester-power and handed over the six shillings for the Hurstville hairdresser.

An hour later it was done. The excellent woman was accommodating in showing Annie how to maintain "the look", and how to push the layered hair into waves while it was slightly damp, and she gave her the bottle of fragrant lotion.

Sublimely happy now, Annie farewelled her long tresses lying unloved and abandoned on the salon floor and felt a delightful sense of freedom as she light-stepped – as Miss Boyle would, towards the railway station, glancing in every shop window but seeing only her new cropped self. The feeling of liberation reminded Annie of the frisky manner in which sheep always spring high with apparent joy immediately after being shorn, and she now understood that exuberance.

The moment Sister Agatha observed Annie Hughs on Monday morning, hanging up her blazer and hat in the lobby, she stared with undisguised disapproval. The focus of her stunned moment of silence was the modern "Italian Boy" haircut.

'Oh, *Annette*! …' Her negative shake of the head shouted *What a disaster!* 'And you used to be such a *nice* little girl!' came her hollow declaration. (Margo suggested later to injured Annie that short hair might have reminded Sister of the sacrifice she'd had to make when taking her vows.)

With an expressive *tut-tut,* a swirl of black habit and the clack of marble-sized rosary beads hanging pendulously from the dagger-like crucifix at her belt, she turned away and left the girl standing there – absolutely *crushed.*

Three elements of her remarks jostled in Annie's brain: a teenage girl, well into her secondary education and considered by convent standards "a young lady", ought no longer to be subjected to the detested term "little girl", nice or otherwise. The haircut – what difference could a new hairstyle make to her established character? "Used to be"! Annie wondered why Sister had not conveyed this surprising generous impression of her before the metamorphosis.

That evening the freckled creature in the mirror reflected the disappointing, unalterable fact that her fair colouring did not evoke the swarthy Mediterranean look and she almost grieved for the amputated plaits. 'Well,' the watery image soothed, 'it'll soon grow again' and with the compensating thought of freedom from the one hundred daily hairbrush strokes and the tedious plaiting, they turned their backs, Annie and her reflection, and fretted no more.

A few days' passing brought an unexpected change. Sister Agatha, regretting her hasty words, fought her nature and smilingly handed Annie a pillowslip stuffed with donated clothing. No doubt she remembered that the Hughs' family was large, the parents contributing significantly by paying fees for four of the children at that time. (The primary included boys.)

Annie felt severely humbled by the charity though, especially after one girl, usually of a sanctimonious mien and who later became a nun, forgot to be pious and laughed derisively. (Compassion, a gradually learnt quality, apparently.) Yet, to be fair, Annie conceded that her struggle with the detested millstone would have evoked comedy as she lugged it across the courtyard and out past the wrought iron gates.

It was a daunting journey, from school to home. Paul and Tony had run on ahead to catch the early train and so, with Josie at her side, Annie lugged her book-laden school case and the lumpy bag along the pavement past the Public School. The children in the playground were delighted by this spectacle and laughed and jeered with the usual chant: "Publics, Publics ring the bell, while the Catholics go to hell." (The Catholic kids reversed it, naturally.)

Finally reaching the railway station, the two sisters stood in the crowded train. Annie kept her gaze lowered against curious stares, all the time wishing to throw the "dratted" encumbrance out the door. At Jannali, she hugged it on her lap in the bus and lastly, like Santa Clause, hoisted the thing over a shoulder and carried it along Oyster Bay Road to welcome home.

The nun's peace offering, conscience-assuaging and ordered by God, had caused humiliation to Annie, but once relieved of the indignity and labour of its transport, recovery was swift. From the contents, under Margo's pleased gaze, the martyr – now, happy recipient – snatched up a white lawn petticoat, lavishly trimmed with *broderie anglaise*, and found that it fitted perfectly. In Annie's estimation, that pretty slip was the acme of elegant underwear, highly deserving of a tiny dot of scent and she asked her mum if she might christen it with: 'a splash of your '*O-dee-kellog-nee* perfume'. (French was never her forte.)

And so, in the recent embarrassing bundle, there emerged for Annie an invigoration of spirit. After all, she mused, who cared about the train gawkers and the pious girl who laughed? And the bag's weight? Only a temporary nuisance. Indeed, in her entire life, Annie Hughs had never encountered a lovelier petticoat ... of the vast multitude observed.

46   The Convent Ball

The school hours were often tiring and sometimes dull, but the hours in the class were not all study, confession, Rosary and Catechism. One brightly renewing spring, the nuns, priests and parents held a meeting and decided to organise a ball for "break-up day" instead of the usual Christmas concert. For weeks, the pupils of the higher classes practised ballroom dancing on the asphalt basketball court and playground, excellent Miss Burns providing the tuition.

The piano, which usually resided in a sort of ante-room at the back of the church where Miss Burns conducted private music lessons, was wheeled out by two men onto the collonaded veranda. There, in response to Sister's alternately pouncing and caressing fingers, and with the benefit of greater acoustics, it yielded up the most delightful melodies. To these stimulating strains and rhythms, the children progressed through the steps of the Barn Dance, Veleta, Waltz, Canadian Three Step, Gypsy Tap and the graceful Pride of Erin.

Although now a teenager, Annie still enjoyed "walking" on her dad's feet. They were engaged in this pleasant pastime one evening about a week before the ball, striding in and out of the lounge room and kitchen, Jack's strong hands holding her steady as they went, and she fervently wished he could dance. Annie turned her face up to him. 'It'd be good if you could come with us, Dad,' she said wistfully.

A low-toned 'Nah,' with a dismissive laugh enforcing the negativity, followed a high-toned 'Me?' And then, 'You'll all be flapping around like a lot of wet hens!' Annie knew, however, that her dad would like very much to be "a fly on the wall". That conviction was later reaffirmed in the admiring, proud looks he bestowed on his children when they were dressed up and ready to leave with Margo.

But rugged, sometimes reserved Jack Hughs regarded dancing with a kind of embarrassment; he considered it a pretentious activity, at least in adults. His opinion of male ballet dancers, for example, was: 'They prance around like a mob of fairies!' He entirely lacked the perception of strength and excellent physical attributes of the dancers, and the sheer hard work.

Jack released his daughter. Paul stepped onto his feet, and then it was Tony's turn. While they were clomping around, Annie grabbed reluctant Paul, who had forgotten to remove himself from the danger of sister-tyranny and began imposing ballroom dancing practice on him. Her tune-humming was the sole accompaniment and did little justice to *Tales from the Vienna Woods*.

On the day of the ball, the convent pupils were sent home at midday to prepare for the grand night. This allowed time for the nuns, priests and some of the parents to remove the desks and to open up the folding doors, which generally sectioned off three classrooms. Thus, a large hall was created, complete with stage and another piano, used when choir practice was held. Forms and chairs were lined up along the walls, and clusters of balloons were hung in every suitable space.

The hired musicians would later take possession of the stage by setting up various musical instruments in readiness to accompany the pianist, Miss Burns. This accomplished and busy lady also was the basketball coach, physical culture teacher and as before mentioned, dance instructor.

Later, when the long day began melting into twilight, mothers would start arriving bearing tea towel-covered baskets of delicious food for the late supper. These treats were the products of hours of careful, creative home-cooking. Margo baked sweet butterfly cakes, enough to fill her large *Bakelite* cake tin.

At home after lunch, Annie sat in the kitchen and submitted her now longer hair to Margo's combing, twisting and final tying up in hideous rags. She began to grow conscious of a sneaking threat of nausea, and the greater the focus, the worse it became. Margo gave her an aspirinand told her to go and lie down. 'It's just the excitement', she said and assured her that the sick feeling would soon pass.

After ironing Paul's snowy shirt, diligent Margo draped it over the black suit hanging up in readiness and then, yielding to weariness, sat down for a quick "cuppa". But even then, between sips, she kept working on the finishing touches to Annie's blue satin ball gown until at last, it hung in its splendour on the wardrobe door.

The gown was indeed a mother-love project. It had been under Margo's clever fingers for a full week and well into the late hours of the previous night. Now, as Annie reclined there recovering from her stomach ailment, her gaze caressed the shining fabric, the flounces, the puff sleeves, the frills around the long, lavish skirt and the exquisite detail of the pink rosebuds embroidered on the bodice. 'What a terrific mum I've got!' she mused.

Later, when Jack arrived home from work, happy as usual with the free weekend ahead of him, he helped Paul to dress. When he positioned the bow tie at the white collar, Annie was quite taken by an impression of an older Paul, a glimpse of the future blond youth in a cadet uniform, for to be a naval officer was his ambition. The reality of eventual separation came to her in an ephemeral wisp of sadness, and she realised how very much they would all miss him while he was away sea-faring.

But God, in His unfathomable wisdom, had other plans for young Paul Hughs.

At the time of the ball, Paul and Tony had not yet reached a secondary level at school and therefore were still attending the convent, but both had been enrolled in the Marist Brothers which

Herb attended. At that time though, there were no senior boys to partner the convent girls, and so the girls danced with each other.

Jack, of course, looked after the rest of the family while Margo, Paul and Annie travelled by bus and train to reach the excited gathering of children and parents, predominantly mothers, outside the hall. Under the shelter of the long veranda, two nuns organised children into a line of pairs, beginning at the entrance farthest from the stage. Suddenly Annie felt the grasp of hands on her shoulders and her adorned person being hastily steered to the front of the line to stand with Gail, a girl of similar height – apparently an important consideration.

The hands belonged to Sister Agatha, and they thrust two bouquets at the startled girls to be presented to the grand lady and gentleman standing in front of the stage. Sister, unusually tense and flustered, gave the girls a quick demonstration of how to curtsy correctly – a memory for Annie to cherish: the big red-faced convent oppressor in her voluminous black habit curtsying, seemingly in homage to the pair of them.

The music, so thrillingly inviting, struck Annie with a bolt of stage fright. She moved forward only in response to a firm Sister-shove. Thus, the two girls entered the hall, their eyes focused on the photograph of Pope Pius X11 on the wall behind the stage, their well-practised slow walk leading the line of children down the hall's length towards the two smiling adults waiting there.

Bouquets presented, the worst was over. Enjoyment could now begin. All the beautifully dressed dancers advanced in procession with the tempo of the music. As soon as every child was inside, the dancing commenced, and the children began waltzing around the hall. Happily swinging along, Annie glanced over at her mum. Margo, in smiling conversation, was nodding to her companion – although distractedly, for her eyes kept returning to the dancers, seeking out her own.

After the dancing, all children attended the photographic session in a detached classroom and then re-entered the hall where trestle tables, covered with cloths, had been spread with the sumptuous supper contributed by the mothers.

Small boys skidded in polished shoes along the floor, and little girls twirled their ample skirts in competition with one another. Toddlers, new to the skill of remaining vertical while in motion, ventured out. Some swayed uncertainly, and others aimed their small steps in headlong staggers towards the groups of now uninhibited children.

The ball was over. Yawning youngsters began leaning against their mothers who were taking jackets and berets out of bags and threading little arms into coat sleeves, preparatory to the homeward journey. The musicians, busy now packing away their magic, imparted nods, smiles and pleasantries to Miss Burns as she gathered up her sheets of music and brought down the brown lid, which put the piano to sleep. And everywhere people were farewelling and remarking on the beautiful evening, the graceful dancing and the delightful supper.

The next day, when Margo and Annie reflected on the occasion, there emerged one sad aspect. It came in the form of the forgotten, hard-working Cinderellas excluded from the ball. Sister Agatha and several other nuns had for weeks worked diligently with Miss Burns, expending much effort and enthusiasm in preparing the children for the exciting event.

Annie recalled other events from which the nuns were excluded: excursions to the museum, the art gallery, the Conservatorium, the theatre for a religious film, and the triumphant basketball final which at least was filmed by a parent for the nuns' pleasure.

Margo lamented that it seemed a most unfair policy that such dedicated women were not permitted to attend the events and reap some well-deserved reward for their efforts. On reflection, she deduced that *that* was the very point – they sought no reward for duty performed.

'Nuns' lives are governed by a sort of asceticism' she explained, 'that came with the vows and black habit when they

427

first entered the convent where full-hearted acceptance was mandatory.'

'Yes, I know that, but they shouldn't have to suffer on hot days all wrapped up in black!' Annie said.

Indeed, the nuns wore habits and head-gear with only their faces and hands testifying to the discomfort of perspiring human flesh enduring beneath the heat-absorbing black tents. It was known, however, that during the summer holidays the nuns went on a kind of retreat at Wagga Wagga, where they stayed in a magnificent old two-storey convent – but they were expected to refrain from speaking for the duration.

'At least they get that six-week holiday at Christmas,' Margo said.

'Yes, but what kind of a holiday is that if they can't talk to anyone?' Annie protested, throwing up her hands.

Over the three years of their association, Sister Agatha and Annie Hughs had many collisions, and it was reasonable to assume that they would never overcome their mutual personality difficulties. Nevertheless, after the night of the nun-excluding ball and the subsequent emotive discussion with Margo, Annie was conscious of a genuine feeling of sadness and admiration for the woman under the wimple.

47 The Bus Driver

It was an endearing quirk of Mr Birtles' nature that he liked to be the bearer of news, of fresh information, to inform people so they would not be deprived. Betraying a touch of human pride, he found satisfaction in evoking wide-eyed dismay, interest and anticipation. In short, to carry such importance that being the first learner of *new* news usually confers. But this time he took no pleasure in it. His face wore pale shock.

'I've just heard at the shop – Clarrie's dead!'

He paused, his lips quivering, and Margo stared, incredulous. A thump lurched in Annie's heart – they knew only one Clarrie.

'The – the bus driver?' Margo asked, and he nodded, gulping back sudden emotion. He had known Clarrie for a long time.

'Can I sit a minute Mrs Hughs?' he asked, stepping towards the veranda chair.

Margo, still staring at him in the mute shock of disbelief, slowly sat opposite. 'What *happened*, Mr Birtles?' Already her eyes were bright with welled tears.

Annie stood there, too stunned to speak but when Tony came running onto the veranda, she found sufficient voice to subdue the merriment of his chirpy greeting. Tony looked from one to the other of them in a mixture of perplexity and round-eyed appeal and became a silent statue, aware that something of great importance had occurred.

Mr Birtles glanced across at him uncertainly. 'Annie love …' he began and, transferring his gaze to the shocked girl, he assumed responsibility for Tony's emotional welfare. 'I don't think he should hear this,' he warned. His eyes locked with Margo's for a few seconds while she absorbed the foreboding dimension of his news and then she took the reins from him and directed Annie to usher Tony into the kitchen for a biscuit.

After a few minutes, Margo left Mr Birtles – still staring at the veranda floor and shaking his head in disbelief – to recover a little. She steered Annie aside, checked to ensure that Tony was occupied, and revealed distractedly, falteringly, that Clarrie had committed suicide. He had driven his car to a secluded bushy location, attached a hose to the exhaust pipe, shut himself and the hose in … and died of carbon monoxide poisoning.

The accretions of life-knowledge sometimes come softly, sometimes with violent suddenness. To Annie Hughs, this was a thunderbolt, a new and horrible revelation too hard to assimilate initially. It was impossible for her to understand the various awful aspects it presented: the premeditation, his actually implementing the plan – attaching the hose with such terrible purpose. The fumes! How long, that last look at the world before relinquishing precious life?

Margo sent Annie off with Mr Birtles under the pretext of a shopping errand, but her eyes, her nod and the accompanying look of concern told her daughter to make sure he reached his gate without incident. Good Mrs Birtles was there waiting. Duty done, Annie continued on towards the shop, her mind fully occupied by Clarrie. 'Walk a mile in another's shoes' Margo often reminded, but how could this terrible thing be imagined? Why did he want to throw away his life? she wondered.

Outside the shop, she dawdled past animated pairs and groups of locals. It seemed everyone was "out and about" and talking. Some of the overheard questions fell in with Annie's thinking: Did Clarrie have children? Where was his home? And her own morbid query attached itself to the list: How did it *feel* to die that way?

It seemed the entire community of Oyster Bay was buzzing with the terrible news, some people speaking in reverential tones, others gesticulating and liberally distributing opinions and speculations. Querying brows were up, and there were many authoritative opinions on *that* particular method of ending one's life. "Surely, life-weary people put their heads in gas ovens or throw themselves over The Gap" was the callous gist. But the big question which trembled on everyone's lips was: Why did he do it?

Upon entering the post office, Annie met dolorous Ruthie, and they came together in mute shock. They heard a few people conversing in whispers and saw bewildered looks and solemn heads shaking and nodding. Somewhat overlooked were several wide-eyed children, all wondering what was going on.

Miss Gilbert displayed genuine grief when she sank, shaking, onto Gumm's bench and wept openly into her hands. By the next day, the stunned population of Oyster Bay had heard all there was to hear of the sad news, the speculation mellowed and much eulogistic comment emerged.

The impact of the bus driver's suicide was severe. Everyone felt something, for Clarrie had been one of them for a long time. He was as much a part of their lives as Mr Gumm, Fast Fred and Mr Quinn, and all the other people who gave that comfortable familiarity to the small community, that blessed feeling of belonging. But now Clarrie was gone, and they were all realising how very much they had always liked him.

Back at home Ruthie and Annie sat forlornly down the yard near the swing. Memory invited a visit to her gallery: the pleasant cadence of Clarrie's voice; his teasing and joking; his broad grinning at the two gigglers with their lipstick, and their winged eyebrows evincing permanent surprise, all clownishly applied by reckless, novice hands. His humorous words came back with sorrowing clearness: 'By the jingoes, there's some good sorts around here!' They thought of the times when he had allowed the penniless pair to pay later. And he was Santa one year at the Community Do when Mr Quinn could not play his usual role, but the kids had all recognised Clarrie's chuckling, throaty laugh, his voice and his stock of worn-out jokes.

Annie remembered something special: Margo one day had told Jack that Clarrie had left his driver's seat and stepped down from the bus to assist her up the steps and escort her to a place, for she was then heavily pregnant. That gentle solicitude was typical of the kind man.

Oyster Bay was not quite the same after Clarrie's funeral. He had been an essential member of the society, but until his death, no one had realised *how* important, and sadly, it appeared he had not revealed to anyone his apparent troubles.

With an encroaching sense of regret for imagined neglect, Annie remembered the cheery bus-driver welcome. She realised that in years past it had never occurred to her to enquire: 'And how are *you*, Clarrie?' When did she ever consider him, or converse with him at all except to berate him for his teasing? And now it was too late.

Sometime afterwards, an unsettling reminder occurred to Annie. One of her many aunts, Dulce, intended taking her to the Empire Theatre in a few days to attend the Borovansky Ballet. The overhanging emotional cloud had removed all thoughts of the excursion, and now that it was near, the young girl hardly wanted to go. But Dulce had bought the tickets, and the arrangement for meeting Annie at the railway station was set. She could not disrupt plans now.

A few days' passing, however, made a significant difference. Other aspects of everyday life claimed moderate importance and soon the school Friday was over. The bell rang to joyful ears, and Annie shoved her case under the desk, removed her tie and hung it up with hat and blazer in the lobby to hibernate for the weekend.

After slipping into the new overcoat Margo had sewn for her, Annie saw with satisfaction that her school uniform had become invisible underneath the blue-grey flecked woollen fabric with its fashionable wide collar and a double row of gleaming blue buttons.

She met Dulce at the appointed time, and after some twenty minutes' train journey they arrived at Pam's home where Beryl also awaited ... all these aunties! Annie thought that it should be her deserving and appreciative mum going to the ballet with her sisters, not her lukewarm self.

There was a moment of thoughtful discussion between Pam and Beryl about the plainness of the coat. Although praising Margo's tailoring skill, they began looking around for a scarf to drape around the collar. Annie felt offended on her mother's behalf by this wish to adorn her lovely overcoat, believing her mum's creation was perfectly suitable to wear to "such a thing" as a ballet without the addition of the frivolous, embarrassing scarf.

Aunty Dulce, her Nursing Sister demeanour a natural attribute, remained neutral in all the fuss as she sat there in her smart suit and lace-up shoes observing all, thinking a great deal, but saying nothing. This was duly noted – they shared a rapport, Annie and Dulcie. The young girl knew that her aunt understood her feelings about the scarf. Nevertheless, she was careful not to show resistance to the accessory, for her generous, culture-conscious aunts were motivated by kindness in taking her to see the highly acclaimed Borovansky Australian Ballet.

After a light meal, they all squeezed into Uncle David's Hillman and surreptitiously in the dimness, Annie poked the imposing scarf down inside her coat. Her uncle drove into the city and despatched the group at the corner of two busy streets near the Empire Theatre, one of the large Sydney theatres that catered for significant events such as visiting ballet companies. (As the population increased, it was becoming apparent to everyone that Australia needed an Opera House!)

Annie's lack of interest aside, the visit to the ballet represented a welcomed break from the heavy load of schoolwork, exams, and the ever-present religious commitment, and especially from sad thoughts of Clarrie. But, having ignorantly underestimated the importance of the ballet, she remained apathetic and expected to be bored out of consciousness.

How wrong she was! Once inside the grand foyer, her apathetic attitude changed. The theatre itself imparted an atmosphere of grandeur. Looking around, Annie noticed the high standard of care every member of the audience had taken in personal presentation, and she understood at last her aunt's careful attention to dress. With this enlightenment, her wiser hands crept up and drew out the blue silk scarf to drape it attractively over the collar.

They found their seats. Annie looked around, and a great many sensations assailed her. There was so much to see, hear and smell, and multiple impressions to savour. The volume and sweetness of the music rising from the orchestra pit; the great curtains grandly bowing aside; the entry of the beautiful dancers in their stiff white tutus; the fluid motion of their tiny tip-toed steps and the leaps and spins with which they seemed to snub their noses at the law of gravity.

Nutcracker and *Swan Lake* were superb – it *all* was and performed with such éclat as to be expected from a company founded by the famous Czech-born Eduard Borovansky. The entire performance was so thoroughly deserving of the lengthy waterfall resonance of clapping flesh, which went on and on.

Annie felt almost plebeian now; humbled by her recent attitude. Although still mindful of Clarrie, she wondered at her misconception that the ballet would be an interminable bore. Contrastingly, she found it difficult to repress the intensity of her delight in the magical performance and afterwards thought and talked of nothing else for several days.

Fortunately, human nature is endowed with a vital resilience, and in Annie's mind, Clarrie had moved aside for the ballet event. But gradually, and with less sharpness of emotion, with the gauzy recall of that day of shock, she picked up the thought-threads belonging to him, and at the same time wove-in her awareness of other day-to-day events.

A few days later, Margo packed a basket with half a dozen carefully wrapped eggs and a bunch of Jack's beautiful squeaky spinach, then she and Annie took the youngest children over to visit the Birtles house, Annie giving young Maree a "piggy-back" for some of the way. It was good to see kind Mrs Birtles again and to hear her exclaim: 'Oh my goodness gracious me! What have we here?'

Mr Birtles greeted them with, 'Aah! Cackleberries and Popeye, eh?' and Margo and Annie knew that he also had rallied.

About a week after that, Annie heard Jack telling Margo, while she was cutting his hair, that he sometimes had good conversations with Clarrie. He said that whenever Clarrie happened to be early and waiting at Como for the train to arrive, he would park the bus beneath the big Moreton Bay fig tree and sit on the low fence of the park to smoke his pipe. Jack was usually glad to join him with a cigarette. He added that he enjoyed their conversations so much that he was always sorry when the train arrived and the horde of passengers hastened towards the waiting bus.

Clarrie revealed to Jack that he had once worked as a brickies' labourer, but an accident with a falling brick wall had damaged his left forearm and weakened it so much that he had to find a less strenuous way to "earn a quid" – bus-driving.

And something else was confided to Jack during those companionable talks under the Morton Bay Fig. The eldest of Clarrie's three daughters, now almost an adult, had polio and although she was a bright and cheerful girl, her disability held her back in many areas of her life.

Jack did not mention, however, that he repaid Clarrie's confidence with his own about "blue baby" Lorraine, for Margo easily became upset at the mention of her dead little one, even after all the intervening years.

Margo paused in her wifely task, sighed and shook her head slowly in that thoughtful, compassionate way so characteristic of her, and remarked, 'Isn't it amazing, the things that come to light after a person dies?'

She put down the clippers, withdrew the cloth from around Jack's shoulders and, brushing his arms with it, she kissed the top of his head, one of the many tender gestures Margo often bestowed upon the man she so loved.

48   The Pie Shop

Jack Hughs was not only a restaurant chef but also a pastry cook. He had been approached by two of the kitchen workers, middle-aged Jewish sisters, with a tentative plan for a partnership in a fish and chip shop, where pies would also be sold – when and if a suitable store was found. The fish and chip division of the business was to be managed by the women, the shop operating under the name the *AJC,* (Abi, Jack, and Chava.)

Margo was pleased with the prospect of a change for Jack. The shift work at the restaurant had never been ideal, and there would be a bonus for Margo in this exciting new plan, in the freedom from the difficult laundering, especially the ironing, of the tall starched hat Jack always had to wear. Although a relatively minor consideration, to be relieved of that arduous duty would be welcomed.

And so, the search for an affordable shop began. For a while, the Hughs talked about almost nothing else but commercial real estate, pie ovens, mangles, benches … and the family looked forward to the day when a shop was found, and the AJC would become a reality.

Years before, Jack's older children had become curious about their father's chef work, and so one day, at his invitation and with Margo's sanction, they visited the restaurant in the city to see the place he talked so much about. Herb, Annie and Paul had travelled, that autumn, by train from Como.

Capable Herb found the street and then the restaurant and led his sister and brother down the steps into a softly illuminated area of tables, all highlighted by snowy cloths and each one centred by a tall lamp and a propped menu. Smartly attired men and women were already seated, their heads turned to one another in conversation, all awaiting a high-class business luncheon.

Pushing open the swinging doors, the three Hughs' children found themselves in the fragrant kitchen. Jack was busily cooking near a large vat, looking the classic chef very much in his white work clothes and tall hat. He turned when one of the women called out, 'Jack, your kids are here,' and, putting down the ladle, smiled broadly and came over to greet them. Another cheery woman, who turned out to be Chava, approached and led the way to the dining alcove at one end of the enormous kitchen.

There the children were treated to Vienna Schnitzel, followed by blancmange and raspberries in glass dishes, daintily elegant on their long stems – quite a contrast from the thick crockery at home. While enjoying the scrumptious food, their keen senses had taken in everything: the warm cooking smells, the crowded benches and shelves and above them, gleaming saucepans and frying pans hanging from beams. They observed the constant, well-orchestrated activity and the frequent deferential consultations with Jack Hughs, and gradually the children came to appreciate their father's importance.

As head chef, Jack supervised all the workers and their tasks in that bustling, busy place. He was responsible for everyone, from the "kitchen-hands" who peeled the vegetables and washed the dishes to the waiters dressed in black-and-white, smartly whisking dome-covered plates of food out through the swinging doors into the dining area with its suitably placed palms trees. The Hughs children viewed Joker Jack from quite a different perspective that day.

It took a long time for Jack, Chava and Abi to find the ideal shop and location. When the fish, chip and pie shop – the AJC – finally became a reality, Annie went with her father during school holidays to help and learn, and to enjoy the excitement of the new venture. The pie oven, installed at a significant cost to space, was more substantial than imagined and there was a mangle, used for the puff pastry, fixed to a high, broad bench – also very dominant in that smallish kitchen.

Annie's first duty was to brush egg yolk onto the dozens of meat pies waiting for their turn to go in the oven. Jewish sisters, Chava and Abi, insisted upon the teenager using their first names, even though in those times it was generally considered a gross impertinence to address an adult so. Chava assigned Annie several tasks, one of which was to cut potatoes into chips.

It was an easier chore than Annie expected for she had the use of a cylindrical receptacle with an interior akin to a cheese grater. There the potatoes were spun and washed to emerge with only slight flecks of skin adhering, each one then placed in a metal cradle. One pull on the handle brought down a cutter, and the chips fell into a bucket. It also was Annie's task to take each half-bucket of raw chips out to the shop. She had the highest yearning to serve behind the counter and was encouraged in this, but a disappointing shyness kept her in the kitchen.

When there was a lull in the frantically busy hours, the girl's thoughts turned to the enticing piano in the sitting room which divided the shop from the kitchen. Under someone else's fingers, the music drifting out might have created a soothing ambience for Abi, Chava and customers. But Annie's musicianship was harshly received.

She overheard Chava's exasperated complaint to Jack: 'It's the same thing already, over and over again! You want I go *nuts*?' Annie felt piqued but realised that even *she* had grown weary of the little piece Margo had taught her, and so could hardly blame the woman for the criticism.

Chava was a good person with a generous nature, gregarious and easy-going, but her high-spiritedness clashed in a bantering way with Jack's strong opinions and his stubborn unwillingness to change them. Chava, equally iron-willed, showed vigorous mental strength when arguing and the two often enjoyed energetic debating sessions.

One afternoon during their late quiet-shop-time lunch, they were discussing the entertainer Liberace who, in response to adverse criticism, was quoted as saying: "What you said hurt me very much. *I cried all the way to the bank.*" (Perhaps the birth of what is now a dead or dying cliché.) Jack voiced a few disparaging remarks regarding the pianist's flamboyant attire – a mode of theatrical dress which excited wide speculation and opinion ranging from condemnation to applause.

Unlike Jack, Chava held a liberal view. Her tolerance and a swerve away from discrimination no doubt stemmed from a consciousness of her own distant origins. She scoffed hotly at Jack's homophobic comments and, deploring the injustice of prejudice – and the penalty of fewer AJC sales – she added, 'Ha! You want maybe I put a sign in the window then: "No poofs!" You want maybe I keep out the Japs and Jerries already?' she asked. But she stopped short, Annie noticed, of adding "Jews".

Chava's mercenary attitude reigned paramountly: 'Money is money! Who cares who hands it over the counter?' The debate ended in laughter but with Chava's last placating word: 'We agree to disagree then, darl.' And off she sashayed into the shop, her manner nonetheless triumphant.

It became Annie's habit, between tasks, to sit on the single step descending from sitting room to kitchen. Resting there that morning, breathing in the lovely smell of pie mince cooking, she began to brood, resenting Chava's addressing her father in so familiar a term as darl. Even her mother, who had the exclusive right, never called him that!

She sat there in morose silence for some time, twirling a tendril of her hair and feeling pressured to say something in Margo's interest but unable to think beyond, 'Please don't call my father darl!' She was trying to summon the nerve to voice it when Chava came through with a bucket for more chips. In passing, she reached down and playfully yanked Annie's hair. 'Move your little bot, darl!' she said ... and Annie smiled and forgave her. After that her ears became ultra-receptive to the "darl" signal and, eventually realising it was accorded to every customer, she stopped fretting but wondered why it had never jarred before.

Occasionally at the AJC, there was time to take a break from the kitchen and wander out into the backyard. It was smaller than the Hughs' chook run and quite narrow with a gate opening onto a lane. There were always a few cats about, superior in their deft treading of the slim paling fence rails – as though the width of each rail measured a foot – and they sprawled on top of the

Chinese restaurant's shed and snooped around the garbage bins in the backyard of the AJC. Annie's hands longed to caress the cats, but they were timid creatures, or proud, and recoiled from her advances.

Chava came out to pick some parsley from the herb garden flourishing in an old concrete laundry trough. When Annie asked her about the cats, she threw a backward jerk of her thumb and said: 'The next-door cooks – they breed them.' She stepped along the brick path to the fly-wire door but stopped abruptly and turned her grinning face to the innocent girl. 'That's what we get when we order *chicken chow mien,* maybe!' (Chava was never an advocate of kosher food.) The frivolity of her remark was confirmed by a wink and, chuckling, she took the parsley inside.

Although Jewish in appearance, Chava was unorthodox in Jewish ways. The sisters had experienced a few brushes with anti-Semitism, but Chava's pragmatic attitude and her incisive judgement of human behaviour enabled her to regard it analytically and dismiss it immediately. She was a big woman, and as Annie watched her jovial retreat with the parsley, the thought occurred that she would soon bring domineering Sister Agatha down a peg or two. That frivolous notion grew into fantasy, which provided solace for Annie whenever she'd had a "run-in" with the nun. Of course, Chava always subdued Sister Agatha, and the girl wished it could really happen that way.

Abi, older than Chava, was quiet-natured, softly spoken and very interested in fashion. She sometimes gave Annie advice concerning the choice and purchase of clothing and jewellery – not that Annie could afford such luxuries, nor did she expect to within the next few years. *Save, save, save* was the wise woman's mantra. 'Quality!' she would aver in warm, gentle tones, patting Annie's hand, as was her habit. 'Buy always the best. Until you can, go without is better.'

The young teenager was grateful for Abi's interest, her advice on many subjects, and especially for helping her to overcome her fingernail-biting habit ... and later, for her first tiny bottle of pink nail varnish.

On the other side of the AJC there was a green-grocery owned by an Italian couple, Lino (pronounced Leeno) and Francesca, (Sweetie Pie to Lino) but, as with the Jewish sisters, they preferred Annie to use only their first names. Lino was a big, generous, smiling sort of a fellow who would *give* you the fruit and vegetables if you were not "pursed". It was generally believed that the shop survived only by his excellent wife's business acumen and the controlling influence of her volatile temperament.

They had a tribe of energetic curly-headed kids and Fran could often be heard chastising them. But just as frequently she would swamp them with praise and customers left the shop wondering about her delusion that she was the mother of perfect children.

Sometimes, Jack, Chava or Abi would send Annie there on small errands. One morning the startled girl heard the crash of glass followed by Fran's husky voice exploding from the room adjoining the shop: 'Ah, mama mia, look-a wattaya *done!*' She was a "kiss-or-slap" mother – her Italian blood had no time for anything between. 'You bloody brats! I sick'n tired-a you always the fighting. Get out-a the front and play on-a the tram lines and don-a come back until dark!'

But by the time grinning Lino had rolled his eyes at Sweetie-Pie's noise, weighed up the tomatoes and handed over the change, she was crooning repentant syllables to the wailing "brats": 'Ooh, my precious bambinos, my *angels!*' There followed the loud "mm-mmph" which accompanied each kissing smack of lips. Some rapid syllables in Italian hinted at maternal worship and forgiveness, and Lino's elevated eyebrows, combined with his nodding and grinning, told Annie that he knew it would be so.

Jack decided to bake a few fruit pies to test the market and sent his daughter to buy a quantity of Granny Smith apples. Lino filled the basket but charged for only half. When realising that the load was too heavy he came around the counter, he grabbed the handle and with his ever-present smile, said, 'C'mon, I take-a the apples to your papa,' and she filed after him through the fish shop and out into Jack's kitchen.

Lino could not stay to be adequately thanked but whizzed back to his unattended shop. Jack's fruit pies were of the same high standard as his meat pies, and they hardly had time to be displayed in the window before being sold. He baked a large one for the Italians and took it into them the next day, and soon a jovial friendship had established itself between Jack and the smiling Italian.

It wasn't long before Jack felt moved to again review his already up-graded attitude of hostility towards migrants. Annie's conviction of this was further supported by his comment to Margo: 'They're really hard workers, you know, those Italians, and terrific family people too.'

After that, his usual prejudicial comments were replaced by positive remarks such as: 'He's a good bloke, that Lino,' (a good bloke having previously been defined as one who did not too often disagree with Jack's strong opinions). 'It'd be good-oh if they were all like him!' he added to appear not wholly swayed towards the bulk of migrants landing on Australian shores.

While Jack was busy making pies, he happened to mention that Margo had never owned a dinner set but always "made do", uncomplaining, with odds and ends of thick crockery and cheap cups and saucers from Woolworths. The next day, without

449

announcement to Jack, one of the generous Jewish sisters put on her best hat and went out, while the other minded the shop. Her mission – to buy Margo a complete dinner set of very high quality – a gift from both of them.

When the revered dinner set was delivered, safely deposited on the lounge room floor and the crate opened, speechless Margo just stared. She hardly dared to believe what her eyes told her, and they soon became wet with emotion.

The set was gracefully beautiful and included many extras. On the back of each piece was the unicorn insignia of Wedgewood and Co. Ltd, made in England, and the name of the pattern, "Pergola". The children swarmed around as the packing paper was dragged out and several pieces of crockery inspected, admired and marvelled over.

After a while, Margo went into the kitchen to clear out a cupboard in readiness for the new dinner set. Joker Jack, waiting for the opportunity, muttered to Herb to go and grab a few of the *old* plates, which happened to be on the table, and to smuggle them back into the lounge room. No one else knew about this as they were all busy carefully carrying plate-by-plate, bowl-by-bowl into the kitchen where beaming Margo arranged them into the cupboard.

Suddenly, a shattering crash burst from the lounge room. Margo paled and cried out: *'OH NO!'* Annie and the rest of the tribe ran in there – glad they had not dropped the plates – and gaped at the shards of crockery on the floorboards surrounding the carpet square. It could not be deduced at first sight that it was the smashing of the old oddments they had heard after Jack had flung them onto the floor. Jack's peculiar sense of humour was a great trial sometimes, his wife often declared resignedly.

Margo's expression was a blend of anger and relief when she saw the pieces of thick crockery and had checked that her precious set was still safe in the box. How then could she thump Jack for his practical joke? He had kept the secret of the surprise and was delighting so much in Margo's pleasure. Soft arms stole around his waist, and after a tender moment, they carried the rest of the beautiful dinner service to the cupboard.

When the crate was empty, Margo released a happy, contented sigh and said to Jack: 'Well, darling hubby, I think we'll have a nice cup of tea now in our Wedgewood teacups.'

After a long, busy day at the city shop, Jack and his teenage daughter travelled by tram to Central, train to Como and lastly by bus (with new driver) to Oyster Bay, but on one occasion the bus had already left so they began walking the mile to home.

Presently, the local terroriser of all kids under the age of fifteen came mooching along towards them, hands in pockets and eyes on the road in front of his bare feet. They were always exposed because he nurtured a strange pride in the twin pairs of webbed toes – as though the oddity signified some evolutionary superiority. Contrary to this, it seemed he worked hard to hide the evidence of any natural physical advantage he might possess – a head of lustrous thick hair, for example, which he never combed – a noteworthy paradox of his nature.

'Here comes the bully,' warned Annie in an undertone as the youth drew near, now wearing whiskers among his volcanic pimples.

Annie stared at him challengingly and in a moment of bravado (and folly) said boldly: 'Hello, Butch!' It was unprecedented! Never, during the entire time of her reluctant acquaintance with "Big-head Butch" had Annie initiated any form of greeting. She did so on this safe and singular occasion specifically to spoil his satisfaction in the positive intention rudely to ignore her and her father.

An icy paternal glare bored into the boy's pugnacious face, and Butch put down his big head, muttered a brief '*lo* to the dusty road and lumbered past. In the shadow of protective Jack Annie felt invincible and smiled happily, savouring the sweet moment of triumph.

But walking along thoughtfully, the smile slowly inverted as the realisation dawned that there may be trouble waiting in an ambush the next time, without her bodyguard, she encountered

Neanderthal Butch with his pushing hands, eyes buried in deep sockets and a vast store of risqué and misogynous utterances at the ready. Doubtless, his disgruntled attitude towards girls had manifested when he realised that they looked at him with the distaste also reserved for toads.

Naturally, Annie Hughs did not love Butch! Apart from the fact that he was physically repellent, always exuding an oniony-sweat odour; despite his meagre stock of words which was dominated by crudities and used as weaponry ... apart from all that, he had once boasted about how he had tortured a rabbit. That incident alone, in Annie's evaluation, classified him as a sadistic "half-wit".

The atrocity amply justified her sinful hatred of him – and how she suffered for it! The shocking details plagued her mind day and night until seeking release from it by mentally consigning him to a maggoty pit lavatory; a petty and childish, but therapeutic device, which did give her some measure of relief.

And so, Annie's holidays ended, and it was back to school until next time. The two weeks spent at the AJC proved a valuable experience for her. She was glad to have had the opportunity of helping her father in the pie shop's kitchen and thereby gaining a greater understanding of how hard he toiled and how long the hours of work and travel were. It also emphasised the respect shown by all who had met Jack while he was baking those delicious pies for the immediate community and, as his reputation grew, for a more extensive area. Typically, he gave it his all and the AJC won custom and acclaim and continued for some time to thrive.

Jack's pies were superb, but free enterprise has always been a two-faceted reality in democratic Australia – eventually, a large bakery opened nearby selling cakes, pies and bread. The AJC could not compete, and after struggling on for some further time, Jack began taking pies home and stuffing them into the refrigerator on top of the previous day's sausage rolls. The prosperous years had passed.

For a short while, Jack was Atlas with all the starry heavens weighing on his shoulders. Worry lines deepened across his forehead and pouches under his eyes betrayed nights of too little sleep. Margo became more tender towards Jack during this lowest point of his life, for he was racked continuously by worry and steeped in self-doubt. Occasionally, he also was subject to long periods of silence, which greatly worried Margo.

Eventually, the pie-making division of the business, which had started out so profitably, became nonviable. Providentially though, it proved to be the much-needed release for Jack which, unrecognised at first, became apparent in a changing attitude.

'Always do your best,' he used to say to his children. No one could have tried harder than tough, resilient Jack Hughs, and although he suffered great disappointment, still he was not beaten. He climbed out of his black pit and began to look speculatively into the future, philosophically using the term "new chapter" often in his discussions with Margo, who voiced enthusiastic encouragement.

Gradually the furrows lifted from Jack's brow and restorative sleep came more readily because he had the spirit, foresight and courage – and valuable wifely support – to try again.

The enthusiasm for the *new chapter* revived Jack's spirit; he turned the negative aspect of relinquishing the pie business into a definite positive – a refreshing change of direction.

After selling the large oven, Jack restored the kitchen to its former arrangement for Abi and Chava, then found steady, well-paid employment cooking for Qantas. An additional benefit gained from this was that his responsibility ended with the shift and allowed more free time for home and family ... and fishing.

Meanwhile, their second refrigerator, no longer large enough for the family, came to the end of its faithful service. Jack replaced it with a tall, elegant electric *Kelvinator*, cream-coloured, which made a nice change from elfin, lettuce and fern green and all the other greens that rendered monochrome the environment in which they lived.

This time, however, Jack had to forgo the defence of his affection for all things verdant. He condescended to admit that he entirely approved of the large, roomy new refrigerator with its full bottom shelf just waiting to receive his bottles of beer, freshly caught whoppers … and his very smelly berley fish bait.

49 Puppy Love

Old Mr Birtles walked over to the Hughs' place one pleasantly warm day wearing overalls that were considerably overdue for retirement – air conditioned, one might say, with holes in areas that were not acquainted with underwear. His voice preceded him through the still afternoon air and presently his features, sun-weathered from hours of fishing in his boat, broke into such smiles as usually accompany the pleasing news.

'Did you hear, Jack?' he repeated as he unlatched the gate and approached the veranda. 'The pubs are open till ten now, y'know. Six o'clock is history – hello Annie love,' he added as just in time she snatched away Pauly's whoopee cushion from a chair.

Jack always kept track of the news and, glad to see his friend, moved the now innocuous chair forward to receive him. 'That's right', he acknowledged, 'and there'll be a lot more happy drunks around now,' he said, inclining his head towards Brownleighs' house next door.

Margo carried out a tray bearing syrupy Johnny-cakes and Jack's home-brewed ginger beer. She picked up the conversation: 'Yes, and fewer pounds, shillings and pence in the housekeeping money for their wives,' she said in a tone of defeat on behalf of womankind, 'and less food on the table for their poor little kiddies.' In Margo's estimation, the new step of extended hours at the discriminatory male "watering hole" emerged as retrograde, yet another blow against women.

Margo's comment prompted Annie to wonder again why men loved beer. Jack had let her try some once, but only two sips went down before taste buds protested. The conversation switched from beer to Donald Campbell's water speed record of 202.32 miles per hour, progressing to the wonder horse Rising Fast and then to the shark that had become entrapped in Oyster Bill's frames … and Annie lost interest.

Their news of the day was not "newsy" to her. There was not a single mention of the opening of Disneyland in California, no feelings of Aussie pride expressed for the filming of "A Town Like Alice" or amazement over Bundaberg's Lucke quads. But it was not a significant concern. In fact, nothing could now surmount a certain new intrigue lately brightening the existence of the blossoming fourteen-year-old.

Margo began collecting empty glasses and plates. In the bustle and clatter, Mr Birtles leaned towards Annie, as if divining her thoughts, and said, "Oh, I nearly forgot, lovie. A young fella at the shop was asking if I knew where a girl named Annie lived up this way … 'pears you've got an admirer!' he joked, oblivious of the cold paternal stare behind him.

Annie sought to hide her sudden elation and was helped in this by a dislike of the hint of conspiracy Mr Birtles' cupped hand

and subsequent wink carried. She shrugged to affect a bored indifference, as though boys enquired about her *all the time*, but she felt the heat rise in her face and turned away from her father's glare. 'He's Greek I think,' Mr Birtles went on, 'or Italian. One of the big mob of migrants that've come over here to help us Aussies populate so we won't perish, as the saying goes.' And then he added, 'Name of Mario.'

Mario! Oh, so that was his name – the crowning jewel of information to add to her treasure chest of facts and impressions. He was tall, aged about sixteen, seemed very shy and was endowed with Adonis-like physical qualities – including perfect white teeth.

They encountered each other only at the local shop and had never even touched hands. But for the thrill of these brief liaisons, Annie would ply Margo every afternoon with hopeful enquiries of her possible need of groceries. She assured her burdensome conscience that if she happened to run into the Divine Personage, it would be only by the most surprising stroke of good luck.

By a remarkable stroke of good luck, Annie succeeded again in the running into ... *Mario*. But as usual, a shy veneer of casual nonchalance suddenly belied the urgent contrivance that had secured their accidentalmeeting. In fact, it became a real "brain-strain" to find something to talk about. At that age, conversation generated by the present state of the weather was limited to 'Nice day!' and 'Yeah, bonzer!' The prospect of further inspiration usually died there, killed off by awkward silence.

Annie stood self-consciously at the counter, a short distance from Mario while Mr Gumm weighed up a pound of sugar, wrapped eggs individually in some torn newspaper (the pre-carton method of at least getting the eggs safely out of the shop) and gently slid loose biscuits into a paper bag.

She risked many sidelong glances that day at the olive-complexioned youth as he flicked through a magazine, noticed a passer-by, checked something in a pocket ... and then he lifted his brown eyes to Annie. She withdrew her gaze the instant he caught it and pretended to be reading Margo's shopping list, but her treacherous blood betrayed full fluster.

After such an encounter, Annie brooded over the unlikelihood that she and Mario were ever going to speak to each other – a timid hello or *tat-ta* hardly passed for a conversation. Moreover, staring at her bedroom ceiling during an even more profound introspective moment, she became convinced of her own foolishness; sure that gorgeous Mario could no more care for freckled Annie Hughs than for that fly up there ... or that–

'*Mum!*Quick! There's a big spider in here!' she squawked.

One afternoon, however, while the grocer was helping Annie to stuff her purchases into the bulging string bag, the Goddess of Love intervened, kindly liberating the purse from her grip, sending coins flying and rolling across the floorboards. Mario at once knelt down and began collecting them for her and, after a moment of paralysis while her excitement conquered mortification, she shyly joined him.

Later, helping her mum in the kitchen, Annie ran the incident through her mind for the twentieth time. She delighted again in the perceived quaint romance of it: both of them crawling about amongst the bags of potatoes, the brooms, mops, buckets, chamber pots, and almost losing each other in the bulk and clutter. *'Oh Mario, Mario! – Where the heck art thou Mario?'* she dramatised to the turnip she was peeling, quite unaware of Margo's amused grin.

The runaway coins had at least got the teenagers past the struck-mute stage. Mutters had evolved into amused comments, and they gradually became coherently conversant and found that their natures and interests were compatible. Before the hour was over Mario had invited Annie to take the train to the city with him on the following Saturday afternoon to see the film *King Henry VIII* … and her psyche rocketed into a giddy state of euphoria.

'Odd choice!' she thought, though. No doubt there were not many fourteen-year-old girls who cared much about King Henry VIII. Impressions gained from who-knows-where, established Annie's belief that he was a detestable tyrant who expediently beheaded wives when he considered them obsolete for reasons pertaining to "greener grass" or for their inability to produce a son, never acknowledging *his* part in the failure, (if failure it was).

Therefore, the film might as well have been about the cartoon adventures of magpies, *Heckle and Jeckle*, or one of Charlie Chaplin's. It mattered to the love-struck girl only to go out with Mario. And so, wildly elated, but applying disciplined calmness, she suggested that he come around on Saturday morning when her father would be at home (and it was hoped, in his weekend good spirits – a crucial aid). Mario readily agreed and after that, all Annie could think of was Saturday and Mario.

Saturday came – and brought a thunderstorm. Peering bleakly out at the nearby saplings bending in the wind she watched and waited, grew increasingly despondent and abandoned all but the faintest of hopes of Mario's appearance. A car shuddered along the corrugated road. Someone wearing a sugar-bag hood splashed past. And then joy thumped in her chest – a figure in a dark mackintosh and *sou'wester* was approaching through the white sheet of rain. It *had* to be Mario. Her school drama lessons came to the fore: 'Oh, how heroic he is! He has fought the raging elements to reach me!'

By the time Mario entered the yard, the capricious wind, surveying Annie with compassion, sent sudden strong gusts to sweep away the rain. Her hero removed the sou'wester from his noble head, and Annie stepped down onto the path to exchange greetings and stand encouragingly at his side.

Paternal Protection loomed in the doorway taking in her friend's foreignness and her audacious proximity to him. Ice-blue eyes bore down into the youth's, luminous and deep brown ... and all at once Mario appeared darker-skinned to Annie. The abundant hair seemed blacker, his nose quite aquiline and accent more pronounced. Furthermore, there was the strong hint in her father's expression that the mellow mood she so counted on was glaringly absent.

A terse and confronting: 'Yes? What do y' want?' followed. The polite young fellow dropped his amiable smile and endeavoured to deliver the short speech he undoubtedly had prepared for this terrifying moment of his life. Annie's eyes stared at Jack's – blue to blue, kin to kin, fervently willing him by telepathic entreaty to take pity and *please comply.*

Painfully, the brave youth stumbled through his request. 'I wish, Sir, I would take – I would *like* I take ...' (poor Mario was *so* nervous he forgot her name!) '... your-your-your daughter to the city – *pictures*, you know ... for to see King Hen—'

'No!' Like the fall of an axe, Jack's answer was stunning in its brevity, and he voiced it thunderously, leaving no room for doubt and absolutely murdering any ideas of an appeal. Without a single backward glance at the gawping object of his desires,

embarrassed, offended Mario strode swiftly away. Annie's smarting eyes followed his retreat … never to see him again.

It mayuniversally be acknowledged that age fourteen is a most challenging time for a child – and challenging for the parents of the new, self-absorbed teen to survive it. During the growing years hormones assert themselves, emotions soar one day and plunge the next into an abyss of depression, often for little or no apparent reason. Annie was thus afflicted. The episode with Mario, humiliating for him and briefly heart-breaking for her, nevertheless proved to be a pivotal point in her understanding of the bottomless depth of parental love.

After Mario's departure, Annie ran into the house, grabbed a handkerchief for waterfall eyes (no tissues then) and somewhat optimistically, sought the solitude of her bed. Solitude? There, the kids were playing the rainy-day game of hide-and-seek: frantically scrambling under beds and slipping among the coats behind the door. There was hesitation. There was panic. There was uncertainty where best to hide as the count neared ten. Time's up! The "com-ing, ready-or-not" warning ignited fresh spurts of stifled laughter and subsequent bursts of boisterousness upon discovery.

Margo came in to hush them, and she listened soothingly to her daughter's miserable complaints regarding the absence of privacy in their household, lack of respect for her spatial needs and the absence of equity and democracy. She ushered the subdued and wide-eyed kids out to the kitchen with the promise of the leftover cake batter in the mixing bowl awaiting their eager fingers.

The banishment of Mario had been a sharp disappointment to Annie lending more intensity to her envy of Ruthie's seemingly limitless freedom. Through Ruthie's accounts, her face rosily vivacious with the telling, Annie had glimpsed a world of city excitement: the vast Central Railway Station; the noise and purposeful haste of busy people and the panorama of trams, buses and cars cramming Broadway.

'There's a kiosk there,' Ruthie had informed her, where you could buy chocolates, *Coca-Cola*, *Smiths Chips* and ice creams. Then, told her, you waited for the policeman's semaphore arms to direct you across the expanse of road and tram lines and that got you to the large department stores. These were quantity-and-quality stores such as David Jones and Marcus Clarks.

The Hughs children had several times been to "Town" with Margo and knew something of the city, but Ruthie, occasionally with her older sister, Gloria, explored – a great deal of difference. She related such sights ... the grand iconic bridge and the harbour with its enormous ships, green-and-cream painted ferries frequently gliding in and out of Circular Quay, and the buildings, then considered high, which hurt your neck after a while gazing up at them.

Ruthie spoke of China town, a fantasy world barely imaginable to Annie Hughs. There were parks, she said, with homeless men sleeping under newspapers; beautiful theatres; the Botanical Gardens ... and everywhere, Ruthie quipped, the boys smiled and whistled at you.

'Well,' Annie thought, 'they certainly would, at Ruthie.'

Presently, Jack came in and sat on his tragic daughter's bed, and she wailed out her attack. 'Dad, how could you be so despicable to him? And to *me*! You never let me do anything ... I'm not a child, y'know – I'm way over *fourteen*! Almost one-and-a-half decades.' (Implied maturity at once annulled by infantile melodrama.)

Jack grinned. "Aah, you poor old thing!' but then assumed a paternal gravity. 'You're only – **only** fourteen,' he qualified chidingly, 'and too young to be going out with boys'. Fatherly pats on the arm helped soften the difficult-to-accept reality of that statement.

'Well, what about Ruthie? She's only six months older than me, and she's allowed to go to the city or the beach and stay all day if she wants. You just don't understand young people,' Annie's voice rose and wobbled. 'Her mum and dad must love her very much,' she whimpered, attempting by force of contrast to make her old-fashioned father realise how possessively he and her mum were inhibiting her progress towards maturity. 'They let her do anything!'

'Yeah well ... but they *shouldn't*. Now listen to me.' Jack waited while she sat up and blasted her handkerchief again. When he spoke, disapproval of Ruthie's parents infused irritation into his voice, 'They don't give a damn, or even know what Ruthie does and—'

'Yes, they do!' she broke in. 'They love and respect her and want her to be happy!' but even as the silly assertion came spluttering out, she recognised the truth of her father's words.

'Aah Annie, *Annie!* ...' There was the quick expiration of breath which expressed so clearly his annoyance that his meaning was not getting across. He reached forward and hugged her. 'Is that what you really think? Look, the reason Mum and I won't let you go wandering around like Ruthie does is that we worry that something bad will happen to you.' He talked her past her tears and sniffles and continued for a while to ensure that she was left with no reservations about her value to him and to her mum.

Flushed and tousled, the troubled teenager looked at him steadily, soberly, and nodded in submissive answer to each querying rise of tone. Gradually, she was able to grasp that precious truth, that wisdom, and to glimpse the anguish of parental fear.

'You'll be fifteen next year and then, too soon – sixteen. The world is waiting for you, love. Just be patient … and be a good girl.'

Everything now was so clear. Annie felt a wonderful sensation of renewed happiness, her love for her father filling her being. She hugged him and breathed the pleasant tobacco smell of him, and held on tightly. 'All right Dad, I'll be a … *a good little girl*,' she mimicked, half-laughing against his damp shoulder.

'Well, come on,' he said gently. 'Mum's got something for you.' And although Annie believed she had transcended childhood (despite recent evidence to the contrary), she allowed Jack to take her hand and, feeling slightly sheepish, went with him into the kitchen.

The "something", accompanied with a piece of warm banana cake and a sweet, cold egg-flip, was a copy of a poem, *Memory* by Zora Cross. Margo had learnt it at school and had always treasured it.

Annie sat at the table and began reading the poem. It was depicted as a poignant retrospection of a twenty-three-year-old woman. When she reached the line, *And while I waited and shook with cold / Through the door tripped me just eight years old...* she suddenly knew the whimsical sadness of leaving childhood.

50 Devoted Parents

As Margo and Jack approached their middle years, they began to feel the heavy imprint of time, for both toiled very hard. In those "old restaurant days", whenever Jack had worked the early shift, and the weather was fine, it had become his pleasurable habit before setting off for Como to treat one of the little ones to a ride on the bar of his pushbike. Margo always placed a pillow over the bar for the small bottom, and Jack, with his protective arms forming a safe barrier around the child, would coast the bike all the way down the hill, before slowing to a stop near Birtles' gateway. It was Annie's duty to run after them and bring her little sibling and the pillow home.

Jack had always left the bike at the station for his return in the evening, but there came a day when he decided to buy a small motor to attach to the bike. It puttered along quite well, and he enjoyed the respite from foot pumping, but after a few months, he decided to avail himself again of the exercise the pedalling gave him. He was also concerned, that the motor would be stolen while he was at work, even though the bike was reasonably safe at the railway station. And so, fitness-conscious Jack Hughs went back to pedal-power.

Sometimes on weekends, as the years wore on, Annie watched her father splitting large rocks, hammering in the chisel with his mallet, shaping slabs of sandstone for his dry-stone wall and garden paths. And when she observed his home-cooking: pasta, waffles, omelettes, or watched him working on improvements to the house, a feeling of admiration would stir her to wonder how he had acquired his numerous skills. It appeared Jack could do anything he set his mind to and he applied not only zeal, muscle and intellect, but also his whole heart to every project he undertook.

Margo Hughs was always a strong woman but not exempt from suffering. Morning sickness plagued her with some of her pregnancies, and she battled a constant weariness. However, in later years when the term "last child" had been firmly affixed to Maree, Margo began feeling and looking quite well and fit.

With the return of vitality, Margo undertook additional work sewing at home (termed "piecework") for the Anglo-American Trading Company, a factory at Ultimo. An impressive power sewing machine was bought for this purpose and installed in the main bedroom of the recent house extensions. She sewed hundreds of children's playsuits, "rompers", which Jack and Annie carried in suitcases on bus and train to the city and then on foot all the way to the factory. With the rompers delivered, the cases were refilled with more cut out pieces of fabric to take home. Eventually, after factory inspection, ironing and packing, the finished garments were dispatched to department stores.

This work, although significantly supplementing the income, proved arduous and taxed Margo's stamina, her tenacious application keeping her up late every night. Seldom was she able to seek the comfort of bed before one o'clock in the morning and her children, snug in their nests, became accustomed to the semi-muted *brr-brr-brr* of the powerful machine behind the closed door of their parents' room. But eventually, it became apparent that Margo had overestimated her capacity to keep up with the demand for completed garments. Not surprisingly her health was affected, and she succumbed to a bout of pleurisy.

Annie was almost fifteen. Jack woke her during the first night of Margo's illness and asked her to make a cup of tea for her mum. When entering her parents' room, anxious and alarmed, the tea slopping a little into the saucer, the girl became even more distressed. Margo was shaking badly, unable to cease the rigor for more than a few seconds' interval. She groaned, and her face creased as the pain assaulted.

Outside the room, Annie gave way to tears of panic, and Jack came out to her. 'She won't die, will she Dad?' her constricted voice squeaked. He hugged her for a moment and imparted calm assurances that her mum would be all right. With a quaver wobbling his words, he told her that he had already walked over the road to ask Miss Gilbert to phone the doctor – who promised to call first thing in the morning.

Distraught Jack, in the tumult of worry and emotion, turned to go back to Margo. Hesitating, while he pocketed his handkerchief, he looked at his daughter standing there wonderingly and advised her to try to sleep. He explained that while he was at work, she was to assume the role of "second mother" and would have to manage the cooking and housework and generally help Herb to look after the family while Margo recovered.

Annie was too young fully to appreciate the big task which lay ahead. It was uncharted territory for her, for Margo had always been in full command on the domestic front. Nevertheless, Annie was glad to take time out of school for her mum's benefit, and there was no thought in her mind of having made a sacrifice because the expected few weeks' interval presented a most timely deliverance from the oppression of Sister Agatha.

Dr Sweeny often visited (doctors *did* in those good old days), but the pleurisy symptoms persisted longer than expected because of Margo's run-down condition. The commencement of her convalescence was a time of extreme uncertainty for her teenage daughter. Small flakes of cold anxiety congregated in Annie's mind and formed an avalanche of worry. Would she be able to cope? Would something terrible happen because of her inadequacy?

She thought of Clivey's near drowning; Pauly's scalding; and Tony's cliff incident. She remembered Josie's shock from the electric jug; the charge had sent her bounding alarmingly through the house. Margo had met those emergencies with the presence of mind she always employed. 'What would *I* have done?' Annie wondered, 'and what sort of a nurse am I going to make if I can't cope with this?' And she drew on her reserves of emotional strength and took up the challenge.

"If Winter comes, can Spring be far behind?" wrote Shelley. The wintery-feel of Margo's illness seemed as long as the bleakest season her family had ever encountered, but eventually, she began to show an improvement, the pain lessened, then vanished and she was at last comfortable.

The Hughs children had all been through the gradations of gloom, worry and depression; the discord of domesticity thrown out of metre and the melancholy of deferred childhood. The first time they saw their mother smile after her long ordeal was akin to the bright sun shining and warming after weeks of cold, grey weather. It imbued them with the sweetest return of happiness and engendered a blissful feeling of normality to the struggling household.

It was August. Margo's front garden was again scented with stocks and jonquils, and in the dappled shade of the lantana, primula bloomed in pink and white tones. The bush between Hughs' place and Martins' was colouring up with the seasonal red-brown of she-oaks and the fragrant golden wattle. Beneath them, amid rocks and other native plants, the purple flowers of the sarsaparilla crawled around under the sheaths of yellow-orange "eggs and bacon" bushes. Shelley was right – Spring was on its way.

Jack sold the power sewing machine. Without the burden of the factory piece-work, Margo gradually became her healthy self again and resumed her usual duties. Jack encouraged his two teenagers to continue to shoulder additional responsibilities, and Paul, Tony and Josie contributed more than was expected of them to assist their mother in every way possible. But with so many children, Margo still had a long busy day, every day. Afterwards, the weight of all that had fallen upon Herb and Annie was made sufficiently evident by the degree of blessed relief both felt in having their mother at the helm again.

Annie continued on at home as her mum's helper, and together they kept the household routine going smoothly enough. However, there came one awful day when they suffered a most heartbreaking set-back: after hanging the washing on the long clothesline, the wire snapped, and many wet things fell to the dirt. (The same catastrophe had happened to Nana Hughs years before.)

It may be a truism that something good often emerges from a mishap. Jack, wholly empathetic, wasted no time in buying and installing a large Hills' clothes hoist – a novelty at that time – and Margo had a great deal of trouble keeping not only her own but a few of the neighbourhood children from using it like a merry-go-round.

As a result of changing circumstances, Annie did not return to school but sought temporary employment at Woolworths. Nerves plagued her before the interview, and so Jack protectively accompanied his daughter as far as the manager's office – the *best* of fathers. Annie worked at Woolworths until old enough to attempt the Nurses Entrance examination.

Not surprisingly, Margo was always the last one to retire at night. Just before switching off the kitchen light she would quietly enter the children's rooms to ensure they were all covered. If any of them were still awake, she'd tucked them in, even when they thought they had outgrown this luxury. Margo's sweet fragrance always evoked pleasure in Annie as she leaned down to impart a good night kiss and to whisper, 'Sweet dreams, dear'. The *best* of mothers.

51 Fast Fred's wintering

The passing of time brought a few more changes to Oyster Bay – a paradise had been discovered. There had been a gradual increase in new homes, and the roadsides were dotted here and there with brown hardwood skeletons of houses in various stages of construction. Some exciting Cracker Nights came and went, each a tacit memorial to Mrs Gracely, and for a while, someone placed flowers against the tall stone chimney; a reminder that the old lady had once lived there and had met a death of unimaginable terror.

There was sorrow, too, for Clarrie the bus driver, Clarrie's suicide leaving a prolonged pall over the whole community. But quite a few weddings had brightened the local people and also much new life, including a daughter at last for Mrs Cheadle, already the mother of four sons. The village had expanded. A baby clinic and doctor's surgery was established near the Community Hall, and there was the promise of a chemist shop soon for Oyster Bay.

Iceman, Fast Fred, began enjoying his retirement, a leisure time of late morning risings and freedom from the responsibility of getting the ice to his customers before it melted. He had become somewhat forgetful though, tending to repeat a remark uttered only minutes earlier, and increasingly he clung to routine, which seemed to give him a heightened feeling of security. For these saddening reasons his daughter, Valda, made room in her home, providing a welcoming, caring environment for the father who had always been so good to her.

Mr Fred's daughter lived next door to Mr Quinn, and this proximity provided Fred with the additional benefit of companionship. The kind old gentleman gently prompted Fred whenever his weakening memory refused to yield up some word or event or person's name. Loyally, he still laughed at the well-known humorous farm-life stories and did not mend the threadbare patches nor correct the new inconsistencies.

Well-endowed by nature with a sociable spirit, Mr Fred spent much of his carefree leisure time in pleasant conversation with anyone waiting for the bus or pausing in their shopping, who had the charity, time and inclination to sit and listen to whatever they had heard yesterday. Chatting to Mr Fred one day, it suddenly occurred to Annie Hughs to ask him his surname, for until then no one in her circle of friends and acquaintances had ever heard of it nor thought to inquire. She was surprised to learn that it was Fredericks.

Ruthie and Annie, one noon, were approaching the shop with their string bags to "do the messages" for their mothers and paused to say hello to Fred and Mrs Tanner chatting on the seat outside. Mrs Tanner "talked posh" and inserted much self-reference into everything she said. It was her way of preserving that sacred division between her eminent self and the common herd. Margo once remarked that she spoke 'with a plum in her mouth'. Annie wondered about this and later, appropriately positioning a Rainbow-ball lolly, attempted speech – and understood.

The large lady, of a sergeant major demeanour, always held in reserve a topical opinion to voice, her political zeal incorporating itself into every conversation. Lately, she had been bemoaning the fact that Australia's population had passed nine million, and militantly she condemned the Immigration Minister for allowing too many foreigners into the country.

'It's a substantial error of judgement for which we ratepayers will be the poorer – you mark my words!' prophesied she who required her every utterance to be memorialised. The woman was saved from being completely objectionable, however, by a spontaneous wit and an appreciation of the ridiculous and also by the occasional local recognition that "Battle-axe" Tanner's character did have a nicer aspect.

Affable Fred was listening, nodding and smiling, his hand resting on the handle of a stroller and Ruthie paused to look pointedly at the green-and-orange striped canvas seat.

'You expecting a little something, Mr Fred?' she joked in her saucy, but a respectful voice.

He sent a quick, puzzled glance to the stroller and then understood. 'Oh!' he laughed. 'Gawd no! Not at my age – spare me that!' and went on to explain that his daughter had just taken young Lennie into the surgery. 'He's got a genial – no, a gentile – gentle – no, a – a *genital* – that's it … a *genital* condition of the foot, the doc reckons,' he said, with a glint of pride in his eyes and satisfaction in the set of his mouth, that he had remembered the term so well.

In their solemn naivety, Ruthie and Annie began to express a token concern for whatever *that* condition was of little Lennie's foot when suddenly Mrs Tanner's clamped mouth spurted, and her belly shook. The girls looked at each other as the florid-faced woman fought in vain to suppress an eruption of laughter. Mr Fred glared at her with cold hostility, and she begged his pardon and wiped a handkerchief over her eyes.

Grandfatherly offence escalated to a blend of disdain and incredulity. 'Well, y' don't hafta laugh about it I don't think, Mrs Tanner,' he said, scandalised. 'Whatameantasay …how would youlike to have a gen— genital condition of the foot, eh?'

A louder eruption followed. But eventually Mrs Tanner summoned the strength to say, in her eloquent diction and upper register voice, 'I would find it most difficult and inconvenient, Mr Fred,' she struggled, 'but I'm quite satisfied with the way God has arranged my anatomy … and I *do* sympathise with little Lennie.'

She rose from the seat, stumbled on the step, emitted a short trill of laughter and entered the store, leaving three astonished faces looking questions at one another.

Returning home, Annie found her mum drying her hair at the stove, and she relayed the conversation, precisely. Margo stared at her through the damp tresses for a second, threw herself back into the chair and fell into body-shaking laughter which left Annie wondering what ailed these middle-aged women. Was it something to do with the enigmatic *change of life* her aunties often talked about? Was there an accompanying change of intelligence … for the worse?

When pressed, and between squeaky explosions of fresh mirth, Margo told her daughter to fetch the dictionary and to find "genital" and then "*congenital*". This Annie did – and at last, understood and appreciated the hilarity.

'Can't wait to tell Jack this one!' muttered Margo as she wiped the towel over her eyes. Belatedly, however, she knew a brief wave of shame for her failure to feel and to express immediate sympathy for the little boy with the troublesome foot.

Time passed. Another spring greeted another summer and for the first and only time during the Hughs' years at Oyster Bay they were faced with the terror of a bushfire. The hot wind had risen early sending the temperature above one hundred degrees

480

Fahrenheit. The fire was racing through the bush on the other side of the bay. Margo, staring out from the back veranda, said quietly, 'Good – *Lord!*' the gravity of her tone and the spacing of the words, a clanging bell to Annie.

Fear rippled through the girl. 'It can't cross over to our side, can it Mum?' she asked, and read the answer in her mother's alarmed silence and rigid stance.

Margo's brow contracted, and after a moment she recollected Annie's presence. 'Kitty's Creek!' she said anxiously, 'It might cross at Kitty's Creek where it narrows.'

That realisation threw her into prompt action. Herb was away, and Jack was at work. Annie and Paul were immediately assigned various activities: to rake up leaves, hose the chook shed and yard, fill containers with water, gather and drench hessian bags and hose the house walls and the piers. The younger children helped too, and as they hurried about their tasks black ashes began falling. Then the *floaties* came down – small, burning gumtree branches borne on the searing wind and as fast as they slapped out each fire with wet sugar bags, new blazes flared up.

There was no point in seeking help for every neighbour was similarly occupied. This was worryingly evident in the decreased pressure of water in the hose, reduced so much that the water spurts no longer reached the house guttering. Surprisingly, and to his credit, Mr Brownleigh spared a few minutes to cast aside his animosity, and he carried two wet hessian sacks over to the struggling family. Margo, fair-minded and with a sense of, 'We're all in this together', acknowledged that his gesture was kind and thoughtful.

Afterwards, Annie heard her mother mutter, 'Oh Jack, Jack!' Working with Qantas, Jack had not known what was happening until receiving the phone call from Miss Gilbert. Margo knew that his anxious return by several changes of conveyance would take a while and so, unaided, she and the children continued their battle to prevent the spot fires from spreading.

Presently, they could hear the clang of the fire brigade arriving somewhere in Oyster Bay but not close enough to help them. Everything was veiled with a tinge of amber; the oppressive sun, a red globe. The smoke seared their nostrils stiflingly. The mercury continued to climb. Margo closed all the windows and both external doors but kept returning inside to ensure that the little ones were sleeping or playing happily with their toys, and to encourage them to drink more water.

Then through the smoke, a figure emerged. Mr Birtles had sacrificed a few precious moments away from the defence of his own home to hurry across to see if the Hughs were coping. His conclusion about Kitty's Creek united with Margo's. He looked in that direction, and then around at the house and yard.

After assessing Margo's position and activities, he waved his arm towards the bay. 'If it gets too much Mrs Hughs, grab all your important papers and things and get the kids into the rowing boat. The tide's full in now – you'll be safe out in the middle.' Margo nodded, gave her thanks and looked at him with round, staring eyes. He turned then and hurried back to his own house where Mrs Birtles laboured with a rake and wet bag.

Annie thought of the chooks and, dramatically expecting that everyone soon may have to run for their lives, asked Margo if she should release them. But Margo shook her head. Her inherent ability to ward off stresses took over and quite calmly she drew on a confident facade and said, 'It probably won't come to that.'

Margo's stoicism aside, to claim later that it had been a stressful event would be an understatement, for the fear had bruised them all badly, but at least the day had not culminated in an evacuation. As often happens during bushfires, the wind changed direction and sent the fire back on itself. The Hughs were left with feelings of gratitude, relief and exhaustion, and also with the more visible choking smoke and depressing sight of burnt-out bush towards the rear of the vacant block between their place and Martins'. There, the boulders the children had often played on were left bare of scrub and for the first time showed their various plateaus, curves and angles.

The Hughs were lucky. Even the army camouflage hut, which Jack had taught his older boys to erect from saplings and branches (a rough copy of those which he helped construct in New Guinea during the war), escaped the toasting because of the hose drenching it had received. Although situated on the vacant block, it was built well away from the bush.

The chooks survived, but the fruit trees and vegetables were severely scorched and dehydrated – though from heat, not from actual flames. Margo learnt later that Martins' pig shed at the end of their backyard had been destroyed. Pixie the pig forever afterwards was fixed with the delightful memory of the day she was permitted to indulge in the luxury of Martins' back veranda, her true status finally recognised.

The worst thing to emerge from the bushfire was the traumatic effect it had on Fast Fred – Mr Fredericks. After Valda had failed to locate him near her home, the word went out, and a search began. He was found a few hours later wandering disoriented across a gully, its bisecting track shortening the serpentine road towards Como, the short-cut local children always took on their way to the Pictures.

Fred's deterioration was quite marked after the fire, and a new "point-the-bone" name was added to his medical records – Alzheimer's disease. After a further few months of loving care doing all she could to cope with the effects of the illness, Valda faced the unhappy decision to have her father admitted into the hospice ward of the picturesque Primrose House near the sighing, crashing sea.

He was smilingly content, Margo was to learn, in the novel surroundings with new ears to hear the wispy remnants of his farm stories. But the epochs of his life, which had always stood tall, dwarfing all other experiences had now become fragments, wearied and disjointed. His old "whatameantasay" had slipped away from his diminishing vocabulary, seeming to take his identity as it went.

And then one afternoon after Valda changed the day of her regular visits, she was surprised to find Mrs Tanner seated at Fred's bedside. 'We liaise twice a week,' the woman explained, feigning conspiracy towards a lighter mood. She stood to leave. 'I'll be in the garden ... should you require a confidante,' she said pressing Valda's arm.

Fred at that moment was attempting to reach his newspaper. Without greeting his daughter, he flung out an arm. 'Here, gimme that paper!' he barked. For a stunned moment, Valda stared back at him. 'C'mon, the paper!' He snatched it from her hand and briskly began turning the pages, entirely disregarding the contents – and his daughter.

Valda watched him through her shocked, incipient tears as he thrashed the pages, and she understood that the gentle, good-natured father she had loved all her life was no longer there.

In the garden, she sought Mrs Tanner waiting as promised on a bench and immediately gave reign to her emotions. 'That's not *Dad* in there!' she sobbed.

Robust, formidable Mrs Tanner reached her arms around the shaking shoulders and replied softly: 'I know, pet ... *I* know.'

52 Towards Sixteen

Television had come to Oyster Bay, and it seemed that everyone was embracing it, some Catholics entirely ignoring the Pope's criticism that it was a threat to family life. Every evening in local suburbs people stood entranced outside electrical appliance stores gazing at the black and white screens, watching the news, comedy, quiz shows – anything that happened to be on. Even advertisements, later abbreviated to "ads", were found to be entertaining.

Jack Hughs succumbed to this almost hypnotic power and bought a seventeen-inch model Pye on four spindly legs. Every night his family hurried through dinner to settle down in time to watch favourite shows, such as *Pickabox*, *I Love Lucy*, the much-acclaimed *Ed Sullivan Show*, and "Westerns", many starring John Wayne. As well, the older members of the family became better informed about everyday news events in Australia and the world, more geographically literate and increasingly aware of the plight of people who did not enjoy Australia's relatively high standard of living.

Annie's knowledge of worldly facts was progressing, but ignorance on some other matters was still painfully apparent. In those days, sexual subjects were never openly discussed; many others, *taboo.* Television was subject to strict censorship, so TV itself was still innocent.

She was working temporarily at Woolworth's variety store. It was midday and six or seven workers of both genders, and of whom Annie was the youngest, had stopped for lunch.

They were seated in the lunchroom (where she first encountered *instant* coffee) all leisurely munching, glancing through magazines. A delicious cream bun was poised in her hand undergoing lustful inspection, and someone began reading out the star signs. When asked hers Annie blithely answered: 'I'm a Virgo,' adding, for the benefit of non-Catholics, 'virgin.' This term had been used every day at school during religious instruction in the context of The Virgin Mary, which the pupils associated only with blessedand divine.

Annie imagined she was making a self-deprecating joke and expected an amused, sarcastic response from one or two of her workmates mocking her capacity to be either blessed or divine … all in fun. Instead, she became aware of smothered laughter. As it grew less suppressed, the girl looked around blankly and wondered at the extraordinary response. (Certainly no one at school had ever reacted that way!) Clarification was required.

'Well …' she began defensively and, assuming a bluffing air of authority to counteract their misguided merriment, she attempted to explain the titles "Blessed Virgin Mary" and "The

Immaculate Conception" of which, in fact, Annie understood very little, '... so I'm a Virgo – or, a virgin!' Well, that indeed took care of their Protestant ignorance!

Liberated laughter filled the room. Astonished, Annie gaped at everyone. A matronly woman, smiling in a constrained, abashed manner, saved her from further "foot-in-mouth" and, casting her eyes floor-wards, took the girl's elbow. She led her to a private corner of the stockroom where she revealed, hesitantly, delicately, the embarrassing implication of Annie's blurted-out "clanger".

Oh! Painful enlightenment! With face afire, Annie thought that now would be a good time to die, and wished for a bottomless crevasse to hurl her ignorant, unworldly self into. Hot tears of mortification ensued, and when, finally, the kind woman's patient, carefully worded counsel had imbued her with sufficient courage, she returned to the Hub of Humiliation to face her merry-eyed workmates. There she sat quietly with her mouth sealed, opening the offensive thing only to stuff in the blunder-inhibiting cream bun, which had so recently suffered desertion.

In subdued retrospect, Annie knew that, along with any other teenager sensitive to ridicule and rejection, she had merely wanted to be accepted and appreciated. While waiting for that blessed concession, she realised that, because of religious ideology or her failure to understand the associated terms, a specific dimension of her mind was veiled in ignorance. Clearly, she had barely negotiated the first rung on the ladder of her ascension into worldliness and could not aspire to equality in that particular sphere where – it dawned on her later – most of the innuendos and jokes went straight over her head. (Following the "virgin" episode, Annie suddenly remembered the embarrassing little book Margo had given her to read some time ago, and now resolved to find it.)

After Annie had been working at Woolworths for a few weeks, one of the boys in the menswear section began paying her compliments, and he eventually invited her to the Saturday night dance. Annie's ballroom dancing lessons prompted her to favour this idea. The "date" was her first formal invitation to go out (Mario long-forgotten), and she could hardly wait to tell Ruthie.

On Saturday afternoon Ruthie called in. Delighted to see each other they hurried into the room Annie shared with Josie. Little sister at that moment, was outside skipping her rope, chanting, 'My mother said – I never should – play with the gipsies in the wood ...', and so their privacy was assured.

Annie burst forth with the exciting news and Ruthie squealed, 'Fair dinkum? Who? *Who*?' and her eyes shone with eager and impatient expectancy.

'Well, I met him at Woolies, and ... and he's nice looking, not very tall, blue eyes, fair hair – well, almost blond, and—'

'Yeah-yeah-yeah,' Ruthie butted in, 'but what's his bloody *name?*'

Annie rounded her eyes – Ruthie *never* swore. Suddenly the actual telling became unexpectedly tricky. 'Well ...' she stalled and looked unseeing at her hands, searching for a way to cushion the revelation. 'Well, it's – actually it's ... P-Percy,' she confessed and looked up at her friend. A stunned second passed and Ruthie's throat emitted a series of squawks, which drew Margo to the door. Smiling, she glanced in and wondered what all the frivolity was about.

With a grimace usually reserved for castor oil, Ruthie spat out the old-fashioned name. *'Percy!* Oh, ga-awd! you're not serious?' Annie nodded. Ruthie's expression of distaste underwent a resigned change then as she lifted her eyebrows and asked, 'Well what's his other name? It can't *all* be ghastly!

Annie braced herself, integrity demanding at least nominal defence. 'It's sort of posh, you know – sophisticated. It's ... it's Cripps,' she said, and then presented the name in its dignified entirety: 'Percival – Clement – Cripps.'

It wasn't long before Annie Hughs, and Percy Cripps were "going steady". After some further months, however, she had detected his single flaw – over-moist kisses which repelled her somewhat and sent her thoughts to the undersides of snails. She had to create cunning and discreet pretexts to dry her mouth.

Eventually, the day arrived for him finally to meet Ruthie (in whom tact, Annie knew, had never found long habitation). It is surprising how quickly familiarity with a name will render it unremarkable. Annie's best friend had become so used to hearing "Percy" punctuating the regular reports of outings that it was no longer hysterically funny and she kindly behaved herself.

But as they sat around socialising in the backyard, Annie realised how quickly her listing "steady" became beguiled. Without conscious effort, Ruthie, by merely being Ruthie, conquered him with the full force of her effervescent personality. They formed an instant bond subjecting Annie's sinking emotions to an unsettling ambivalence. She was yanked from this reverie, however, by Margo's unexpected call from the house.

'Oh *bugger!*' Annie muttered, reluctant to leave her boyfriend to Ruthie's increasing familiarity and the hypnosis of her musical "little girl" voice and bewitching smiles. Annie silently grieved over it, for it seemed now that any delight he might have found in her was relegated to an inferior second by the force of contrast before him.

Indoors, detained by the untimely mind-dulling task of stirring custard so that it wouldn't burn while Margo attended to a salesman, Annie risked a brief sneak-peek through the kitchen window, but the custard's inclination to stick held her prisoner.

Valiantly, while stirring, she tried to use mind power, to tether her thoughts to the reality that Ruthie was her best friend, to gain mental comfort in the delusion that her own character was above jealousy and not prone to petty insecurity. Indeed, she was a tier above the sly temptation to check again on the laughing pair. In fact, so soothing was her complacency that she zipped over to the window only two times more.

When at last Annie was free to hurry out and retard the advance of this new alliance yeasting away there between her happy friends, a sour feeling of her own mean-spiritedness encroached. This sensation philosophically suggested a withdrawal from the competition in favour of heeding the maxim regularly delivered on the wireless by famous singer Doris Day: *Que sera, sera.*

After smilingly acknowledging Annie's return, Percy drew her into the conversation regarding the "Woolies" group's planned trip to the Sydney Stadium to see the celebrated singer Johnnie Ray. Her nobler instincts – and a lesser feeling of her being corralled anyhow – dictated that they invite Ruthie – and to that idea, Percy responded too eagerly.

'I should've kept my stupid mouth shut!' Annie mumbled to the ground.

'Oh, *fab!* I can't wait!' Ruthie tinkled with the natural vivacity which so often became her chief charm. Suddenly, Annie's feelings of fond sisterhood were supplanted by sensations of intense resentment.

Annie responded with faked enthusiasm, but as her attachment to Percy was not yet entirely severed, her heart sank fathoms. 'I wish to God Ruthie would just vanish,' she thought. How very fine the line that separates friendship from rivalry!

53 Heartthrob Johnnie Ray

In some respects, Ruthie and Annie had always been alike, but as the years passed they began to differ more widely in their preferences – for film stars and singers, for example. Annie admired Kathryn Hepburn and Elizabeth Taylor, while Ruthie intended one day to bleach her hair in faithful emulation of Marilyn Monroe. The friends were becoming opposites.

A similar difference extended to "heartthrobs". During a shopping excursion in the city one morning, the young girls paused to watch a newsreel featuring "The Mississippi singing sensation, Elvis" as he belted out *'You ain't nothin' but a hound dog'.*

Annie's reaction was swift: 'Sissy name! ... sounds like elves. What was his mother thinking? He certainly is handsome, though', she conceded, yet sniggered at the pelvic swivels and earthy grunts, dismissing both as corny theatrics. And when he several times thrust forward his hips ("Elvis the pelvis") it struck her that he was just another "nine-day wonder".

Ruthie though, drew excitement from the performance; sighed and swooned and thought he was second only to God. Annie was no puritan, but she began to believe that her own attitude was abnormal. Some days later, however, hearing Elvis sing *Love Me Tender,* she paused by the wireless to listen – and melted with the magic.

On the other hand, Johnnie Ray, the practically deaf American singer, songwriter and pianist, had Annie turning up the volume whenever she heard him sing *Cry* or *Such a Night* or any of his other songs. Naively, she saw him as a fantastic yardstick from which all "pop" singers should be measured and longed to see him perform.

The eagerly awaited day dawned. The hours moved on, and the enticing kitchen smells filled the house: from breakfast toast to evening rissoles frying, and then fragrant *Lifebuoy* soap and cosmetics and freshly ironed clothes.

The weather was seasonal for March. The lovely firmament of early sunset began sending out its golden "hooroo" glow over the hills of Oyster Bay. Annie stood leaning on the front gate, watching out for Ruthie to come walking down the road, her skirt swinging. At intervals, she rearranged the gathers of her own three-tiered skirt over the two circular starched petticoats. She checked to ensure that the cardigan partner of the twin-set was correctly draped over her shoulders. Teenage girls, at that time, regarded cardigans as mere accessories and inserted arms into sleeves only if the weather turned cold and forced that mode upon them.

Presently, Mr Birtles came ambling along on his evening walk. He was a merry-natured, grandfatherly person. With no children of his own, he evinced a kind interest in the Hughs kids.

Correspondingly, Annie often considered him a sort of composite of the real grandfathers she had lost.

'Hello, Annie love,' he said. 'Gawd, you're done up like a sore toe! Lipstick and earrings now, eh? ... *and* high-heels!' He shook his head at her new white shoes as though seeing again the tiny-tot sandals little Annie used to wear, marvelling at all the years gone by since their first meeting during the war. He strolled over to the gate and leaned on the fence. 'Where are you off to then, lovie?'

'Well, as a matter of fact, I'm going to see Johnnie Ray,' Annie said excitedly.

'Is that so? And who's he when he's alive?'

'Oh, come on Mr Birtles! You've heard him singing on the wireless, seen his picture in the paper. You *must* have.'

He was smiling knowingly. 'Well, 'course I have. I was just teasing, y' know. Actually, the missus and I were listening to him just this morning singing *Walkin' in the Rain* ... or was it *Walkin' My Baby Back Home*?' He frowned at the pebbles as the little memory test once more reminded him of age and time rapidly passing, but tossed off the sensation with, 'One of them anyhow.' And then, an afterthought, 'Funny how the yanks call girls "baby" isn't it? *Baby!* Like they never grow up – girls, I mean. Good songs, though eh? He's at the Stadium, is he? So how are you going to get there?' he asked, and his eventual pause enabled the

497

girl to cease the nodding which had covered the first three questions.

'Oh, I'm waiting for some friends, one of them has a van. And Ruthie's coming too,' Annie told him, deliberately brightening her tone – for her own psychological benefit.

Sydney Stadium, "the old tin shed", was the usual place for visiting celebrities such as Frank Sinatra, Nat King Cole and Frankie Laine, who drew larger crowds than could be accommodated at the Tivoli. In discussion with Ruthie the previous day, Annie had vowed never to react the way most flutter-hearted girls did when "clapping eyes" on her idol. Ruthie scoffed: 'Ha! Who are you trying to kid? You'll yell as loud as the rest of the mob.'

From the cheap, up-the-back seats (the bleachers) where the small "Woolies" group was seated, they watched and waited in terrible anticipation for Johnnie Ray to appear. The delay, a strategy to increase suspense, worked well. When at last the police escorted the running singer with his backup vocalists down to the square "ring", everyone went wild.

Music is undoubtedly a people-uniting medium. Crowd hysteria has always been fodder for newspapers in which photographs are liberally displayed, especially those depicting girls crying because of an intensification of emotion beyond their ability to cope. Now, Ruthie and Annie were experiencing a degree of the phenomenon. Tears flowed as they jumped up together and became merely two more noisy cells in the colossal animal body termed "crowd", and for many months afterwards, Annie cringed at the memory of her display and knew she would never trust herself again.

The screaming continued as the almost-deaf singer walked around the ring, turning to face in turn every aspect of the audience, and in the attitude of a revered evangelist, raised his arms, subduing the crowd sufficiently to allow his voice to be heard. And then, a surprise – from his right ear he removed a hearing aid, held it high, and with a broad, heart-racing attractive smile, his husky American drawl playfully announced: 'I don't *haaave* to listen to *you!*' More screaming, and then he just stood there as though a statue, waiting. An expectant church-like quietness descended. The music rose and, hands on the microphone, the charismatic teen idol, Johnnie Ray, began to sing.

The crowd listened, entranced by *Walkin'my Baby Back Home*, *The Little White Cloud That Cried* and others. But before his finale, *Cry*, the song that had topped the hit parade for three consecutive months and which everyone had been waiting for, he suddenly ran down off the "stage" and approached a girl in the front row. With arms extended, he helped the astonished teenager to her feet, and not only did he embrace her, but he kissed her very well. The crowd cheered and whistled. Every girl in the stadium surely longed to be the one in his arms

Sometime later, Annie read in the papers and heard on the wireless news that "Mr Emotion" Johnnie Ray had been mobbed at Sydney airport by a crowd of four thousand fans and, with shirt and trousers torn, had been rescued in a state of semi-consciousness. But she was reminded of something her father always said: 'Don't believe everything you read in the papers.'

Jack Hughs dismissed the report as 'just another crummy publicity stunt.' He asserted, in effect, that Johnnie Ray had become merely a product of his creators – as Hitler was of Joseph Goebbels' propaganda. Jack believed that Johnnie Ray's apparent charisma was owing to the God-like persona the manipulated audience had been groomed to believe him to be; that as an individual he was just another good singer – a good one, he allowed.

Annie understood her father's point of view and reserved judgement on the dramatic news report. However, she also knew what she had seen and felt: the magic, real or contrived; the mania power, and the potential danger of being drawn into such a mass of worshipping people. Nevertheless, this great experience of hers was a singular one never to be forgotten. Annie was well-satisfied, and by the time The Beatles came to Australia she had no inclination to become another throbbing cell of the "crowd animal".

54 Growing Up

The following Saturday Percy visited again, and then
Ruthie arrived. Sitting companionably on the front veranda, they
spent the first half-hour drinking *Coca-Cola* and munching *Smith's
Chips*, happily re-living the excitement of Johnnie Ray's
extraordinary performance. But other less ecstatic topics emerged,
submitted to comment and departed, and gradually Ruthie and
Percy surrendered to the magnetic draw of eye contact.

Ruthie's print dress and her shining eyes, Annie noticed
admiringly, were in perfect harmony with the blue of the sky. And
Percy! Annie had never known him to be quite so attractive in his
tanned, blond way. Was it a trick of atmospherics, Annie wondered
in some wordless, quixotic way, which enhanced the beauty of the
two teenagers? Or was it the power of love?

The first twist of adult pain began insidiously to declare
itself, distorting Annie's senses. With elbows on knees and hand
under chin, she let her ponytail flop to the side, curtaining the
disturbing view of them. She looked at her free hand and inspected
the fingernails at last delightfully growing and gleaming with
bright colour, but they held little interest now.

Presently, Annie began to resent this perceived disregard
for her existence. It was blatantly rude of them … but oh, how
absolutely, helplessly drawn to each other they were! This

realisation filled her mind with envious wonder, for Annie had never felt quite thatbesotted over anyone – except unattainable Johnnie Ray!

So preoccupied were they, and so utterly superfluous had become her own company that Annie selected to remain silent, taking refuge in deep thought. She understood in some wordless way that this was how it always would be – Ruthie, the flame to every moth of their future life as friends.

Annie Hughs did not possess the emotional stamina or inclination to compete for the attention of any boy and believed that such necessity rendered the prize unworthy of the effort – hence expendable. Therefore, her self-placating attitude was: if so destined, let Ruthie become Mrs Cripps and mother of all the little Cripps!

Annie was very thoughtful for the rest of the day and went early to bed, spending much time staring at the window and the silvery phosphorescence of the rising full moon, hearing the goodnight ticking of late grasshoppers and the distant lonely howls of a dog.

At intervals, she glanced at Josie's lovely First Holy Communion outfit Margo had made. The diminutive bridal-like apparel was hanging on the wardrobe door, the veil fluttering up now and then with a busy breeze and hovering like a moon-white ghost. And dear little sister lay curled up there in her bed dreaming no doubt, about her big day tomorrow.

At the last hour of the twenty-four, as Annie turned her thoughts over again and punished the pillow, she sought to draw comfort from the memory of Johnnie Ray as he sang a particular line in "Cry": *Just remember, sunshine can be found behind a cloudy sky.*

With weary resignation, she acknowledged the approach of the first fracture in her happy childhood with Ruthie, which nevertheless, was destined to widen as their lives diverged. Annie sought to retreat, to glean a kind of solace from the bitter-sweet fact that she was soon to leave home to move into the Nurses' Quarters at St George Hospital. There, her beloved aunt and valued mentor Sister Dulce Carrington awaited to "show her the ropes" ... and there, later, Annie would meet Christopher and finally come to understand the wild, ecstatic, *I-love-everyone* happiness of falling in love.

The years of 1957 and '58 had been memorable. Everyone was startled by Joern Utzon's vision of Australia's future Opera House. A campaign was born to promote equal pay for women workers, most of whom were receiving only seventy-five percent of the amount paid to their male counterparts. As well, the basic wage went up by ten shillings, and some found it easy to dispose of this extra "half-quid" during the newly extended hours for hotel closing.

The world sadly farewelled Humphrey Bogart, but Bill Haley and his Comets still had teenagers rocking around the clock. Some people were fearful of the "bodgie and widgie" cult as it's notoriety increased, but on a happier note, the relatively small transistor radio exploded into popularity and become an extension of many a teenage arm. Australians were proud of the latest Holden, a station wagon, though expensive, costing £995 – and prouder still of our "coat hanger" Harbour Bridge, just turned twenty-five.

At home, Herb and Laura announced their engagement. Margo and Jack, wearied by years of tolerating the troublesome neighbours – *her* complaints and *his* drunkenness – decided they would sell the house … but then Paul became ill.

He was a happy, good-looking, God-loving youth with the best of life beckoning. By the power of contrast, Annie saw herself as unworthy, perceiving her own character as willful, doubting and analysing. She now regarded unquestioning Catholic obedience, not as a virtue, but as a flaw.

Annie had prayed that Paul would beat the disease, that some natural defence would shrink his tumour and allow her brother to recover. But the cobalt treatments at the Royal Prince Alfred Hospital did not halt the insidious spread of cancer. Margo,

Jack, Herb, the children and everyone else in the extended Hughs family were thrown into an abyss of despair when, finally, Paul was admitted to St George hospital.

At a private, late afternoon revisit to the Woronora Cemetery; to the grave Paul now shared with baby Lorraine, Annie realised the cruel irony. From conception to birth the creation of this precious human being had taken nine months ... and it took nine months for cancer to destroy him.

She grew blazingly angry. 'Hey God, you took the wrong one!' she railed. 'He was the best of the lot of us ... *I'm* the doubter. I'm the bloody sinner,' she sobbed. 'You should've taken me! Y' hear me, God – *if* you're there at all? It should've been ME!'– and her shouted profanity ascended through the treetops to the magnificent gilding heavens.

There is a strong correlation between the paramount events of being born and leaving home. Both are within the natural order of things. Both are to some degree painful, but equally, they initiate progress – the ability to orientate to a new environment and the freedom to grow and to prosper.

Annie Hughs stood on the cliff and gazed out over the river, sparkling in the morning sun. A multitude of memories assailed her: there, a group of scallywag "river kids" pelting mud balls; farther up, a launch full of sun hats and happiness; closer to the wharf, a canoe and a green rowing boat.

The breeze brought the heady fragrance of nearby wattle-bloom and of salty water visiting from the sea. And Annie thought of Jack and his oysters, and Margo's regular warning to them: 'Stay away from the cliff!' Even her own child-voice came echoing to her across the years: 'Mum, Mum, I can *swim*!'

And there, most poignant of all, was Paul … enshrined forever in his sister's memory, her waning faith now undergoing the severest of tests.

Childhood was gone. Annie turned and saw the rising, curling chimney smoke and knew that her mum was baking a "going-away" cake. The girl-woman stood firm-footed on the sweet, but the uncertain threshold of her adult life and felt a tremor of apprehension for that which lay ahead, but also sorrow for all she was to leave behind.

Annie had suffered the pain of family deaths, and yet she realised now with full force that despite this, Oyster Bay had become her "Pearl of Great Price". Good times had been polished and entrusted to memory and small irritants smothered with layers of nacre so that even they would occasionally gleam in her treasury of recollection.

She loved the river and the green fibro house that had evolved with the family. She deeply felt the loss of her brother, and of everything she had ever known as far back as the war years and towards a future of peace. And so, Annie would leave it all behind but with the knowledge that always with her would remain the memory of Paul and the love shared with siblings and with her dear mum and dad, wherever she happened to be.

"And in the end the love you take

is equal to the love you make."

The Beatles

54633679R00285

Made in the USA
Middletown, DE
05 December 2017